The Medieval Experience

God Measuring the World. *Illustration from a French moralized Bible of the thirteenth century.* (Bildarchiv des Österreichischen Nationalbibliothek, Wien)

THE MEDIEVAL EXPERIENCE: 300–1400

Jill N. Claster

PROFESSOR, MEDIEVAL HISTORY
DEAN, WASHINGTON SQUARE AND UNIVERSITY COLLEGE,
NEW YORK UNIVERSITY

New York University Press. New York *and* London.

Library of Congress Cataloging in Publication Data

Claster, Jill N.
  The medieval experience: 300–1400.

  Bibliography: p.
  Includes index.
  1. Middle Ages—History.   2. Europe—History—
476-1492.   I. Title.
D117.C6   940.1   81-14094
ISBN 0-8147-1384-x
ISBN 0-8147-1381-5 pbk.   AACR2

10 9 8 7 6 5
Manufactured in the United States of America

To—and for—my
beloved daughter Elizabeth
(1961–1974)
whose book this is

Contents

Preface

This is a book about our European beginnings—the experience of over a thousand years which, by convention, we call the Middle Ages. The time-span covered is from the early decades of the fourth century to the closing decades of the fourteenth. But since no historic period is so neatly bounded—and the Middle Ages least of all—the book begins with a brief prologue on the founding of the Roman empire and closes with an epilogue on the dissolution of the medieval unity in the fourteenth century.

The book is designed to be a first guide to the medieval experience. It was written with my own college students always in mind, with the intention of providing them, and others like them, with a thoughtful, useful and, it is hoped, provocative introduction to the European Middle Ages. The book was undertaken also out of a desire to convey a sense of the unique creativity of the medieval period.

When the term "medieval" was first used (in the fourteenth century) to apply to this long stretch of time, it was chosen intentionally to impart a negative image—a picture of an unchanging landscape. And so it occasionally still does, even now, when we know better. It is assuredly true that during much of those thousand years the physical aspects of life were exceedingly difficult, and life itself was precarious. And yet, despite the many wars, the epidemics, famines, and the widespread illiteracy, there were always people who struggled to improve the quality of life, who were inventive, who kept alive a body of learning, and tried to make the world beautiful. There is much inspiration to be found in the medieval experience.

xi

The Middle Ages is the formative stage in the development of European civilization and a common European culture. This book concentrates on western Europe, although not exclusively. At the beginning of our period, in the early fourth century, most of Europe—that part which lies north of the Alps—was still a backwater of the Roman empire, much of it inhabited by nomadic or semi-nomadic German tribes. The center of the world was the area surrounding the Mediterranean Sea. As the culture of the early Middle Ages began to evolve, the Latin West maintained its complex ties to the Mediterranean and to the other two civilizations that developed during the medieval centuries: Byzantium and Islam. Both Byzantium and Islam are therefore included, first to provide some understanding of how they arose and to describe their main characteristics, and then to provide some understanding of how they influenced western Europe.

The chronological framework of the book is divided into three parts: the first concentrates on the centuries of transition from the classical world of Rome to the Germanic, Christian culture of early medieval Europe; the second part concentrates on the Carolingian Empire and its aftermath—a period sometimes known as the "first Europe"; the last period is the full flowering of medieval Latin culture.

Although it is certainly true that each age flows into the next and that, as an historian of the ancient world remarked, "there are no periods in history, only in historians," these now familiar divisions of the Middle Ages have their own special themes and are distinct from one another. They are also useful because they help give shape and coherence to a period whose events do not naturally or tidily organize themselves around a single, or even major, topic, as the age of the Reformation, for example, or the Enlightenment. There are nonetheless two themes which run throughout the entire Middle Ages and which are followed through the book: the development of Europe into a predominantly Christian society, and the continuity of Rome and Latin culture. The book thus begins in Rome and ends with the transition from the Middle Ages to the Renaissance of the fourteenth century—a period which had as a dominant feature the longing for the Roman past and the wish to recreate the Roman empire.

The pictures which accompany the text were chosen with great care to illustrate the history. It is in a good medieval tradition, because the manuscript illuminators understood very well the educational and artistic value of a picture on a manuscript page. All in all, they were chosen to give texture to our understanding of the Middle Ages and to draw attention to the ingenuity and beauty which flourished even in the harsh environment of medieval Europe. It is hoped that this book will dispel any lingering doubts about the creativity, and the variety, of the medieval experience.

Acknowledgments

Many people gave me valuable assistance with this book, and it pleases me now to express my gratitude: to Professor Moshe Barasch of The Hebrew University of Jerusalem, art historian and good friend, who read the manuscript in its early stages and generously gave me scholarly advice and needed encouragement; to my colleague, Dr. Tina Stiefel, whose knowledge of the medieval field and fine literary taste improved the manuscript; to my graduate student, Maricel Presilla, who worked with skill and unfailing good humor to find just the right illustrations and assist with many necessary details; to Nancy Kirk Fogelson, who gave more than her time and good editorial judgment, and deserves more than this space permits; to Professor Francis E. Peters, longtime colleague and friend at New York University, for my education in Islam and for *bona exempla*; to Professor Robert R. Raymo, whose devotion to medieval studies is an inspiration; and to Professor Lucy Sandler of the Fine Arts Department at New York University for teaching me to love medieval manuscript illuminations.

Of my former students, now dear friends, four merit special thanks for their important contributions to this book: Dr. Thea Browne, Dr. Tamara Greene, Dr. Vito Caiati and Sheila Rosenzweig, who read the galleys. Above all, my gratitude to my husband, Judge Millard L. Midonick, for his loving patience and his unfailing support and kindness. I am grateful also to the staff of the New York University Press for their courtesy and help, especially that of Despina Papazoglou, and to Nat LaMar for his talented and tolerant editing.

Acknowledgments

I hope that all my students will know how much this book owes to their interest, the joy they have given me, and their friendship—most particularly those who were in my classes in 1973–1974. Because I live daily with the remembrance of my daughter's extraordinary courage, spirit, and love, the book is dedicated to Elizabeth, of course.

The Medieval Experience

Prologue:
The Romans and the Founding of
Their Empire

The Roman Empire was the culmination of a long series of conquests which began in the fifth century B.C. and continued until nearly the end of the first century B.C.

When these wars of expansion began Rome was an insignificant rural village, its government a republic founded by a small group of families who had formed themselves into an aristocracy. The republican constitution was modified over time, but the most important body was always the Senate, whose members were drawn from the aristocracy. Hesitantly at first, but then with increasing determination, the republican armies conquered the western and the eastern Mediterranean. It was an expansion "the like of which," as a Greek historian of the second century B.C. observed, "has never happened before." By the middle of the first century B.C. Rome had annexed Italy, Spain, North Africa, Gaul, Greece, Asia Minor, Syria, and Palestine.

Although nearly all the lands along the Mediterranean littoral ultimately became Roman territory, the government remained at least outwardly much the same as it had been when Rome was small. The real power, however, had passed from the senators to the generals who fought Rome's victorious foreign wars. The strains and expenses of the seemingly endless wars, the difficulties of governing the new territories, and the strength and independence of the generals all conspired to destroy the republic. During

Roman Patrician with Busts of his Ancestors (ca. 30 B.C.). *According to Roman tradition, aristocratic families kept and venerated the busts of their ancestors. "For,"* *as the historian Polybius wrote, "who could not be inspired by the images of men* *renowned for their excellence, all together as if alive and breathing?"* (ALINARI/ EDITORIAL PHOTOCOLOR ARCHIVES)

the last one hundred years of the republic, from 133 to 31 B.C., there were civil wars in addition to the foreign wars. The battle which finally brought these wars to an end was fought in and around the Bay of Actium off the Greek coast in 31 B.C. On one side were the Roman general Mark Antony and his queen and ally Cleopatra, ruler of Egypt. On the other side was the young Octavian, grandnephew of Julius Caesar, champion of the Roman Senate, later to become Augustus, the first Roman emperor. Octavian's victory ended the civil wars, added Egypt to Rome's possessions, and, above all, brought peace to the Mediterranean world.

Octavian had won complete control of Rome and of the Mediterranean. Yet within a few years of Actium he announced that he had returned the state from his own power to that of the Senate and the Roman people. In gratitude, the Senate accorded him the title Augustus, or "honored," which from then on was used by all Roman emperors. Even though Augustus claimed that he had restored the republic, his long rule (31 B.C.–14 A.D.) was actually the beginning of the imperial period of Rome's history. The government he worked out was a delicate balance between the emperor and the Senate. The greater power by far belonged to the emperor since he retained command of the army and navy, control of the imperial finances, and was supreme law giver. But Augustus kept alive the forms of republican government and indeed fanned new life into the Senate. All his powers were voted him by the Senate, and he shared with the senators much of the administrative business of the empire. Augustus said of himself that he ruled as *Princeps*, or first citizen, and his system, known as the principate, lasted for the first two hundred years of the empire. The principate was more than simply a clever political device. Augustus' respect for the republic and the Senate in the early days of Rome's greatness was genuine, and throughout his reign he encouraged by legislation and every other means a return to the "customs of the ancestors."

The customs of the Romans during the early days of the republic were those of a rural society and were shaped both by the demands of a farmer's life and by the difficulties the Roman state had in surviving during its early centuries. The Romans were surrounded by neighbors who coveted their land, and the Romans had to fight hard and work closely together with no thought of personal advantage. Roman history is filled with stories of the selfless devotion of heroes like Cincinnatus, who left his plow in the middle of his field to defend Rome and, when the fighting was over, returned to pick it up and go on with his farming. Three institutions mattered to the Romans: the family, the state, and the gods who protected home and country. These institutions were at the heart of everything, and it was the special responsibility of the first families, the senatorial aristocracy, to maintain and transmit the traditions which would ensure their continuation. In the most literal sense Roman society was conservative, deeply rooted in the soil.

In the third and particularly the second centuries B.C. Rome's expansion had brought her citizens into close contact with the Greek world and with a culture that was different and far more advanced than her own. The home of classical Greek civilization was Athens in the fifth century B.C. The Greeks themselves crossed over to the eastern Mediterranean in the armies of Alexander the Great—and they stayed. In Egypt, Syria, Palestine, Asia Minor, and central Asia they built cities which became enclaves of Hellenic civilization. When the Romans went East and encountered the thoughtful and beautiful culture of the Greeks they succumbed (as who has not?) to the civilization that has been described as "the finest flower of the species that ever came to bloom." Roman philosophy, art, and architecture "grew up" under the influence of the Greek achievements. Alongside their education in Latin, upper-class Romans learned Greek and studied the literature and sciences in their original language. Greek teachers and philosophers came to Rome; Greek statues were imported (or plundered), Greek architecture was imitated, and Greek refinements were adopted. "Not a little rivulet . . . but a mighty river of culture and learning" the Roman philosopher-statesman Cicero called it, and there were many who feared that Rome herself would drown in it and that the ancient way of life would be lost.

With the founding of the empire, however, came a reaffirmation of Roman values which for a long time had lain dormant. The Romans believed that winning the empire had been destined by the gods, but that it nevertheless had been won against formidable odds. "Such a toil it was," wrote the Roman poet Virgil, "to found the Roman people." The obstacles were overcome—so the Romans believed—because of the special characteristics they associated with the heroes and way of life of their early republic. From the Augustan era on, those qualities that were distinctively Roman were emphasized in art, literature, and propaganda. They are most beautifully expressed in the *Aeneid*, the epic poem written during Augustus' lifetime by Virgil (70–19 B.C.). Few poets have ever been as widely read and as well-loved as Virgil. And from Virgil, more than any other writer, the ideas about Rome and the Romans were transmitted to the later empire, to the medieval centuries, and to us.

The story of the *Aeneid* begins with the close of the war between the Greeks and Trojans, immortalized by Homer in the *Iliad*. Aeneas is a Trojan, and when the Greeks destroy his city he is given a mission by the gods to set out for Italy in order to found the Roman people. The *Aeneid* has many levels: Aeneas' wanderings are an allegory of Rome's expansion, and the fact that the poem begins with the Trojan War, the most hallowed event in Greek history, is a way of acknowledging Rome's ties to the Greek world. But Aeneas is most decidedly not a Greek; nor is he any longer a Trojan. His destiny, which is Rome's destiny, is to found a new nation, and his traits are those the Romans most valued in themselves. Aeneas is described throughout the poem as "pious" and to the Romans piety meant reverence for the gods and devotion to the family. Aeneas is also courageous, not so much in the physical sense (though he is that, too), as in the moral sense. He possesses the courage to make difficult decisions, a quality that is softened by compassion and loyalty to his companions on his journey.

Aeneas is not a flamboyant hero, but an infinitely human one. His sufferings and failings are quite real. He is dogged by adversity on his travels; he complains often about his fate and has to be reminded by the gods that he was chosen for a special task. His piety is tested constantly, and as he takes each difficult step his character is strengthened. In one moving episode of the poem Aeneas falls in love with Dido, a Carthaginian queen, and is tempted to remain with her. The gods have to come to tell him that he must continue his mission, if not for his own sake, for that of his son and future decendants. "Italy must be my love and my homeland now," Aeneas tells Dido, and so "he remained obedient to the divine command, and with many a sigh, . . . returned to his ships."[1]

The Romans knew that others, the Greeks foremost among them, possessed talents they themselves did not have in abundance. They knew that others, as Virgil wrote, could "hammer forth more delicately a breathing likeness out of bronze, . . . plot with their gauge the movements of the sky." And they recognized that their own abilities were of a different order. "[Y]ou, Roman, must remember," Aeneas' father tells him, "that you have to guide the nations by your authority, for this is to be your skill, to graft tradition onto peace, to show mercy to the conquered . . . ." For the two hundred years of the principate the Romans "guided the nations"—and did it remarkably well.

The empire they governed was bounded by the Atlantic Ocean, the Rhine-Danube Rivers, the Black Sea, the deserts of Africa and Syria, and the northern Euphrates. Augustus established the boundaries, and his advice to future generations was not to go beyond them. The only additions in two centuries were Britain, part of the land lying between the Euphrates and Tigris rivers, and an area north of the lower Danube. (The last was abandoned because, as Augustus had predicted, it was too difficult to defend.) Within the empire lived an extraordinarily heterogeneous population that included Italians, Spaniards, Celts, Africans, Greeks, Syrians, Egyptians, and Jews. Although in theory the empire was one world, in reality it was a house divided.

One fundamental division was the cultural distinction between the East and the West. For the most part, the populations of Italy,

1. This and the following quotations in this section are from Vergil, *The Aeneid*, rev. ed., trans. W. F. Jackson Knight (Baltimore: Penguin Books, 1960).

Spain, North Africa, Britain, and France had been brought into the orbit of Roman power at a cultural level lower than that of Rome itself. Under the imperial government, the Romans embarked on an extremely successful mission of cultural diffusion: The Latin language, Roman education, and Rome's cultural monuments—literary and architectural—were disseminated with amazing rapidity through the western provinces. In the Eastern Empire the situation, as we have noted, was very different because there Greek culture had been firmly entrenched before the Romans arrived. The language of the educated classes was Greek, and the dialect of the traders and businessmen throughout the East was a form of Greek. Although Roman law, the Roman soldier, and the Roman trader all went East, it was never in any fundamental sense Latinized.

The transmission of Greek and Latin culture was primarily an urban and upper-class phenomenon. The Greek cities of classical antiquity had a tradition of independence and self-government, and the Romans allowed it to continue and encouraged this tradition in the new cities they founded. Each city had its own senate or council, composed of the richest men. They were responsible for seeing that the city ran smoothly, and they were invited to fund, out of their own pockets, such civic projects as public contests, new buildings, and religious festivals. The wealth of these city fathers was in land. In fact, ownership of a large amount of land was requisite for holding public office, but although they owned country villas, their political lives took place in the cities. The elite of the Roman Empire were not unlike the British aristocracy of the nineteenth century: landed gentry, raised to be public officials, well-educated in the classics of Greek and Latin literature and in the art of speaking well. Theirs was a privileged existence that inspired a strong loyalty to the city and the empire; and within the aristocracy, the distinction between those from the eastern and western cities became blurred during the principate.

A wide gulf, however, separated the city dwellers from the vast majority of people—some ninety percent of the population—who lived and worked on the land. Although Egyptian and Syrian peasants, Gallic and Spanish farmers, and Berber nomads were

7

all considered Romans by the government, each group clung fast to its local dialects, local religions, and local customs. Even so, none was immune to a process of Romanization, however slowly it took place. Many entered the Roman army where they learned Roman ways. They had to deal with Roman tax collectors, do business with Roman traders, and they saw all around them the outward signs of Roman rule.

The entire empire was interlaced by a great network of paved roads, and even at the farthest frontiers there were cities, aqueducts, and temples. Administrators, soldiers, aristocrats, farmers, and merchants all followed the milestones along the roads to travel from one part of the empire to another. But not even the great Roman roads could surpass travel by sea. The heart of the empire was the Mediterranean, and the Romans sailed from the Straits of Gibraltar to the Nile and the Black Sea, bringing their ideas and their goods with them. More than ever before, they did so during the first two hundred years of Roman imperial rule. It is therefore not difficult to understand how the Romans came to believe that their empire was the fulfillment of the destiny that Jupiter foretold at the beginning of the *Aeneid*. "To Romans I set no boundary in space or time. I have granted them dominion, and it has no end."

During the first two hundred years of imperial rule East and West were successfully and, by and large, peacefully, ruled from Rome. Edward Gibbon, the great historian of Rome's decline and fall, wrote that the rule of certain emperors in the second century was in fact "the only period of history in which the happiness of a great people was the sole object of government." This is a very seductive statement, partly because it is so well–written, and partly because there is truth in it. For two centuries the internal problems that existed were obscured by peace and prosperity.

PART ONE ⌘

THE EARLY
MIDDLE AGES:
THE FOURTH TO
THE LATE EIGHTH
CENTURY

There is no precise date to indicate the change from the ancient to the medieval period, but after 300 A.D. two new factors assumed crucial importance in the formation of the character of the Middle

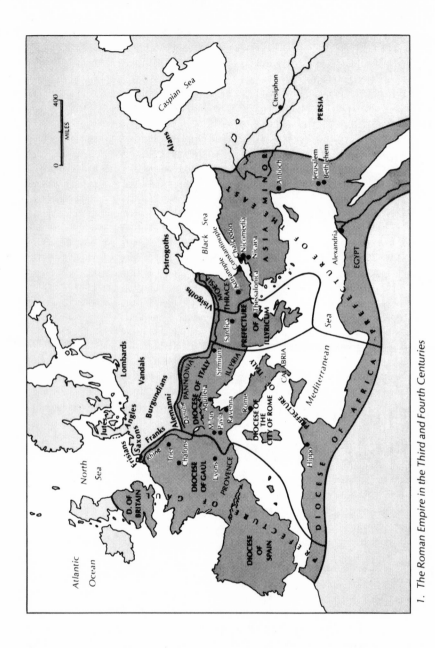

1. *The Roman Empire in the Third and Fourth Centuries*

Ages: the conversion of the Roman Empire to Christianity and the influx of Germanic peoples into Europe.

The fourth century, beginning with the reign of Constantine and ending with the reign of Theodosius the Great, was the first stage in the creation of medieval civilization. During the course of that century the problem posed by the steady growth of Christianity within a polytheistic society was resolved. At the close of the century and on into the next, the empire coped, as it could, with the German invaders and their settlements. It is the blending of these new peoples and the new religion within the framework of classical civilization that gives to the fourth and fifth centuries their special character as an age of transition.

The following centuries, from 500 A.D. to 800 A.D., were a uniquely creative period during which three great civilizations were formed on the foundation of the Roman Empire: Byzantium, Islam, and Christian Europe. Each developed a rich culture distinctively its own, yet each drew strength and inspiration from the same source—the Graeco-Roman civilization of classical antiquity.

1

The Mediterranean World in Transition: 300–500

The Background to the Reign of Constantine:
Crisis and Recovery in the Third Century

During the third century, the peace that had characterized the principate was replaced by chaos and upheaval in all areas of the Mediterranean. This was the century about which Edward Gibbon wrote that the empire "appeared every day less formidable to its enemies, more odious and oppressive to its subjects." The problems which confronted the empire are so tied together that it is difficult to place them in order of importance. Each problem exposed another weakness and each weakness created yet another problem, until it seemed the empire could not possibly recover.

To begin with, Rome was beset by invasions on all frontiers. Barbarian tribes living along the boundaries of the empire broke through the Roman defenses, and for the first time the security of the empire was threatened from within. The pressure of the barbarian invasions exposed a weakness in the Roman military system. The Roman army was a stationary army, and each legion was permanently posted to a province. In the first century, the officers and the majority of ordinary soldiers had been Romans or Italians whose loyalties were first and foremost to Rome. In the second century there began a gradual change in the makeup of the army, and commanders as well as soldiers were recruited from the provinces. Their loyalties were therefore more local than Roman. When the frontiers were overrun in the third century, the legions quickly became aware of their increased importance for defense and seized this opportunity to reject imperial authority. Sometimes whole provinces seceded, at least temporarily—even so Romanized a province as Gaul. At best, the legions demanded more pay; at worst, they put forward their commanders as emperors.

The lack of a fixed method for selecting the emperor was one of the single most serious flaws in the Augustan system. Since Augustus claimed to restore the republic, he could not at the same time establish a hereditary monarchy. The way succession generally worked during the principate was that the emperor designated his successor and the Senate approved the choice. Sometimes the nominee was a member of the emperor's family, sometimes not. This was a process in which no constitutional principle was adhered to—only arrangements that on the whole proved satisfactory. However, in the third century the legions took it upon themselves to create, and murder, emperors at an extraordinary rate. Soldiers elevated their own commanders to the imperial purple and the consequent wars among the legions, coupled with the foreign wars, drastically undermined Rome's political and economic stability.

The government needed huge sums of money for defense so

taxes were raised continuously and collected more strenuously than ever before. The two main taxes were a poll tax and a land tax. The latter was the more important source of revenue, and the government insisted that increased amounts be paid, whether land was actually under cultivation or not. Exactions were unequal, and it was the small farmer who felt the burden most acutely. As his taxes went up he had to borrow to pay them, and if he could not repay his loan he finally had to turn over his land to creditors. Many small farmers were thus forced either to become sharecroppers, or *coloni,* on someone else's land or to flee to join the ranks of the urban poor.

Spiraling inflation in the third century was coupled with a decline in commercial activity. Cities could not collect enough taxes

Roman banker depicted with two of Rome's poor (3rd c. A.D.). *This relief dramatizes the social ills brought about by a system of excessive taxation, and particularly the fact that some new taxes levied during the later Empire had to be paid in agricultural products and manufactured goods.* (DEUTSCHES ARCHAOLOGISCHES INSTITUT, ROM.)

15

to meet the expenses of municipal services, and the imperial government insisted that cities take over more responsibilities just when they could barely afford to continue their normal functions. The wealthier members of the councils and senates were first asked, and then forced, to make increasingly larger personal contributions; and many tried to leave their cities because they simply could not meet these demands.

During the early empire Roman towns had been unfortified, except for those close to the frontiers and, here and there, some walled towns. In the late third century the emperor Aurelian (270–275) built a massive wall around Rome, and most other cities followed suit in building walls and fortifications. Such measures, of course, were yet another expense. They were also positive evidence of a new defensiveness and fear spreading through the empire—a lack of confidence in the ability of the government to protect its citizens and maintain order. Order was finally restored and the empire was rescued, but in the process the empire was radically altered.

The first stage in arresting the turmoil was accomplished by Diocletian (284–305), who had risen through the ranks of the army and had been elevated to the imperial throne by his legions. The irregular way in which Diocletian had become emperor and the fact of being faced with an administrative machine in a state of collapse made clear to him the absolute necessity of finding a system to provide for the smooth succession to power. The wars had also made clear the need for securing tight control over the provinces and for establishing an administrative center in the East, where the frontiers needed careful watching. Diocletian worked out a formula which divided the empire for administrative purposes among four rulers—two in the East and two in the West, with varying levels of responsibility. He chose Nicomedia in Asia Minor as the eastern capital from which he ruled.

Diocletian doubled the size of his army and changed its organization. He replaced the stationary legions with smaller mobile forces located within the provinces, and the frontiers were guarded by semibarbarian soldier-farmers. The fifty provinces were divided into over one hundred areas, called dioceses, and the civil

Diocletian and his three imperial colleagues in battle dress. Porphyry sculpture, San Marco, Venice. (FOTOTECA UNIONE, ROME)

and military commands were separated to prevent a concentration of power in the hands of any one individual.

The security of the state was of paramount importance, and for that there was a continuous need for large sums of money. Diocletian's solution was to turn the state into a huge tax-collecting machine and impose a rigid system of taxation upon all. In order to curtail inflation, provide a steady income to the state, and feed and supply the army Diocletian attempted to fix prices for goods and necessary services throughout the empire. To keep the econ-

17

omy running he forced citizens to remain at their jobs and keep their land under cultivation. Yet his attempt at regimentation worked less well than he wished because he could not fully control the movements of his subjects. Nor could he control the fluctuations in agricultural supply and demand which dictated prices with greater effect than any imperial edict. With all its problems, however, the system begun by Diocletian and continued by his successor, Constantine, arrested the disintegration of the empire.

The price exacted from the Roman people for the recovery of the fourth century was high; and they paid with the loss of personal freedom and opportunity. The government and its subjects were well on their way to becoming estranged from one another. Diocletian's rule was completely autocratic, based on his control over the army and a highly centralized bureaucracy. His nomenclature, in contrast to that of the early emperors, is very revealing of the change which had occurred in the conception of the imperial position. Augustus had considered himself *Princeps inter pares*—first among equals. Diocletian chose to have himself called *"Dominus,"* or "Lord." Remote from his subjects, the emperor now ruled from a splendid palace, his every move carefully guarded, his court run by a formal etiquette designed to keep his subjects in awe of him.

Rome's Internal Problem: The Growth of Christianity

Diocletian retired in 305 A.D. One of his last official acts before giving up the throne was to institute an empire-wide persecution of the Christians. This was a desperate and ultimately futile effort to wipe out the group which, though small, appeared to have become a state within, and opposed to, Rome.

The official Roman policy toward Christianity had passed through several phases since the founding of the religion at the beginning of the empire. In general, the Romans had accepted the huge variety and range of religious groups that existed along with Christianity in the early empire. One thing only the Romans

demanded from all their subjects: worship of the gods and god-
desses of the official Roman pantheon. The Romans believed it
was the duty and responsibility of the government, as it had been
from the earliest period of Rome's history, to make certain that
the deities who protected the state were propitiated. It was the
government's duty to keep the gods in the right relationship to
Rome by building and tending the temples and carrying out public
sacrifices. To the ancient pantheon the imperial government added
the worship of the deified emperors. These official deities were
intended to inspire devotion to the empire and foster a sense of
continuity with the past, and it was incumbent upon all who lived
under the protection of these gods to sacrifice to them on public
occasions as a demonstration of loyalty to Rome. For pagans, such
worship was presumably easily performed. It is inherent in poly-
theism that there would be no conflict between worshipping at
a shrine of Asclepius, the god of healing, and then at a temple
dedicated to Rome and Augustus. And the Roman government
was readily prepared to grant licenses to carry on their cult activities to the followers of the Egyptian goddess Isis, the Persian
Mithra, the Greek Asclepius, and a host of others.

Only the Jews had asked for, and received, exemption from
worship of the Roman gods. When Rome had conquered the
province of Judaea in the last days of the republic, the Jews had
attained a unique position in their relations with the Roman government. They agreed to pay heavy taxes to Rome and offer
prayers in their temples on behalf of Rome and the emperors, in
return for which they were freed from the obligation of sacrifice
to the pagan gods.

Since Christ and his first followers were Jews, it is not surprising
that it took the Roman government several decades to understand
that a new and distinctive religion had broken away from its
Jewish background. The earliest known persecution of the Christians occurred under the emperor Nero in 64 A.D. when Christians
were blamed for a huge fire which destroyed an entire area of
Rome. It is not absolutely clear why the Christians were chosen
as the scapegoats for this fire, though the small community in
Rome had begun to exhibit qualities which the Romans intensely

disliked. The Christians had not asked, as the Jews had, for official recognition of their religion, nor did they ever ask for any of the privileges the Jews had received. Instead, they organized and behaved as a secret society—sufficient of itself to turn the Romans against them. The early church drew its membership primarily from among the lower classes, which made it appear socially disreputable. All sorts of stories circulated about the secret rites practiced by the Christians, among them that they sacrificed infants. Since Christians were not charged with specific crimes during their persecution by Nero, the precedent was thus established that simply to confess to being a Christian constituted a crime.

The imperial policy set forth early in the second century was that Christians were not to be hunted down, but when, for some

Three Boys in the Fiery Furnace (2nd c. A.D.). *Scene of Christian martydom painted on the walls of the Catacomb of St. Priscilla in Rome, one of the places where the early Christians buried their dead. The theme of the three youths burned in the furnace was taken from the Old Testament and used by the Christians as a symbol of faith strengthened by persecution.* (FOTOTECA UNIONE, ROME)

20

reason, they were brought to the attention of the local provincial magistrates they were to be required to make public sacrifice to the Roman gods as proof that they were not Christians. If they refused, they could be persecuted. Until the mid-third century persecutions were sporadic and local, which does not detract from the fact that Christians were at various times and in various places persecuted and subjected to cruel tortures in an attempt to force them to recant. But here there is an interesting paradox: With each successive persecution the church was strengthened, and nothing is truer than the axiom that "the blood of the martyrs was the seed of the church."

Martyrdom—indeed, the *seeking* of martyrdom—is in the most literal sense the way of the Cross, the perfect imitation of the life and death of Christ. The works of early Christian writers are filled with examples of the horrors perpetrated upon the Christians to force them to deny their religion: "Some were scraped, racked, mercilessly flogged, subjected to countless other torments too terrible to describe in endless variety, and finally given to the flames." And yet, "[a]ll the time," the writer continues, "I observed a most wonderful eagerness and truly divine power and enthusiasm in those who had put their trust in the Christ of God. No sooner had the first batch been sentenced, than others from every side would jump on to the platform in front of the judge and proclaim themselves Christians."[1]

The first full-scale imperial persecution of Christians was proclaimed by the emperor Decius in the midst of the chaos of the third century (249–250). This was during a period when popular hostility toward the Christians ran very high because they were not supporting the state in a time of crisis. But once again the pursuit and harrassment only served to demonstrate that the Christians could neither be wiped out nor forced in large numbers to recant. By the time of the next persecution, under Diocletian in 303, popular sentiment towards the Christians had softened. Romans were less attached to imperial policy in general, and they had come to admire the Christians' willingness—even eagerness—

1. Eusebius, *The History of the Church from Christ to Constantine*, trans. G. A. Williamson (Baltimore: Penguin Books, 1965), pp. 337–338.

21

to die for their religion. Nevertheless, the persecutions continued for several years after Diocletian retired.

In 305 Diocletian abdicated, as did his senior colleague Maximian in the West. Each emperor's junior colleague then moved up to become the senior ruler or Augustus. The new Eastern emperor was Galerius; the new Western emperor was Constantius, father of Constantine. Then his junior colleagues (or caesars) had to be chosen, and Galerius opposed the choice of Constantine as one of the caesars. The imperial position was not intended by Diocletian to be hereditary—he himself had no sons—and Constantine was very young. There were also other political intrigues surrounding the succession to the highest positions in the imperial government. But the succession which Diocletian thought he had provided for, and which excluded Constantine, lasted only a few months. Constantius died in Britain in 306 and Constantine, who was with him, won the immediate support of his father's legions. The Army proclaimed him Augustus for the West and since his father had held the title, Constantine's acceptance of it benefitted from a certain aura of legality. Immediately, there were other claimants for the imperial throne, but after several years of complicated military and political jockeying for power, there remained only one major rival in the West—another so-called emperor, Maxentius. The decisive battle for imperial power took place in 312 near the Mulvian Bridge, which spans the Tiber River in Rome.

The Conversion of Constantine

There are two slightly differing accounts of the events of the night preceding the battle, but the import is the same: In a vision Constantine saw the sign of the Cross and heard the voice of Christ saying, "In this sign you shall conquer." The next morning he had the Cross or the first two letters of Christ's name—it is uncertain which—placed on the banner he carried at the head of his army when he marched into battle. Constantine's victory gave him the Western Empire, and in gratitude, or perhaps as his end

Head of Constantine, the first Christian emperor (307 A.D.–337 A.D.). (METROPOLITAN MUSEUM OF ART. BEQUEST OF MARY CLARK THOMPSON, 1926)

of a bargain with the God of the Christians, he promulgated the Edict of 313, which made Christianity a legal religion, officially sanctioned.

Constantine's was not the first edict of toleration for the Christians ever written, but it was the first ever enforced. The persecution begun by Diocletian in 303 had actually been ordered stopped in 311, but this had been more of a short-term reprieve than a cessation—until Constantine's decision. The imperial edict not only enforced toleration, it granted the Christians many privileges. Constantine himself gave money for the building of churches, land confiscated from the Christians was restored to them, and, when possible, Christians were favored by the imperial household. All this happened despite the fact that Christians were a small minority in the empire: It has been estimated that only about one-tenth of the Roman population was Christian at the beginning of the fourth century, that Christians were primarily in the East, and that the majority came from the urban lower classes.

The precise reasons for Constantine's legislation of peace towards Christians will never be known; and the nature and extent of his personal spiritual commitment to Christianity is an even greater unknown. His mother, Helena, had been a devout Christian, canonized by the church because she claimed to have found the relics of the cross on which Christ died. Constantine's father, Constantius, had been a pagan, however, and there is no satisfactory proof of whether or not Constantine was ever baptised in the faith he legalized. However, it may well have seemed to Constantine that if allowed to flourish Christianity could become an important unifying force in the empire.

In a world recently torn apart Christianity remained cohesive. Again and again the church had demonstrated that it had tremendous staying power and, on the whole, a fiercely loyal membership. The Christian communities looked after the welfare of their own; even their opponents had to acknowledge that the Christians cared for their widows and orphans, the poor and sick, and often ministered to non-Christians in need. The stresses and dislocations suffered particularly by the poor during the third century made them responsive to the solace offered by Christ's message of love and peace. People were drawn to the Christians, who were demonstrating a new way to behave in a world that had become quite cruel. On the whole the Christians showed the generosity of spirit that Christ had preached: "If anyone impresses you to go a mile, go along with him for two; and from one who wants to borrow from you do not turn away." (Matt. 5:41–42)

The continued growth of Christianity came to be the single most important fact of religious life during the third century. Its chief competition came from the mystery cults that flourished in the Eastern Empire. These cults, many of them very ancient, were often salvationist and stressed some kind of external revelation.

They became exceedingly popular, and by the time of Constantine one in particular, the worship of the sun god, had won large numbers of adherents principally among the soldiers and including Constantine himself in his early years. The mystery cults were discrete and exclusive entities wherever they existed in the empire, usually requiring a membership fee, social position, and an education. In contrast, Christ's death and resurrection held out the promise of salvation for everyone, excluding "neither Jew nor Greek, . . . bond nor free, . . . male nor female. . . ."

The spiritual content of Christianity was in marked contrast to the minimal religious experience offered by the worship of the gods of the Greek and Roman pantheon. This contrast is best illustrated by the pagan temples, which were singularly beautiful on the outside but notably spare on the inside. (The worship of the gods was thus external in both the literal and figurative sense.) The early Christian churches were built in exactly the opposite way, to draw people into the inner and spiritual experience of the religion, thus reminding them that Christ's kingdom "was not of this world."

The Organization of the Church

Christianity's problem was that it had to exist in the real world, and to that end it perfected its organization. By the age of Constantine the main lines of development had been clearly marked. The most important authority of the church resided in the bishops. In the earliest Christian communities there had been no distinction between bishop and priest, and the two titles had even been used interchangeably. By the middle of the third century, however, the bishop had come to be head of the largest church in a diocese where there might also be many smaller congregations, the latter directed by priests. Most often the episcopal churches—those headed by bishops—were in the provincial capitals of the empire; as Christianity expanded, its organization closely followed the pattern of Roman civil provincial administration.

The special role of the bishop was also given a spiritual basis—

the belief that he was the successor in authority and spiritual power of the original Apostles, who had in turn received their special powers directly from Christ. The text for this belief is in the Gospel of St. Matthew, where Christ says to St. Peter, "Thou art Peter, and upon this rock I will build my church; and the gates of hell shall not prevail against it." (Matt. 16:18) The ordination—or installation—of a new bishop is the ceremony by which this spiritual authority is passed on, in perpetuity. Although priests are also ordained, they do not receive the full apostolic powers of the bishop—another distinction between bishop and priest as different orders of the ministry.

As the powers of bishop and priest evolved and became differentiated, a distinction was also being made between the ministry and the congregation. The first followers of Christ regarded themselves as the community of the faithful to whom the second coming of Jesus had been promised; but as the expectation of the Day of Last Judgment was postponed, the church evolved its role as the instrument through which ongoing individual salvation might be attained. More specifically, this salvation could only be attained through the sacraments or rituals of the church. There were three sacraments in the early church: baptism, the Eucharist, and penance. Baptism was the act by which converts were cleansed of their past sins and born anew into the Christian faith. The Eucharist was, and is, the central ritual of Christian worship: It recalls Christ's Last Supper with his Apostles when he said "this is my body" and "this is my blood" over the bread and wine. Penance was the sacrament through which the Christian confessed and undertook punishment in return for God's forgiveness of sins. As the sacraments were formulated, the office of those specially ordained to perform them took on an increasingly sacred character.

There was, finally, a hierarchy developing among the bishops themselves. The bishops of those churches which could actually trace their founding to an Apostle were regarded as particularly prestigious. These included, for example, the bishops at Rome, Ephesus, Antioch, and Alexandria. The idea that the bishop of Rome was supreme above all other bishops had begun to be accepted by the western bishops by the time of Constantine and was based on several factors. The church at Rome was the only apostolic church in the West, and it furthermore had a double apostolic tradition: the belief that St. Peter had founded the church and that St. Paul had visited Rome and been martyred there. That St. Peter's Church was in the imperial capital gave it additional prestige. The final elaboration of the idea of Rome's spiritual supremacy was, as we shall see, a development of the mid-fifth century.

"The Foxes that Spoil the Vines": The Problem of Heresy

One of the major internal problems confronting the growing church was that of heresy. In Christian terms, a *heresy* is a religious opinion which does not conform to the established doctrine of the church; it is a doctrine put forward in the name of Christianity but declared to be an error. Heresy as an issue in the history of the Christian church is linked to the very heart of Christianity.

The single word which best describes and explains the core of Christianity is *orthodoxy*, which comes from the Greek and means "right belief." The essence of being a Christian is maintaining the "right belief." This emphasis on orthodoxy itself rests on the belief that Christianity is a God-given revelation, complete and perfect. But although the revelation is divine, the expounding of it—the work of defining Christian doctrine—is a human affair, an ongoing process subject to error and to change. The core of the revelation is contained in the Gospels and in the teachings of St. Paul, but since there was sometimes great variety of interpretation, the problem was to determine the "right belief." This became the work of the bishops who, as successors to the Apostles, were believed to be divinely inspired and guided. Until the reign of Constantine, the bishops met in small, local councils to resolve disputed issues. When a doctrine was accepted, it became orthodoxy; when rejected, it was branded a heresy.

During Constantine's reign a dispute arose which was important in and of itself and because of the precedents that were established by its resolution. This controversy was called "the Arian dispute," from the name of the leader of the movement, a priest in Alexandria named Arius. Arius' doctrine was one of the first attempts to deal with the many theological difficulties posed by the concept of the Trinity and the belief in the Incarnation of Christ. The difficulties began with the question of the relationship between God the Father and Christ the Son and proceeded to the problem of how Christ's divine nature (as the Son of God) and his human nature related to each other.

Basically, Arius insisted on the difference between Christ's divine nature and the nature of God. At the same time he also rejected the full humanity of Christ, an argument which, if carried to its logical conclusion, robbed Christ's suffering and Crucifixion of its meaning for mankind. Arius' doctrine was put forward in 318 and was immediately refuted by the bishop of Alexandria, Athanasius. By the time Constantine became emperor in the East the church was sharply divided over the Arian controversy.

From Constantine's point of view, the church's unity was essential, and he determined to take a hand in resolving the dispute. He therefore called the first ecumenical council of the church at Nicaea in 325. The council pronounced Arianism a heresy and formulated the orthodox position of the church, the Nicene Creed, which asserts both the full divinity and full humanity of Christ. The fact that Constantine actually presided over the Council of Nicaea set a precedent for imperial control over future church councils. The bishop of Rome absented himself from Nicaea, but Constantine's supremacy over the Eastern bishops, and their acceptance of his role, defined their relationship from that time on and precluded the growth of an independent church in the East.

It was one thing to declare Arianism heretical, but quite another to eliminate it. The heresy flourished until nearly the end of the century, and before it died out in the East Arian Christian missionaries began the conversion of some of the German tribes near the eastern borders of the empire. Thus, although the Arian heresy did not spread among the native Roman population in the West, it was the form of Christianity adhered to by many Germans when they invaded the Western Empire in the fifth century. The

Western church was, in fact, quite free of the particular heresies which divided the Eastern church in the centuries after Nicaea.[2]

The heresy which arose in the Western church at the time of Constantine and which affected Western Christianity for more than a century was Donatism. Named for its leader Donatus, it began in the North African church at the end of the imperial persecutions and arose from the problem then facing all Christian communities: Whether or not to take back into the church those members who had renounced their faith to save their own lives.

The decision of the majority of Christian communities—and supported by the bishop of Rome—was to restore everyone to the fold, but Donatus believed that the church was a church of saints and that those who had been traitors therefore did not belong. There were serious consequences of the Donatus position. Among the recanters were priests, who had surrendered the Holy Scriptures to save themselves. Donatus believed that the sacraments performed by such priests were invalid due to the deficient character of the celebrants.

Although Donatism was declared heretical early in the fourth century, it continued to grow in North Africa, where it flourished as an independent church. It was not finally eliminated until the fifth century, and then only with great difficulty. The Christian church's main spokesman against the Donatists was St. Augustine (354–430), who propounded its doctrine as related to the central issues of Donatism. The Christian church, Augustine maintained, is universal and not a church of saints; and the sacrament is a divine miracle and therefore independent of the character of the person who performs it.

The Church's Final Victory

Even with its organization and a rapid increase in its membership in the aftermath of Constantine's Edict of Toleration, the church's complete victory over paganism was by no means assured.

2. The two major Eastern heresies, Nestorianism and Monophysitism, will be discussed in the context of the Eastern empire in the next chapter.

30

Constantine had established a hereditary dynasty; at his death in 337, he was succeeded by his son. Constantius II (337–361) continued his father's favorable policies towards the Christians and even encouraged those who sought advancement in the government to convert to Christianity. But in the years 361–363 Julian, called "the Apostate," ruled the empire. Although born a Christian, he was educated as a philosopher in the Graeco-Roman tradition and sincerely believed that the world was waiting to be delivered from Christianity. Julian's beliefs, though larded heavily with mysticism, reflected those of many Roman senators, who clung tenaciously to the paganism of their forebears. Julian closed the churches and tried to restore paganism to its former position. His policy was a failure; Julian knew it, and there is a story that on his deathbed, as he breathed his last, he said, "Pale Galilean, thou hast conquered."

The final stage in the church's victory over its pagan rivals is summarized beautifully in an exchange of letters between a Roman senator and one of the greatest of the church Fathers, St. Ambrose. The specific issue dealt with a pagan Altar of Victory before which the Roman senators had offered sacrifices each time they met, according to tradition since the founding of the republic. The altar had been removed by Constantine's son, replaced by Julian, and after his death, removed again. In 384 the Senate made a plea for the altar and the paganism it symbolized. It is Rome who speaks:

"Let me use my ancestral ceremonies," she says, "for I do not repent me of them. Let me live after my own way . . . I do but ask peace for the gods of our fathers, the native gods of Rome. . . . What matters it by what kind of learned theory each man looketh for the truth? There is no one way that will take us to so mighty a secret. All this is matter of discussion for men of leisure. We offer your majesties not a debate but a plea."

←————————————————————————————————————

Ivory relief, commemorating the marriage of the daughter of the pagan Senator, Aurelius Symmachus. *The scene illustrates in its form and content the classical revival of the fourth century and the resistance of the Roman aristocracy to Christianity. The general composition recalls the great age of classical art in the early empire. The standing figure is believed to represent a priestess sacrificing to the pagan god, Bacchus.* (CROWN COPYRIGHT. VICTORIA AND ALBERT MUSEUM)

31

And St. Ambrose replies:

"Why cite me the examples of the ancients? 'Tis no disgrace to pass on to better things. . . . I suppose that back in the good old times of chaos, the conservative particles objected to the advent of the novel and vulgar sunlight which accompanied the introduction of order. But for all that, the world moved. And we Christians too have grown. Through wrongs, through poverty, through persecution, we have grown; and the great difference between us and you is that what you seek in surmises, we know."[3]

The final edicts making Christianity the only religion of the empire and outlawing paganism were promulgated by the emperor Theodosius the Great (379–395). Theodosius was a fervent, if not fanatical, Christian, and by the final three years of his rule he had succeeded in making the boundaries of the church and the boundaries of his empire coterminous. If the marriage between Christianity and the empire had its full share of problems, it had also a certain inner logic. Throughout the fourth century both empire and church, each in its separate sphere, had been moving steadily towards centralization and absolute monarchial control. Each in its own way was also becoming an increasingly elaborate, hierarchical institution.

In 390 Theodosius had an obelisk brought from Egypt to Constantinople. On the four sides of its base are reliefs showing the emperor in various scenes. The way in which Theodosius is depicted is a perfect illustration of the changes in the fourth century: He is represented in almost superhuman form. Whether he is shown receiving tribute, presiding over games, or with his family, he is portrayed as the summit of the hierarchy, which conveys more eloquently than words the concept of the imperial office. Thus the absolutism of the emperor, begun by Diocletian and Constantine, was strengthened under Theodosius by its final Christian transformation.

3. E. K. Rand, *Founders of the Middle Ages* (Cambridge, Mass.: Harvard University Press, 1928) pp. 16–17.

Theodosius' Obelisk. *This side of the monument shows the emperor Theodosius watching games or chariot races in the famous Hippodrome in Constantinople. The Obelisk still stands in the city renamed Istanbul.* (HIRMER FOTOARCHIV)

The Founding of Constantinople

Few—if any—rulers in history have made a single decision as critical for the future as Constantine's determination to legalize Christianity. Constantine also made a second decision of almost equivalent consequence—the founding of the city of Constantinople.

Throughout the fourth century the main resistance to Christianization came from the Roman Senate. It began when Constantine declared his intention to convert Rome from a pagan to a Christian capital. Though its members were no longer drawn exclusively from the old republican aristocracy, even the new members had absorbed the traditions of the Senate and, to the senators more than to anyone else, the concern for Rome and the care of the ancient gods who protected Rome were inextricably linked.

Confronted with senatorial resistance and influenced as well by his desire to win the entire empire, Constantine left Rome for the East. In 324 he defeated his former colleague, the Eastern emperor Licinius. Very soon afterward he solved, for over a thousand years, the problem of a capital for the East. As its site Constantine chose an ancient Greek city, Byzantium, which he dedicated in 330 under the new name Constantinople. This was in every sense a perfect choice: The city on the Bosphorus commanded, as Istanbul still does, both Asia and Europe. Moreover, the surrounding mountains and water made it naturally easy to defend and, fortified by the addition of a massive wall, it became almost impossible to invade. Control of the entrance to the Mediterranean and Black Seas soon made Constantinople the wealthiest city in the East. The Eastern Empire was able to survive and thrive due to the enormous revenue from the trade which flowed into and out of its capital. And, above all, because Rome had not done so, Constantinople became the Christian capital of the empire.

It was not Constantine's intention to create a permanent division between the East and West; the cultural separation had, after all, existed long before the founding of the empire. But Constantinople became both the symbol and the epitome of a transformation which took place in the East during the centuries following Constantine's death. Although it was not truly the "new Rome," as Constantine liked to call it, Constantinople was a Roman imperial capital, ruled by Roman law and in its beginnings, Latin-speaking, Roman-minded emperors. It was also a city essentially Eastern and distinctly Greek in culture. The leaven which, over time, turned these ingredients into the new amalgam of Byzantine civilization was Christianity.

Constantine's plan in founding Constantinople had been to have joint rulers for East and West. He had hoped, by dividing the administrative work, to hold the empire together and, until the end of Theodosius' reign (395) that hope was fulfilled. But Theodosius' last three years as emperor (during which he happened to rule alone) were also the last three years that the Roman Empire at its greatest extent was held together.

Rome's External Problem: The Germans

In 395, the year of Theodosius' death, the German tribe known as the Visigoths moved into the Western Empire. Soon afterward, and with astonishing speed, the provinces of the West began to fall into German hands. The Germans were by no means a new problem to the Roman government, but by the end of the fourth century the problem was different and, finally, overwhelming.[4]

Our record of the Germanic tribes before their first sustained contacts with Rome is very meager. The slow migration of these nomadic peoples from their homeland in Scandinavia had begun in about 1000 B.C., but it was not until the second half of the first century B.C. that the Romans came face to face with them for the first time. They had no written language until late in their history, so there were no Germanic recorded sources until long after their final settlements in Europe. The later chronicles they wrote provide us with some information, as do the Roman historians, but even with the help of archaeology and linguistics our picture is far from complete. Added to this is the difficulty of conveying in a single sentence the hundreds of years of wandering before the tribes reached the Rhine or the Danube Basin.

In the course of their long migration the Germans had pushed before them yet another group of nomadic peoples from the same Indo-European parent stock—the Celts. The latter settled primarily in Gaul (to the Romans they were known as Gauls) and the British Isles shortly after 400 B.C. From Gaul they moved southward into Italy (once in 390 invading even Rome itself) until gradually the Romans were able to contain them in the north. In

4. The term "German" is actually the name of one particular tribe but is conventionally used to refer to the group of related tribes.

49 B.C. Julius Caesar conquered Gaul, bringing the heart of western Europe into the framework of Roman civilization, and bringing Roman power right up the German settlements east of the Rhine.

In the next generation, when Augustus established the empire, he made one disastrous attempt to push the Germans further to the northeast as far as the Elbe River. When that failed, he established the Rhine-Danube as the permanent boundary of the empire. From then on, it became imperial policy to maintain that boundary.

The Germans facing the Romans across the Rhine were by now no longer completely nomadic. They farmed, although their primary occupation was hunting and raising animals, which meant that the population was scattered rather than concentrated. They lived in small, unwalled, village communities, and their largest political and social unit was the tribe. The Germans were good fighters, and one of the essential relationships in their social system was that between warrior and tribal leader. The Germanic tribes closest to the Roman border became familiar with Roman civilization. In the early fourth century some of these were even encouraged by the government to enter the Western Empire gradually and in small numbers because the Germans were needed as workers on large estates or as recruits in the army. This latter capacity explains why so much of the defense of the empire against the German invaders of the fifth century was carried on by other Germans.

The slow and normally peaceful movement of Germans into the empire had been seriously interrupted during the third century by the invasions of the most warlike of the Germanic tribes. These had caused a great deal of devastation, but by the reign of Diocletian the Rhine-Danube border had been restored intact and, although at enormous cost, the Romans were able to maintain an equilibrium between themselves and the Germans for many decades thereafter.

At the end of the fourth century that equilibrium was again violently disturbed by the advent of the Huns. Pushed out of

China, they were the first in what was to be a long line of invaders from the East. The Huns descended, fiercely and seemingly out of the blue, upon the Western Empire. Their ability to fight on horseback awed and finally defeated the Ostrogoths, who were the first German tribe the Huns encountered in their westward move.

The Visigoths, who lived along the lower Danube and seemed to be next in the Hunnish line of march, begged the Roman emperor Valens to be allowed to cross into the shelter of the Roman frontier, and in 376 he permitted the entire tribe to enter Thrace. Two years later, dissatisfied—apparently with good cause—with the treatment they were receiving, the Visigoths turned against the Romans, defeated them at the Battle of Adrianople (378), and killed Valens. Although subsequently given land in Greece by emperor Theodosius, the Visigoths remained there only until Theodosius' death in 395 when, led by their king Alaric, they began their march into the Western Empire in search of better land.

At that time Honorius, who had inherited the West from his father, was young and incompetent (as was his brother in the East) and the defense of the West was directed by a German (probably Vandal) general, Stilicho. As the Visigoths approached Italy, Stilicho made the decision to withdraw a large number of the legions stationed along the Rhine and move them southward to give Italy better protection. This was a critical and indeed fatal decision (which cost Stilicho his life) because several German tribes immediately broke through the border and crossed into the empire. From 406 onward the German problem ceased forever to be an "external" problem, and within less than thirty years Roman territory in Gaul, Spain, and North Africa had been occupied by German tribes.

The Visigoths were the first to found a kingdom within the empire. As other Germans poured into Gaul, the Visigoths continued their march into Italy, and in 410 they sacked Rome. Their attack on the capital was psychologically more than physically damaging, and its effect was heightened because the emperor was forced to abandon the city for the relative safety of Ravenna. The Visigoths marched throughout the Italian peninsula, then turned northward into southern France, and by 418 the emperor was ready to concede to them what he no longer had the power to refuse—land in western Gaul. From there as a base, the Visigoths spread southward across the Pyrenees into Spain.

The second major Germanic kingdom was established by the Vandals in North Africa in 429. Such was the wanton destruction of their long march through Gaul and Spain on the way to North Africa that the term *vandalism* derives its meaning from their name. The kingdom of the Vandals was particularly important because from it a fleet was built which threatened imperial naval power and trade in the western Mediterranean. And in 455 the Vandals sacked Rome.

The third important settlement before 450 was made by the Burgundians in the Rhone Valley. By this time Gaul—of all the Western provinces it had suffered the most from the constant fighting and plundering of the fifth century—had been overrun by German tribes.

Until now the Huns had been kept out of the empire by a monetary tribute which was being paid by the Eastern emperors. In 450 the emperors stopped payment and in 451 the Huns, led by Attila, invaded Gaul. They were defeated by an army carrying the imperial standard but composed mainly of Germans, and the next year they marched into Italy where, according to tradition, Attila was persuaded by Pope Leo I to leave. It may have been the pope who persuaded Attila to turn back, but it is more likely that his army had been so decimated by a plague raging at the time that he could not have continued. In either event, the sad reality is that there remained no Roman power of any consequence in Italy for Attila to conquer. There were, instead, roving bands of Germans and Huns who supported puppet-emperors. In 476 Odoacer, a German (or perhaps Hunnish) general, deposed the twelve-year-old boy Romulus Augustulus who was, as it turned out, the last Roman emperor of the West. This is a sorry and empty gesture which can hardly be said to have caused the decline of the Western Empire.

The Contrast Between East and West

The question, of course, is why Roman power in the West should have succumbed so quickly and so completely. The answer can best be understood in terms of the differences between East and West on the eve of the Germanic invasions. The Eastern Empire suffered its own German problem but was nevertheless able to survive—often against great odds—until 1453. The East had one fortunate, if accidental, advantage: It had only the lower Danube to defend against the Germans, while the Western Empire had the entire length of the Rhine and the upper Danube to protect. Furthermore, the Eastern emperors were skillful at persuading or paying the Visigoths, Ostrogoths, and Huns to go westward after they crossed the Danube. Since the majority of tribes were, to begin with, massed closest to the Rhine, the West suffered the full force of the invasions.

The critical factor, however, was the difference in resources on which the two halves of the empire could draw at the beginning of the fifth century. The contrasts, in fact, go back to a much earlier time. At the founding of the empire the East had been far more populous and far more urbanized than the West, and had already developed important centers of industry and trade. Although the emperors of the first two centuries, following the Greek tradition, had founded many new cities and had encouraged industry in the West, this gap was never closed. The East had been, from the very beginning, the economic heart of the empire, and its power to recover remained always far greater than that of the West.

There were also larger reserves of manpower in the East, and the general state of agriculture and of the peasantry was healthier by far than that of the West. (As long as Constantinople retained control of Egypt, a substantial part of the Eastern Empire was fed from the grain produced there.) The West was faced with a shortage of manpower at precisely the moment when it required enormous reserves of manpower for its army and the cultivation of the land. Gaul was the most populous of the Western provinces, but its population was still only one-third that of Egypt, the most densely populated province in the East. And Gaul, the richest Western province, had also suffered the greatest devastation and depletion of human and economic resources during the German invasions. Besides the lack of human power, the West was now in the throes of its most serious food shortage, just when food was most urgently needed. (The major source of grain for the Western Empire had been North Africa, but that supply had been cut off when the Vandals had settled there.)

The peasant in the West had been in an extremely difficult position well before the fifth century, and this now worsened considerably. The marginal existence of many small, independent farmers had been depressed by the extraordinary financial needs of the government during the third century. The government had pressured everyone in the attempt to collect taxes in coin and in kind, but the greatest pressure, as we have seen, had been sustained by the small farmer. Quite simply, if he could not pay the increasingly heavy requisitions placed on his land, he had to abandon it or sell it for very little. This was a situation which profited the wealthy who were able to buy land cheaply, so that in the end, the rich landowner grew richer and the poor were often forced to become tenant farmers simply in order to survive. This trend, already marked during the third century, worsened during the fourth and fifth.

The displaced peasant in the West had one other very limited choice—that of moving to the city. But there was a sharp contrast between the cities of the East and the West. In the East many were still flourishing centers of trade and industry, viable and self-sustaining. (This is a generalization for which there are exceptions, but it is basically true that the economic life in such cities as Constantinople, Antioch, and Alexandria was sufficiently healthy to contribute to the vitality of the empire.) Many of the Western cities, on the other hand, had never derived wealth from industry or trade and were primarily administrative or educational centers. They had been created for those purposes, and they were usually controlled by landowners, not merchants. When the rural population went to the cities the influx created an economic strain on the cities which they could ill afford. The cities throughout the empire had been expected to support public works: repair or build roads and buildings, maintain public education, and carry on local administration. Under the combined pressure of this declining economy and the German invasions, the cities of northern Gaul, Spain, and North Africa began to shrink in size and purpose. One of the sadder consequences of this was the attrition of a fine system of education in the northern cities of Gaul.

There were some Western cities which survived into the Middle Ages. This is especially true of the Italian cities and port cities such as Marseilles, but their ability to recuperate from the invasions was severely limited and therefore slow.

The Effect of the German Invasions

The end of this first stage of the German invasions saw the breakdown of imperial authority in the West, but two important facts should be borne in mind in assessing the effects of these events. First, the Germans entered a world which politically and economically was far different at the end of the fourth century from that of the empire at its height in the second century. Without question, the Germans accelerated the changes but the alterations that were going on in the empire had begun long before they came. The other fact of great consequence is that the breakdown of imperial authority was not synonymous with the demise of the civilization of the classical Roman world.

Although the year 476 has often been assigned to mark the so-called fall of the empire, it is useful as a date only in signifying the end of a process which had been ongoing for nearly seventy years. Imperial power in the Western provinces had begun to recede as early as 406, when the Germans overran Gaul. From then on, the withdrawal of Roman legions and Roman authority presents a spectacle much like that of the withdrawal of the British from their colonies in this century (except that the fate of the native populations in each case was different). Throughout the West the story was the same. Roman protection was gradually removed from northern Gaul and Spain in an effort to save Provence and Italy from invasion. During the early decades of the fifth century all Roman legions had been withdrawn from Britain, leaving that island vulnerable to the Germans, who immediately moved in. The boundaries of the empire continued to contract steadily. St. Augustine who, during his life (354–430) witnessed the Vandal invasion of North Africa, recorded the fact that there were simply not sufficient legions to defend the cities, which fell to the Vandals with almost no resistance at all. (This alone is a remarkably telling fact, because the Italians for centuries had depended on the grain raised in Africa.)

The main resistance to the invasions centered in Gaul and Italy, and in both provinces the cities which were able to do so undertook their own defense, directed principally by the church officials. The bishops, who most often came from the aristocracy and had been educated for public service, moved into the power vacuum left by the Roman administration. In an earlier age these prelates might have been prefects of their cities, and since they belonged to a class accustomed to civic responsibility they assumed it naturally. The Germans who had been Christianized before they entered the empire were Arian, and therefore heretical Christians. The difference in belief between the orthodox Romans and these heretical invaders created an impassable gulf and the resistance of the orthodox church to the Germans took on the character of a holy war. Meanwhile, the role assumed by the bishops had the important effect of strengthening the power of the local churches and the clergy throughout Europe.

The Developments within Christianity in the Fourth and Fifth Centuries

Christianity and Classical Culture

There seems to be almost a neat balance between the contraction of imperial authority and the expansion of the church's power. Under the pressure of the German invasions the Roman emperors relinquished their control of Western Europe, and many imperial traditions passed to the ecclesiastical hierarchy. Meanwhile, Christianity was also incorporating many of the cultural traditions of the Roman world, and there the difficulties confronted by the church were considerable. Christianity's relationship to Roman culture—both *whether* and *how* to relate a Christian view of man and the world to Roman civilization—was part of the larger problem of Christianity's relationship to the world itself and to "the treasures on earth." This was a religious concern of a profound nature.

From the beginning, there was a world-rejecting strain within Christianity based on Jesus' words: "My kingdom is not of this world." The act of Christian conversion necessitated rejecting all worldly ties, and everything in the history of the pre-Constantinian church confirmed and strengthened this belief. "The man who loves father and mother more than me," Christ said, "is not worthy of me; . . . he that wins his life will lose it, and he that loses his life for my sake will win it." (Matt. 10:36, 39) The early Christians saw themselves as aliens in a world set against them, and this sense of their own estrangement was quite realistic. They also saw themselves as pilgrims and voyagers through the world while not really being part of it.

There is also an anti-intellectual strain in Christianity which stems from the conviction that faith, unencumbered by intellectual knowledge, is the main path to God. "Hath not God made foolish the wisdom of this world?" St. Paul wrote to the Corinthians, for "faith should not stand in the wisdom of men, but in the power of God." (I Cor. 1:20; I Cor. 2:7) Faith, pure and simple, nurtured mainly by the Gospels, was the principal way of coming close to God, and the "wisdom of men" was worse than useless. It is therefore not surprising to find that the initial Christian reaction to classical culture was to reject it completely. "What has Athens to do with Jerusalem?" asked a Christian writer, Tertullian, at the end of the second century. "Avoid completely heathen books! . . . for what do you lack in the word of God that you shall partake yourselves to these heathen tales?"

The early Christian communities were composed mainly of the poor and the uneducated; and although there was always a sprinkling of the literate among the membership of the church, these were a small minority during the early centuries. By the second century, however, the most vocal among this minority were writing in defense of Christianity and addressing themselves to educated pagans. To do this, they needed at least the forms and styles of classical literature. As church doctrine was expanded, Christian writers came to rely on the discipline and vocabulary of ancient philosophy, and then to recognize that many of the ideas had considerable value. In the Western church before Constantine the problem of how to relate to pagan culture had not yet become a central issue; but the circumstances of the fourth century—the legalizing of Christianity, the rapid increase in church membership, the change in the social composition of the church, the onset of the German invasions, and the weakening of Roman power— brought the problem sharply into focus. By the time Christianity finally became the only religion of the empire, the resolution of this conflict had assumed paramount importance for the future.

During the fourth century the most creative and talented people in the empire were drawn to Christianity, and educated upper-class Romans began entering the church in large numbers. These were people who were not ready, or even able, to forsake Athens because they had come to Jerusalem. They recognized, furthermore, that Christianity was expanding into a world which had an ancient, rich, and pervasive cultural tradition the future of which was in jeopardy. These Roman converts also belonged to the social class which had for centuries valued classical training as necessary equipment for making one's way in the world. Since Christianity had within it an anti-pagan, anti-intellectual tradition, the problem of how—and whether—to reconcile classical culture with Christianity created painful conflicts for educated adult converts. This was not an academic problem, but one whose resolution could come only out of intense personal struggles.

Among the educated Romans who entered the church during the fourth century, three in particular were so influential in shaping the nascent Christian culture that they have been designated the Fathers of the Latin church. These were St. Jerome (340–420), St.

Ambrose (339–397), and St. Augustine (354–430). (The fourth
Latin Father, Pope Gregory the Great, lived two hundred years
later.)

St. Jerome

The career of St. Jerome illustrates the intensity of the conflict
between Christianity and pagan culture as well as the resolution
of it. Jerome's parents were wealthy upper-class Christians, and
he had been given a traditional Roman education in order to become a professional scholar. Talented and well-trained, Jerome
was deeply devoted to classical literature, and like his parents he
became a Christian convert. (It was not yet customary for infants
to be baptized at birth.) As he matured, Jerome became more
devoutly religious and the aspect of his own nature which was
sorely tempted to reject the world began to emerge. Jerome always
had been at odds with the world since he found corruption wherever he looked. His many letters reveal him to have been a crusty,
difficult man who railed against the sin and corruption that he
saw all around him.

The turning point in Jerome's life came when he dreamed that
God had turned him away from the gates of heaven because he
loved pagan books. In this dream God told Jerome that he was
a Ciceronian, not a Christian, and Jerome vowed never to read
the classics again and retreated to the Syrian desert, where he lived
for five years as a hermit. But Jerome discovered that he could
neither erase his love of learning nor tolerate the solitary life. He
went to Antioch for a time, then to Constantinople, Rome, and
finally to Bethlehem, where he lived out his life and where he
turned his immense erudition to the task of translating the Bible
into Latin. (There had previously been only two poorly done Latin
translations of the New Testament.) Jerome knew the Hebrew
and Greek languages of the Old and New Testament, and his
translation, the *Vulgate*, eventually became the authoritative Latin
Bible. Also, his commentaries on the Biblical texts were studied

Death of St. Jerome. *A fifteenth-century manuscript illustration of the death of St. Jerome in the desert. Note that the saint is dressed as a hermit. The Belles Heures of Jean, Duke de Berry.* (METROPOLITAN MUSEUM OF ART, THE CLOISTERS COLLECTION, 1954)

throughout the Middle Ages. Jerome's use of his classical scholarship in the service of Christianity summarizes the resolution of the conflict and the medieval synthesis in the larger framework. The study of classical literature was continued and the intellectual discipline involved valued so long as these could serve the Christian purpose—and without endangering the new Christian society.

St. Augustine

The single most influential church Father was St. Augustine (354–430). One is tempted to write, "In the beginning there was St. Augustine," because there was scarcely a problem confronting Christians and Christianity to which he did not address himself. Throughout the Middle Ages the discussions of the Christian way of life and of man's relations with God began with Augustine, and for nearly a thousand years Augustinian ideas, though debated and somewhat modified, were not seriously challenged.

Augustine was not, in his youth, particularly "saintly," and his road to Christianity was long and arduous. This is recorded in his spiritual autobiography, the *Confessions*, one of the greatest masterpieces of Christian literature. Augustine was born in Thagaste, a small town in the Roman province of North Africa. His father was a pagan, but his mother, Monica, was a Christian, and she expended great energy in trying to persuade her son to be baptized in his youth. Augustine seems to have been close to accepting Christianity until he attended school at Carthage, where he studied the classics and prepared to become a professor of rhetoric. It was the study of classical philosophy that turned him away from Christianity, and in this same period, when seventeen, he took a mistress by whom he had a son. During his period of studying and teaching at Carthage, Augustine became attracted to Manichaeanism, a heretical mixture of Eastern paganism and Christianity. Augustine remained an adherent of Manichaeanism for ten years, although he found it increasingly unsatisfactory.

In 383 Augustine left North Africa to go to Italy to teach first in Rome and later in Milan. In Italy he became deeply involved in the main current of philosophical speculation of the time, until he heard St. Ambrose preach. St. Ambrose was then the most influential preacher in the West and although the two had little personally to do with one another, Ambrose's sermons had an important effect on Augustine. He was already moving in the direction of Christianity and in 386 he had a revelation in which a child's voice told him "to take up and read." He knew then that he was meant to "take up" the Christian Bible: Soon afterward he was baptized. In 388 Augustine left behind his wife and son in Italy (his son died at the age of eighteen), and returned to North Africa, where he spent the remainder of his life. He devoted himself to the church, becoming first a priest and then bishop of Hippo.

In the years before he had accepted Christianity, Augustine had gone through a personal religious quest that is interesting as a human experience and interesting also because it illustrates, to a degree, the intellectual approach to God. But in the end, Augustine's conversion was an act of faith, a jump across that chasm that separates the "wisdom of men" from the "power of God." Before his conversion Augustine had been trained in and had taught the classics. He had been steeped in Greek and Roman philosophy, and he did not reject that education. Instead, he saw it as useful, and he viewed classical learning as a necessary preparation for the study of the most difficult and precious book of all—the Bible. Augustine outlined a course of learning for Christian students which began with the classics and led up to Biblical studies and the writings of Christian authors; and his plan became the model followed whenever possible throughout the Middle Ages.

Although Christianity had been made the only legal religion of the empire at the end of the fourth century, paganism had by no means been wiped out. In 410 the Visigoths sacked Rome, and the pagans raised a great hue and cry against the Christians, arguing that if Rome's gods had not been deserted, the city would have been protected. Among the Christians, too, many felt insecure and perplexed by the attack on Rome. By then Christians believed in the eternity of Rome and prayed for its safety and continuance. Even St. Jerome wrote, "If Rome be lost, where shall we look for help?" In response to the pagan attacks and the Christian doubts, Augustine wrote *The City of God*. In this monumental work he addresses himself to the specific issues raised by the sack of Rome and then goes on to formulate the Christian view of history and man's relationship with God.

In *The City of God* Augustine points out to Christians and pagans alike that everyone deserves adverse treatment at God's hands. In fact, given man's nature, it is God's justice that man suffers during his lifetime on earth. In the Augustinian view, we are the product of an historic event—our exile from the Garden of Eden. The act which no man can escape is Original Sin, which led to this fall from grace. Since the Fall, our nature is defective; we are born in sin and cannot, by our own powers, redeem ourselves. The framework of Augustine's idea is the theme of the two cities, a heavenly City of God, and an earthly city. The City of God represents eternal life which, in Augustine's words, is "the highest good" to which we can aspire; it is the salvation of the soul. Each individual has a history and a destination, and that destination leads one toward or away from the salvation of his or her soul—toward or away from the City of God. What is therefore important is not a series of external events, but the course and outcome of man's inner struggles to reach God. If we are not saved, we are then condemned forever to the earthly city and to an eternal death.

Since man cannot overcome his defective nature by himself, salvation depends on God's grace. Baptism is the sacrament which cleanses man of sin when he becomes a Christian; it is a gift from God. Throughout his life man needs a series of God's gifts to keep him from sin; and he needs God's grace in order to choose to do good rather than evil. Augustine discusses the thorny problem of man's free will and God's predestination of man's actions. This is a problem which has been debated endlessly—both for itself and as it relates to the Augustinian position. In Augustine's view, man needs God's grace in order to choose good over evil: Man has freedom of choice, but this freedom can come only from God's grace. And grace is not something which can be earned: If it could be earned—by doing good works, for example—it would no longer be a gift. The church later modified Augustine's position by stressing the value of doing good works for salvation, but his interpretation of man's nature remained the essential medieval view. The classical world had believed that man was free in the sense that he was not hampered by his own nature. It was also believed that good and evil were forces external to man which therefore could be overcome, if one so desired, by placating the gods or by understanding them in a rational way. The great change introduced by the Christian view is that man is disabled permanently by original sin, that good and evil do not exist outside man (in other words, they are internal), and that human life is thus a constant struggle—if God has so predestined it—to overcome the evil within all of us.

Augustine wrote about many of the issues confronting the church in his lifetime. He struggled against heresy; and he advocated, as St. Jerome did, a life of withdrawal devoted to the contemplation of God. Although he lived in a monastic community of his own founding, Augustine was an active participant in the world and was greatly concerned with pastoral care. A brilliant and complex man whose personal life was often a torture, he lived through one of the most difficult, even tortured, periods in the history of the world. He saw the Vandal invasion of North Africa, and he died just as the Vandals were surrounding Hippo, the city of his bishopric.

The Church and Secular Power

The third Latin Father, St. Ambrose (339–397) addressed his efforts to yet another problem—one which emerged during the fourth century precisely *because* the Church had been legalized. Ambrose came from an aristocratic Gallo-Roman family, and his father held the high post of prefect in Gaul. Although well-educated and famous for his scholarship, Ambrose's greatest talents lay in administration. In Milan he displayed such skill as a civil administrator that he was elevated by popular acclamation to the bishopric of that city, although he had not yet even been ordained a priest. Once elected, Ambrose directed his abilities to strengthening the church and forwarding its independence. Through his actions and his own ecclesiastical theory he played a special role in formulating the position of the Western church in relation to secular power.

When Constantine converted to Christianity, most of the bishops, particularly those of the Eastern church, were so pleased to have a Christian emperor that they accepted Constantine's authority as having a divine basis which permitted his interference in the internal affairs of the church. We have seen that it was the emperor and not a bishop who presided over the Council of Nicaea, and this precedent was accepted always in the Eastern Empire.

Soon after Constantine's death, however, the church in the West began to move in exactly the opposite direction. What had begun as a tendency to resist imperial interference in church matters now was taken a giant step further by Ambrose. On two occasions he rebuked the emperor Theodosius from the pulpit, denouncing aspects of imperial behavior that he considered unchristian. On one of these occasions, after Theodosius had been responsible for a massacre at Thassalonika, Ambrose refused to allow the emperor to enter the church until he had repented because, as Ambrose put it, "the emperor is within the church, not over it. . . ."

At about this point the nature of the relationship between the church of Rome and the secular government becomes a continuous theme in medieval history, and there are two parts to it. The first is the way the Western church is itself governed, the second is the struggle of the Western church to maintain its independence from secular authority. By the mid-fifth century the supremacy of the bishop of Rome had become fully articulated and generally accepted by the Western bishops. This Petrine doctrine, as it is called, is based on the passage in St. Matthew regarding the apostolic power of all bishops: "Thou art Peter, and upon this rock I will build my Church, . . . and I will give unto thee the keys of the kingdom of heaven." (Matt. 16:18–19). The bishops of Rome maintained that this passage meant that Peter had been singled out by Christ to be the supreme pontiff in Christendom. In the mid-fifth century Pope Leo I (440–461) summarized the papal position in a sermon in which he first quoted the key biblical passage and then went on to point out that Peter "was ordained before the rest in such a way that . . . we might know the nature of his association with Christ."

At the very end of the fifth century, Pope Gelasius I (492–496) had formulated a theory of the relationship between papal and imperial power that is essentially an elaboration of Ambrose's position. According to the Gelasian theory, the world is ruled by two powers, the secular and spiritual, and of the two, "priests carry a weight all the greater because they must render an account to God even for Kings before the Divine Judgment." To develop such a theory in support of an independent and supreme papacy was one thing; to put it into effect was quite another, and the outcome of the struggle was dependent on the real power of the papacy at any given time in history.

With Leo I as pope in the mid-fifth century and Gelasius as pope at the end of it, the bishops of Rome were in effect governing the city of Rome. At that time there was no longer an emperor in Rome, and the defense of the city, and even much of Italy, was organized by the pope. (We have already noted how bishops in Gaul, for example, filled the void as Roman imperial power in the West contracted under German pressure.) In this way the church assumed many of the secular powers of the Roman government, absorbing the political traditions and to some extent the organization of the Roman Empire. This was not a development that ever proceeded smoothly, however; for a century after Gelasius there were weak popes, and the political circumstances in Italy and Europe generally precluded any further advance of papal authority.

The Origins of Monasticism

There were, as there always have been, those Christians who took literally Christ's statement that his kingdom was not of this world. For these individuals any reconciliation between Christianity and the world was simply not possible. At the very end of the third and the beginning of the fourth centuries a movement arose in the Eastern Empire which stemmed from the world-rejecting impulse in Christianity. Men appeared in the deserts of Egypt, Syria, and Palestine who had given up the earthly aspects of human existence to await the end of the world. The spiritual roots of this movement were not new, but its impetus came from the particular circumstances of the fourth century. The movement to leave the world was both a rejection of the secular life and a protest against what they considered the changed position of the Christian church after Christianity had been legalized. The desert saints, as they are often called, wanted to recreate the conditions of the early Christian church, when to be a Christian meant rejecting the world. The movement began when the persecutions of Christians stopped because the opportunity for martyrdom had thereby been removed. The desert saints, also known as anchorites (from the Greek word *anchoresis,* meaning departure) went off to seek a new kind of martrydom, one which they inflicted on themselves. These were the founders, unknowingly and unintentionally, of the most important and enduring manifestation of the world-rejecting spirit—the monastic movement. The word *monasticism* (derived from the Greek word *monas,* meaning "alone") was used to describe their way of life because these early monks chose to live in solitude. They sought martrydom and purification by practicing an extreme form of asceticism.

The ascetic, whatever his or her religion, assumes that man has two natures—spiritual and material—that are in conflict. The ascetic also believes that the pure, spiritual state can exist only when the material part of one's nature has been overcome. The three chief asceticisms practiced by the anchorites—ones which have become the essential features of all recorded monastic rules—are fasting, poverty, and celibacy. In the life of Christ there were many examples of fasting, and his teachings contained many exhortations to poverty. In most of the stories of the desert saints one passage in particular is nearly always quoted: "If thou wouldst be perfect, go and sell what thou hast, and give to the poor, . . . and come and follow me." (Matt. 19:21) The most important and most difficult asceticism was celibacy, for which St. Paul was the major early spokesman. In Paul's teachings, sexual purity was singled out as the greatest Christian virtue, though marriage was permitted to those who could not manage to remain celibate. "It is good for a man not to touch a woman. Nevertheless, to avoid fornication, let every man have his own wife." (I Cor. 1:1–2)

53

The Daughters of Eve

In the lives of the desert saints the struggles against the temptations of the flesh played a very prominent role, and the Devil often appeared in the guise of a woman. It is in these struggles of the anchorites to remain sexually pure that we find expressed the extremely negative Christian attitude toward women. Women were regarded as the daughters of Eve in the worst sense, which meant they were considered to be the cause of all man's difficulties. Had it not, after all, been for Eve, Adam would not have been tempted, and their exile from the Garden of Eden would not have occurred. Since God created Eve from Adam's rib, so the argument went, she was therefore inferior to Adam, and she was also spiritually weak—incapable of controlling her emotions, a temptress to be resisted. The ascetic ideal in Christianity was promulgated by men primarily for men, and chastity is at the very center of it. Marriage was considered necessary for the propagation of the human race, but the celibate life was the higher good, and women were the stumbling block to that life.

There existed a duality in the Christian attitude toward women throughout the Middle Ages, however, partly because Christ's attitude toward women was very positive, and there is nothing in his example that would foster a negative view. We know that women were accepted in the early Christian communities on equal terms with men; nevertheless, the teachings on celibacy emerge from the very first, and with them the negative view of woman. One medieval historian writing about women said they were either "in the pit or on the pedestal," and both in theory and everyday life this seems indeed to have been the case. For women also, celibacy was held out as the highest virtue, and the women most prized were virgins and widows. As the monastic life evolved, women were encouraged to enter monastic communities and the female religious played an important role in medieval society. Even so there were always fewer women monastics than men, and it was always believed that the prayers of monks carried more weight with God than those of their female counterparts. None of this, of course, was in accord with the belief that in the sight of God all were created equal; nor did it accord with the value placed upon women as wives and mothers in early medieval society. This negative attitude remains firmly in place, however, throughout the Middle Ages.

As if fasting, poverty, and celibacy were not enough, the desert fathers inflicted merciless self-punishment to purify themselves. Many lived for years in the open, exposed to the extremes of heat and cold in the desert; still others lived in tiny caves hewn out of rock in which there was not room to stand. They competed with one another in practicing austerities. St. Simeon Stylites, who lived chained to the top of a column for thirty-seven years, found

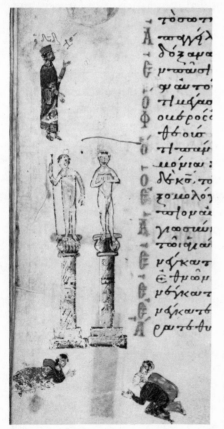

A scene from an illuminated Greek manuscript showing two Pillar Saints. *These desert saints did not live in isolation. They attracted a great deal of popular attention, as demonstrated by the three kneeling figures at the base of the columns.* (THE BRITISH LIBRARY)

one of the more picturesque austerities to inflict upon himself. The archetype of the desert saint was St. Anthony, who lived as a solitary for twenty years in the Egyptian wilderness, and then early in the fourth century (ca. 305) founded a colony in which the hermits lived close to one another rather than in strict solitude. These early ascetics did not follow rules of any sort, nor did they share a communal life. This was a later development that came about in the early fourth century, as a contribution of St. Pachomius, who organized the first communities of ascetics in Egypt. Pachomius' rule permitted many of the ascetic practices, but tempered them by labor, both to sustain the community and to curb excessive austerities. Later in the century St. Basil, a Greek who had visited Egypt and Syria, founded monasticism in Greece; and his rule, far more than that of Pachomius, emphasized the importance of communal living. The monks shared a common house, ate, worked, and prayed together. Thousands of individuals entered the Pachomian and Basilian monasteries during the fourth and fifth centuries, although they did not displace the hermits who continued to seek the solitude of the desert.

Monasticism was introduced into the West in the mid-fourth century through the *Life of St. Anthony* written by Bishop Athanasius, who had opposed the Arian heresy. The *Life* immediately became popular, and it inspired widespread imitation of the saint. St. Jerome and St. Augustine were also very instrumental in encouraging the spread of monasticism in the West. St. Jerome, as we have seen, lived as a hermit in Syria. After his return to Rome late in the fourth century he was particularly active in encouraging women to join monastic houses—an idea which seems to have gained considerable popularity among wealthy Roman women. In his later years, Jerome established a monastic community in Bethlehem, where he lived the remainder of his life. Augustine founded a monastery in North Africa; and he also wrote a rule for a women's monastery directed by his sister.

Through the late fourth and fifth centuries monastic communities (as well as groups of hermits trying to recreate the life of the desert saints) sprang up all over western Europe. The popularity of the movement is, in fact, quite astounding: It spread through

Spain, North Africa, Gaul, and reached Britain and Ireland. There were some problems, however, in transplanting monasticism in its Eastern form to Europe. For one thing, the more vigorous climate made it virtually impossible to imitate the lives of the desert saints, and certain changes had to occur. The ascetic, anchorite ideal remained always strong in Eastern Christianity; but the individuality of the Eastern monks, their solitariness, and their austerities were not really in harmony with the emphasis on organization in the Roman church. The adaptation of the monastic spirit to the Western church did not come until the following century, with the second stage of the movement.

With hindsight it is possible to see that the last decades of the fifth century in the West were in all ways the end of the first stage in the change from classical to medieval civilization. The main ingredients were now present: the church securely in place, the Germans settling in Europe, the beginnings of the monastic movement, and underlying all, the legacy of Rome. In the next period of European development the difficult question of how these ingredients would relate to one another would begin to be answered. The problems were not worked out in a vacuum, however. What took place in the West is part of the history of the entire Mediterranean world, so it is necessary now to turn to the changes which occurred in the East.

~~~ 2

The New Civilizations Emerge

The Byzantine Empire

The fourth and fifth centuries were an age of transition for the East as well as the West, but for each the nature of this transition was altogether different. The Western Empire suffered violent disruptions in the transformation from classical to medieval civilization while the East gradually, and without dramatic upheavals, became the Byzantine Empire. In the West imperial rule was terminated in Rome. By contrast, an unbroken succession of rulers occupied the throne at Constantinople from the founding of the city in 330 until its capture by the Ottoman Turks in 1453. From first to last the Eastern emperors used the title "Emperor of the Romans," and to a certain extent the Byzantine rulers were justified in their insistence on the title, because their empire began as the living continuation of the Eastern Roman Empire.

Although through the length of its history it is always possible to see the Roman behind the Byzantine, by the sixth century a new civilization had evolved in the East, having taken its name from the Greek city of Byzantium, on whose foundations Constantinople was raised. Constantine's site for the city was, as we have seen, economically and strategically perfect. It was also perfect in a symbolic sense because the spiritual foundations of Constantinople were Greek, and the cultural history of the Byzantine Empire derives from the classical world of Greek antiquity. Byzantine religious and political history, however, go back to the time of Constantine's dedication of the Eastern capital.

It is not easy to discern all the steps in the transformation from Roman to Byzantine, but one of the clearest and most important was the political separation of the eastern and western halves of the empire. Constantine's hope was that his new capital would help preserve the unity of the empire, but whether his goal was ever realistic is highly debatable. In any event, the division of the empire following the death of Theodosius in 395 and the subsequent German invasions in the West mark the fork in the road. From then on, East and West moved, figuratively as well as literally, in quite different directions; yet the theory that the empire was one world did not change.

As Western imperial power gave way to the Germans, the emperors at Constantinople began to consider themselves the only legitimate rulers of the entire Mediterranean. They regarded themselves as the successors of Theodosius (and specifically, his successors during the three years when he ruled alone). In their view, German control of the Western provinces was temporary until this territory could be recovered and the empire reunited under the emperors at Constantinople. The first attempt at recovery was made before the end of the fifth century, soon after Odoacer had deposed Romulus Augustulus. The Eastern emperor Zeno followed a time-honored Roman policy and sent barbarians to fight the barbarians in Italy. His agent was the Ostrogothic tribe led by its king, Theodoric.

Byzantium and the Recovery of the West: The Ostrogoths in Italy

The Ostrogoths were the first Germans defeated by the Huns (in 375), and they were kept in subjugation until 453. In that year Attila died and the Hunnish kingdom fell apart, releasing the Ostrogoths from their bondage. The Ostrogoths were then allowed to become allies of the Eastern emperor and to settle in Thrace; and as insurance of their good behavior they sent their king's son, Theodoric, as a hostage to Constantinople. Theodoric had been raised and educated at the imperial court, and when he in turn became king of the Ostrogoths in 483 he was even granted a Roman title. Despite this surface friendship, by 489 the Ostrogoths had begun causing trouble in the East; but Zeno persuaded Theodoric to lead his tribe instead to Italy in order to drive out Odoacer and restore imperial authority over the peninsula.

Theodoric began his conquest in 493, and within four years he had killed Odoacer, wiped out his armies, and established the Ostrogothic capital at Ravenna. This kingdom lasted only until Theodoric's death in 526, but however short-lived, it is an important chapter in the transition from classical to medieval civilization in Italy.

Theodoric's Kingdom

Theodoric faced the problem of how Germans and Romans could live together—once the fighting was over—with intelligence, tact, and a degree of genuine understanding of the value of Roman institutions. The Goths lived under their customary Germanic laws, but Theodoric permitted the Italians to maintain their own laws and their own civil administrations. Toward the Roman

Senate he showed great respect, and he called on members of the senatorial class for help in establishing his administrative system at Ravenna. During most of his reign Roman officials willingly helped Theodoric, and all civil posts were filled by Romans. One in particular, Cassiodorus (ca. 480–575), was prominent in Theodoric's government, and he chose the Latin word *civilitas* to characterize Theodoric's rule. This term was intended to convey to the Romans what in fact was true—that Theodoric wanted to restore and maintain Roman civilization rather than destroy it. Cassiodorus tried to help Theodoric to Romanize the Goths, and his *History of the Goths* was intended to make them more acceptable to the Romans. For the most part, Theodoric's rule was indeed acceptable to the Romans.

The army during Theodoric's reign was exclusively Gothic, and the king rewarded his soldiers for service by giving them lands he confiscated from the Romans, a practice followed by all the German invaders. This latter policy does not seem to have been a source of great dissatisfaction to the Romans, since though Theodoric claimed one-third of their estates, most of the land he confiscated had already been engulfed by previous invaders or had become public property. Theodoric and the Ostrogoths were Arians and they remained so, but even this does not seem to have caused conflict until late in Theodoric's reign, and then it was a symptom of political friction rather than religious antagonism. On the whole Theodoric was on friendly terms with the Catholics and they with him—a toleration born of mutual respect.

The Ostrogoth ruler was devoted to preserving Roman civilization, and underlying his strong desire to do so was the consciousness that the old Roman order was slipping away and that classical culture and learning were in danger of being lost. His court at Ravenna became an artistic and intellectual center that attracted writers and scholars who shared Theodoric's concern. Cassiodorus, in the preface to a book he wrote on religious and secular learning, might well be speaking for all of them:

" . . . inasmuch as a peaceful affair has no place in anxious times, I am driven by divine charity to this device, namely, in the place of a teacher

61

to prepare for you under the Lord's guidance these introductory books; through which, in my opinion, the unbroken line of the Divine Scriptures and the compendious knowledge of secular letters might with the Lord's beneficence be related . . . In them I commit to you . . . the words of men of former times, which it is right to praise and glorious to proclaim for future generations. . . ." [1]

After the collapse of the Ostrogothic kingdom, when his public career was over, Cassiodorus devoted himself to the collection and preservation of classical and Christian manuscripts. He established a monastery in southern Italy, Vivarium, that was dedicated to copying religious and secular texts, and his library preserved many literary works that might have been lost. The copying done at Cassiodorus' monastic community provided a model for later monasteries to follow.

The other famous scholar at Ravenna during this time was Boethius (480–524), who planned to translate all the works of Plato and Aristotle into Latin. Although he did not live long enough to come close to his goal, the translation he made of Aristotle's treatise on logic was the only Aristotelian text available in Europe through much of the Middle Ages. Boethius was found guilty of treason against Theodoric, and not all of the circumstances of the case against him are known and none of them is clear. But during Boethius' confinement in prison he wrote the book for which he is best known, the *Consolation of Philosophy*. It is an extraordinary work, moving and affecting because the sadness that engulfs the author at its beginning is a universal part of the human condition and because the process by which Boethius himself was consoled has the power to bring genuine comfort to his readers. The *Consolation* is intellectually interesting because the philosophical arguments at its core are derived from Greek philosophy, and particularly from Plato. For the Latin Middle Ages this work was extremely important because it was one of the very few sources of Platonic philosophy.

In spite of Theodoric's encouragement of scholarship and the

1. Cassiodorus, Senator, *An Introduction to Divine and Human Readings*, trans. Leslie W. Jones (New York: W.W. Norton, 1969), pp. 67–68.

arts in an effort to Romanize his people, the Ostrogoths and Romans were never merged. The sense that there were two worlds, however close, is graphically clear in the contrast between Theodoric's tomb and the churches at Ravenna from the same period. The tomb is a massive, round mausoleum, and the only light that relieves its stark interior emanates from an opening in its dome. The technical facility of its structure is Roman, but its overall feeling is far more primitive. In its own way it is truly impressive, yet it conveys the feeling of having come from a world altogether different from that which produced the exquisite, jewel-like interiors of the churches.

The Tomb of Theodoric at Ravenna. (ALINARI/EDITORIAL PHOTOCOLOR ARCHIVES)

In the last years of his life Theodoric incurred the enmity of the Byzantine emperor Justin I (518–527). Justin feared that Theodoric was usurping far too much imperial power in Italy and that Theodoric had plans—as indeed he did—to expand Ostrogothic rule to Gaul and Spain. The emperor therefore issued laws prohibiting Arians from holding public office, and he also actively plotted to overthrow Theodoric, involving in his plan the pope and many Roman Catholic aristocrats. Theodoric retaliated by taking the pope prisoner along with other prominent Catholics, among them Boethius, whom Theodoric executed. However, Theodoric died (in 526), leaving no male heir and no strong Ostrogothic ruler to follow him. A year later Justin died and was succeeded by one of the greatest of all Byzantine emperors, his nephew, Justinian I.

The Age of Justinian

Justinian's long reign from 527 to 565 was a major turning point in Byzantine history. His achievements and failures were equally grand and they affected the course of Byzantine history for centuries. Justinian had a rare talent and liking for hard work. He was well-trained in the law, and he trained himself to be a theologian during the course of his reign. He was sometimes a brilliant ruler, although his sense of the majesty of his office drove him to his major failures as well as to his major successes. The age of Justinian was at once the culmination of two hundred years of development and a new beginning for the Byzantine Empire.

All along, one of the most characteristic features of the Byzantine Empire had been the autocratic position of the emperor. In his conception of the monarchy Justinian looked back to Constantine, during whose reign the Eastern political theory of absolutism had originated. This theory was first formulated by Constantine's biographer Eusebius, who believed that Constantine was the Vicar of Christ on earth, divinely appointed to fulfill his task as Christian emperor. Constantine was therefore called the Thirteenth Apostle, and from the fourth century on, all Eastern emperors were believed to rule by divine right. In theory if not always in fact, the Byzantine emperor was the supreme ruler, supreme law giver, commander-in-chief of the army and navy, and head of the church. This last power was based on the doctrine of Caesaropapism enunicated by Justinian, which quite simply means that the emperor was at the top of the religious hierarchy in the Eastern church, and equal to the pope in power, though not spiritual authority.

Justinian's feeling for the imperial purple was shared, and sometime outdone, by his wife the empress Theodora, who was by any standard one of the most extraordinary women in history. She was the daughter of a bearkeeper at the Hippodrome in Constantinople and had been an "actress" (perhaps a euphemism for prostitute) before Justinian had fallen in love with her. The idea that Justinian would marry this woman caused quite a stir in the imperial household, and in fact, the marriage had to be postponed until the death of Justinian's aunt, who was adamantly opposed to it.

The marital partnership of Justinian and Theodora was a firm and productive one largely because the empress was a woman of intelligence and considerable courage. There exists a mosaic portrait of her in a Byzantine church in Ravenna and, although it is stylized, her beauty—particularly her large dark eyes—and the force of her character emerge very clearly. In 532, a series of political riots occurred in Constantinople, and to Justinian and most of his supporters there seemed no alternative except to flee. But not to Theodora, who shamed them all. In essence, she told them that all of us have to die, and that when someone has been a ruler, it is impossible to step down and live in exile. "I agree with the old saying," she said, "the [imperial] purple is a fair shroud." And so they remained, the riots were quelled, and Justinian continued a long and ambitious reign.

Justinian's Western Conquests

For Justinian, nothing could more fully exalt the glory of his reign than the glory of restoring the historic frontiers of the empire. His

The Empress Theodora and her Attendants. *Detail of a mosaic panel in the Church of St. Vitale in Ravenna (mid-sixth century).* (HIRMER FOTOARCHIV)

first and greatest ambition was therefore to recover the Western provinces. Furthermore, the time seemed perfect because the East was extremely prosperous and the imperial treasury was well-filled. In the two hundred years since its founding, Constantinople had become one of the wealthiest cities in the world. Luxuries from all over the East—silks from China, carpets from Damascus, spices from India—were imported by Constantinople and then exported to other cities in the Mediterranean or along the Black Sea. Raw materials were imported and the guilds of artisans and craftsmen, whose industries were thriving, fashioned articles of gold and silver and wove beautiful fabrics for their own highly successful luxury trades. All commerce into and out of the city and all industry was carefully regulated by the government, and the taxes flowed into the imperial treasury with abundance.

Justinian had a huge army and navy, most of which was at his disposal because he had solved—or so he thought—the vexing problem of the eastern border of the Byzantine Empire. The eastern question had required regular attention since the late days of the Roman Republic when the Romans had fought the Persian Empire (then called "Parthia") and had been defeated. Augustus had established the Euphrates River as the boundary between Rome and Persia, and it had been Roman policy to maintain a balance of power with Persia. The Persian Empire had been an ancient and great power, fairly equal in strength to Rome, and peace with Persia was essential because the main Byzantine trade route to India and the Far East wound through Persian territory.

In 531 Justinian signed an "endless peace" with Persia which turned out to be all too finite, but at the time Justinian believed he had secured the eastern frontier. Two years later his brilliant general, Belisarius, set sail for the West. Belisarius' first campaign was against the Vandals, and it was a quick and total success. Within a year he had recovered North Africa and returned in triumph to Constantinople. Two years later the campaign to restore Italy was begun, but the Ostrogoths were exceedingly difficult to defeat, even in the absence of a strong king. It took twenty years of campaigning before Italy and Sicily were brought under imperial control. Justinian also recovered parts of Visigothic Spain but none of the other Western provinces, leaving his great dream only partially fulfilled.

Ravenna now became Justinian's capital in the West. From there his representative (called the Exarch) controlled Italy, and a separate administration was established for Sicily and North Africa. The Roman population of Italy was not overjoyed at having the imperial government so close at hand. The long years of fighting had caused terrible destruction and had left Italy weakened, exhausted, and hostile to its rescuers. Moreover, the representatives of the Byzantine government in the West were foreigners. Thus, however tenaciously Justinian clung to the belief that his house was only temporarily divided, in reality East and West had become thoroughly estranged.

One of the clear indications of this estrangement was the disappearance of the Greek language in the West. In the early empire, Western education had been bilingual, children were urged to learn to read Greek before Latin, and all the Greek texts were studied in the original. During the late third and early fourth centuries Greek began to disappear, except among a few intellectuals who learned it as a foreign language. St. Augustine complained of the difficulty he had in learning Greek as a solitary occupation, and at Theodoric's court at Ravenna Boethius had hoped to translate all the works of Plato and Aristotle into Latin because he recognized the danger of their extinction. Few Greek texts had ever been translated, and when Greek finally did disappear so did Western Europe's direct knowledge of the culture and learning of the classical Greek world.

The loss of the Greek legacy was incalculable. Through most of the Middle Ages, Europe had neither Homer nor Euclid, little Greek philosophy, almost no Greek science or medicine, and not a single Greek play or history. However, the loss of Greek in the West does not mean that there was lack of communication between the Byzantine East and the Latin West. Although there were periods of infrequent contact, Byzantium and the West were never total strangers to one another, as we shall see. The linguistic barrier was difficult to surmount, but this was essentially a symptom of the estrangement between Greek and non-Greek. For by the time Justinian ascended the throne a new culture had formed on the shores of the Bosphorus.

The New Synthesis

All the elements present at the time of Constantine had undergone a new synthesis—part Christian, part Roman, part Oriental, and, at its core, Greek. Hellenism pervaded all the other influences, and it did so because in the East the Greek heritage had remained continuously alive and exceedingly adaptable. It had been adapted to the Oriental world when Alexander the Great had marched East, and it had been adapted again during the Byzantine period. Pericles would have found much in the Byzantine world quite strange, but he also would have recognized that it shared with fifth-century Athens two characteristics in abundant measure: "the love of what is beautiful" and "the love of things of the mind."

The "love of what is beautiful" is most surely reflected in the building that will stand for all time as the symbol of the Byzantine Empire and Eastern Christianity—the church of Santa Sophia at Constantinople. The first church of Santa Sophia was built by Constantine but was destroyed in the fires that accompanied the riots of 532. It was built anew by Justinian, and a vivid description of it was recorded by Procopius, the historian of Justinian's reign: "The church has become a spectacle of marvelous beauty, overwhelming to those who see it, but to those who know it by hearsay, altogether incredible. For it soars to a height to match the sky . . . adorning it [the city] because it is a part of it, but glorying in its own beauty. . . ."[2]

Structurally, the most impressive part of the church was the dome which, placed above a row of glass windows, seemed not to be supported at all but simply to float in the air. The

2. This and the following two quoted passages are from Procopius, *Buildings, Book I*, trans. H.B. Dewing and Glanville Downey (Cambridge, Mass.: Harvard University Press, 1940), pp. 13 and 27.

The interior of Santa Sophia. *The Byzantine Church was converted into a mosque by the Muslims after the Ottoman conquest in the fifteenth century. The original mosaics were whitewashed and Christian symbols were replaced with Islamic motifs—some of which can still be seen, though much restoration of the original building has been done.*
(HIRMER FOTOARCHIV)

70

interior was so beautiful that it nearly defied Procopius' descriptive powers:

[W]ho could recount the beauty of the columns and the stones with which the church is adorned? One might imagine that he had come upon a meadow with its flowers in full bloom. For he would surely marvel at the purple of some, the green tint of others, and at those on which the crimson glows . . . And whenever anyone enters [Santa Sophia] to pray, . . . " Procopius continued, "his mind is lifted up toward God and exalted, feeling that He cannot be far away, but must especially love to dwell in this place which he has chosen.

Justinian undertook a vast architectural program, and two of the loveliest Byzantine churches may still be seen at Ravenna; but of all the buildings he commissioned, Santa Sophia remains the most impressive.

Santa Sophia mean "holy wisdom," and the church is a particularly fitting tribute to the "love of the things of the mind" because one of the most striking traits of the Byzantine Greeks was their intense curiosity about religious matters. The intellectual drive associated with the classical world was woven into the fabric of the Hellenized Christianity of Byzantium. The Byzantine Greeks were true descendents of the Greeks to whom St. Paul preached in Athens, who "took him, and brought him into the Areopagus, saying, 'May we know what this new doctrine, whereof thou speakest, is?' . . . (For all the Athenians, and the strangers who were there, spent their time in nothing else, but either to tell or to hear some new thing.)" (Acts 17:19–21)

One receives the clear impression from reading the Byzantine historians that the discussion of new Christian doctrines was as popular with the Byzantine Greeks as the discussion of politics is with us. This is borne out by the fact that from the late fourth to the seventh century, the major doctrinal disputes within Christianity were for the most part localized in the Eastern Empire and were of fundamental importance to the political fortunes of Byzantium.

The theological problem which led to the two major heresies had to do with the attempts to explain the relationship between

Christ's two natures—one divine, the other human. One doctrine, Nestorianism (after Nestorius, its chief proponent), insisted on the distinct separation between God and man in Christ. The other doctrine, Monophysitism (the belief in one nature), insisted almost completely on Christ's divinity to the virtual exclusion of his humanity. These controversies were fanned by ecclesiastical rivalries in the Eastern church, by the loyalties of provincials to their bishops, and by provincial hostility to Byzantine control.

Just before the founding of Constantinople, the two most eminent rival bishoprics in the East had been at Antioch and Alexandria. During the fourth century the church at Constantinople was officially elevated to a position in the hierarchy above that of Alexandria and Antioch and second only to Rome. The bishop of Constantinople was identified with imperial religious policy, which meant insistence on doctrinal uniformity as determined by the emperor and the bishop. Thus the rivalry between Antioch and Alexandria now expanded to include Constantinople.

In 431, a council at Ephesus condemned the Nestorian heresy with the result that many Nestorians, rather than relinquish their belief, chose either to move to eastern Syria or to leave the Byzantine Empire entirely. The latter group of Nestorians settled in Persia and from there sent missionaries to India, Central Asia, and China. At the same council in 431 the bishop of Alexandria put forward his belief in Christ's single nature, and when this too was condemned, national sympathies in Egypt were aroused in support of the bishop. Monophysitism was again condemned at a council in 451, and instead of leaving, as the Nestorians had chosen to do, the Monophysite church solidified its position in Egypt and Syria.

By the time Justinian came to the throne, the Monophysite church was firmly entrenched in the Eastern provinces. Justinian's problem in dealing with this heresy was complicated by several factors. He wanted a unified orthodox church, but he hoped to find some middle ground so as not to arouse further resentment against the emperor. At the same time Justinian wanted papal support for his reconquest of the Western provinces, but the pope would accept no compromise with the Monophysites. To add to imperial problems, Theodora was sympathetic to the Monophysites and gave them her protection. None of Justinian's attempts at conciliation was successful, though he became a theologian himself in trying to work out a compromise. In the final years of his reign Justinian resorted to persecuting the heretics, but this succeeded only in intensifying the hostility toward Constantinople in the Eastern provinces.

Along with his building program, the most successful and important of all Justinian's undertakings was the codification of Roman law. The Roman legal tradition was already a thousand years old when Justinian became emperor, but it is not longevity that accounts for its uniqueness. The real genius of Roman law is that in its historical evolution it became a reasoned and reasonable system which transcended local customs and provincialism. This is not to say that it was perfect or that its blessings fell on "the just and the unjust" alike. (It upheld slavery, for instance.) Nevertheless, the Western world's conception of the law and proper legal process was contained in Roman law.

The Roman law that became the basis for the legal systems throughout Europe (except in England) in the later Middle Ages, and that was venerated until well into the nineteenth century, was revised, explained, and compiled by Justinian's jurists. We can safely say that Justinian saved for the West and incorporated into the East what otherwise would surely have been lost; for although the German tribes themselves sometimes adopted aspects of Roman law and often allowed Romans to use their own laws, they made no attempt to maintain the Roman legal structure as a whole. At the close of the eleventh century the West rediscovered Roman law through the discovery of Justinian's code, and a complete inheritance was thereby wholeheartedly accepted.

Justinian has been praised for his lasting achievements yet severely criticized because his reach far exceeded his grasp. This was particularly true of his attempt to recover the western provinces, since this left the Byzantine Empire drained of its financial resources. The disasters that followed Justinian's reign were due partly to his expenditures and partly to the fact that he overlooked the real dangers to Byzantium along its eastern frontier.

Throughout the remainder of the sixth century and on into the seventh, Justinian's successors were at war with the Persians. There were intermittent periods of peace, but these respites were temporary and the army had other problems to cope with at the same time: The Slavs and a barbarian tribe, the Avars, were attacking the Danube border. The concerted thrusts of three enemies nearly swept away all the eastern and Balkan provinces of the empire. By 628–629 Byzantium was able to defeat the Persians and the Avars and to exert a measure of control over the Slavs, who settled permanently in the Balkan peninsula. But the price of victory was high. Not least among the costs to Constantinople was the disaffection of many of its subjects. The heretical provinces had already been alienated, and their resentment was increased by the long years of warfare, the loss of population, and by heavy taxation.

Islam

The Background in Arabia

One of the most difficult problems caused by the warfare was the fact that Byzantine traders were deprived of the use of their major trade route from the East—the sea route that ended at the Persian Gulf and then went overland, partly through Persian territory, to Antioch or Damascus. Of necessity the traders found an alternate route that they began using in the sixth century—a route that went around the coast of Arabia and up the Red Sea. There were several ports to choose from, but the one most often used was Jiddah, which was linked to the city of Mecca. From Jiddah, Byzantine goods were picked up by caravans from Mecca and carried through the northern Arabian desert to Gaza or Damascus.

Because this route through Arabia was essential to the economy, the Byzantine government spent time and money in securing political influence among the Arabs; but the Persians were not far behind, and Arabia became an economic battleground between the two empires. The hostility between Persia and Byzantium thus reverberated in a part of the Near East that until the sixth century had been relatively little exploited or explored.

Most of Arabia was inhabited by nomadic tribes, the Bedouins of the desert, and neither Byzantium nor Persia made any attempt to control these peoples or to penetrate the desert. Instead, they directed their energies to winning control over the trading centers along the coasts of Arabia and over the seminomadic tribes along the edge of the desert closest to Byzantium and Persia. The effect on Arabia was to give a great spurt to the economy of the caravan and trading centers.

In the fashion of imperialist countries, Persia and Byzantium tried to win allies through religious conversion, with important consequences for the religious life of Arabia. Individual Arabs, and even a few tribes, converted to Christianity. Some converts were Orthodox, some were Monophysites, and more were Nestorians due to the proximity to Syria. There were also communities of Jews in the caravan cities, so that the Arabs were familiar with Judaism as well as Christianity.

Muhammed (570–632) and the Religion of Islam

When Muhammed was born in Mecca in 570, his birthplace had become the most prosperous of the caravan cities and therefore the one most closely linked to the Graeco-Oriental world. But although greatly influenced by the outside world, Mecca was still tied to the traditional social and religious life of Arabia and was governed by the tribal society that characterized the life of the Arabs of the desert. Membership in the tribe was determined by blood descent and the life of the individual was subordinate to the interests of the group. This close community was necessary for survival in the desert, but in the more open society of the commercial city it began to break down. Each tribe worshipped its own deities—objects in nature believed to be inhabited by divine spirits. The one object worshipped in common by all Arabs was the Kaaba, a huge black stone enshrined in Mecca. There was no sense of monotheism implicit in this, but because the Kaaba had religious significance for all the Arabs, Mecca was an important pilgrimage center.

For a long time it was believed that Islam, the new religion preached by Muhammed, was a religion of the desert. It is now quite certain that Islam was not "born of the desert" but of the city. Muhammed's genius—or inspiration—lay in the fact that he gave to what was becoming a new and different world a new and different religion.

Muhammed's father died before his birth and his mother six years later. Although his guardians helped him begin a commercial career, he had a difficult time until his marriage (in 595) to a wealthy widow who engaged in the caravan trade. Muhammed worked hard and was successful, but his adult years were dominated by his need for contemplation and by his concern with the social problems that had arisen in the changing society of Mecca. He spent long periods in the solitude of the desert until 610, when he received his first revelations and began to preach.

Muhammed believed that his revelations came from God, who spoke to him through the angel Gabriel. The revelations came over many years and were dynamic as the circumstances of Muhammed's life and mission changed. The heart of Islam, however, is unchanged still and is contained in the five so-called pillars of Islam—the five obligations incumbent upon a Muslim. The first obligation is a profession of faith, the belief that there is no God but Allah and that Muhammed is the final prophet. The remaining four are the duties mandatory for a believer or follower to perform: prayer five times a day at specified hours; the giving of alms; fasting during certain periods; and undertaking a pilgrimage to Mecca.

The essential duty of a Muslim lies in following the laws of his or her religion. These are recorded primarily in the Koran, which contains all Muhammed's revelations; they are also contained in a body of tradition, the *Hadith*, which is a record of the Prophet's sayings and practices that are not in the Koran.

Muhammed believed that God had chosen him to be the last, or the seal, of a line of prophets that had begun with Abraham and included Moses and Jesus (whom Muhammed accepted as a prophet, but not as the son of God). He believed the Jews and Christians had strayed from the religion which God had first revealed to Abraham, and that it was his mission to bring them back to the Word of God. Having begun to preach in 610, his first disappointment in the ensuing years was that the Jews and Christians failed to convert to Islam. His second disappointment was that he was totally rejected by the authorities at Mecca; but his career reached a turning point in 622, when he and his followers were expelled from Mecca and moved northward to Medina, another somewhat less prosperous caravan city.

The year 622, the year of the Hegira, or flight, is the year 1 of the Muslim calendar. This was a turning point because during the period which followed, Muhammed Arabicized Islam and developed its political foundations. The Arabs who converted to Islam were brought together by Muhammed into a theocratic community modeled on the Arab tribal structure with one important difference: Membership was based, not on kinship, but on the acceptance of Muhammed as God's prophet and one's belief in the revelations. The Koran contains laws that pertain to all aspects of political, social, and economic life, and these are as binding on Muslims as the laws that pertain more strictly to the religious side of life. There is, in fact, no distinction.

During the years in Medina, Muhammed prepared for his return to Mecca, which he intended to make his holy city. He directed his followers and the people of Medina in raids on the caravans from Mecca and, in 630, on Mecca itself. Two years later, after establishing Mecca as the center of the new religion, Muhammed died.

The Expansion of Islam (632–733)

Although it is difficult to be exact about the extent of Arab conversion to Islam at the time of Muhammed's death, the best estimate places it at about one-third of the peninsula. Immediately following Muhammed's death some of the converted tribes withdrew from the Islamic community, but a series of short wars brought them back under Muslim leadership and, thus united, the Arabs began their wars of conquest.

The invasion into Byzantine and Persian territory began as raids but soon gathered momentum and direction. By 643, Arab armies had won control of Syria, Palestine, and the Persian Empire up to the borders of India. During the same period another Arab army captured Alexandria (whose harbor contained most of the Byzantine navy) and then the remainder of Egypt. From Egypt the Arabs went westward across the Libyan desert to the Byzantine province of North Africa, which they also easily captured. They then turned inland and defeated and converted the Berber tribes of the North African desert. After their initial contacts with the Byzantine navy, the Arabs built their own navies and began successfully attacking the Byzantine islands in the eastern Mediterranean—Crete, Rhodes, and Cyprus.

In a second wave of expansion in the early eighth century, the Arabs in the East went across central Asia to the borders of China and down into northern India, all the while attempting to capture Constantinople both by land from Asia Minor and by sea. In the West the Arabs and Berbers crossed the Straits of Gibraltar into Spain, where they defeated the Visigoths. (A small number of Christian princes managed to retreat to an area south of the Pyrenees where they established a small kingdom which survived to become the base from which the Christian reconquest of Spain began in the tenth century.) After conquering nearly all of Spain, the Arabs crossed the Pyrenees into southern France.

In 717–718, the Byzantine government was finally able to turn the Muslim fleet away from Constantinople by using a secret weapon, "Greek fire," an incendiary device that was shot across the water to burn the Muslim ships. They also gained sufficient strength to drive the Muslims out of Asia Minor, and not many years later, in 733, a Frankish army led by the Mayor of the Palace, Charles Martel, defeated the Muslims in central France and pushed them back across the Pyrenees into Spain. Although Charles Martel became a great hero after the Muslim retreat, it is probably true that the Muslims had overextended themselves in the West

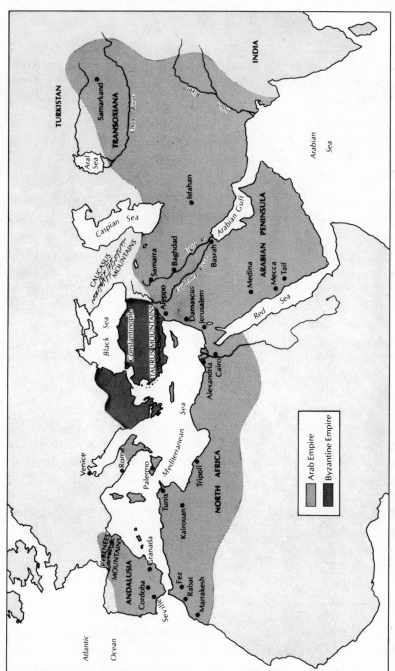

2. *The Expansion of Islam in the Seventh Century*

and could not have held southern and central France. But within the semicircle from Spain to Aisa Minor, the rest of the Mediterranean was—and for centuries remained—securely under Muslim control.

The Caliphate

One of the chief internal problems in Islamic history was—and is—the problem of the caliph, the successor to Muhammed. Since Muhammed was God's final prophet, he could not be succeeded in that religious capacity, but a successor had to be chosen to direct the Islamic community in every other way. Muhammed had not designated a successor, and only one daughter survived him. The first four caliphs (from 632 to 661) were Arabs who had converted early and had been personally close to Muhammed. In 661 the caliphate was established at Damascus and became a hereditary dynasty under the Umayyads, who were also Arabs. In the mid-eighth century two important changes occurred. The first was that the Umayyads were overthrown and a new caliphate was established at Bagdad under the Abbasid dynasty. Soon afterward there were other revolts within the Islamic Empire, and although the Abbasid caliphate lasted until the mid-thirteenth century, the Abbasids did not rule the entire Islamic world. By the end of the tenth century there were several caliphates within Islam—the principal ones at Cairo and at Cordova in Spain as well as other lesser ones.

The second—and by far the more important—change was that from 750 on, beginning with the Abbasids, the rulers of Islam were no longer Arabs. These rulers were Muslims in belief, but ethnically they might be Persians, Egyptians, Spanish, or any of the other peoples who converted to Islam. The terms *Arab* and *Islam* are often used interchangeably, and this creates a certain amount of confusion. Arabic is the language of the Muslim religion, and it became the international language for the remarkable culture created in the Islamic world from the Straits of Gibraltar to China. People today who call themselves "Arabs" are not pri-

marily—nor even likely to be—people who were born on the
Arabian peninsula. This began to be the situation as early as the
Middle Ages, once the political control of Islam was taken out of
Arab hands. Islamic culture evolved slowly at first. Its real growth
began during the late eighth and the ninth centuries under the
Abbasids, and contributions to it were made by Christians and
Jews living within the Islamic countries as well as by those who
professed the religion of Muhammed. The considerable impact
of Islamic culture on Western Europe that came about in the
eleventh and twelfth centuries will be discussed later.

The Cause and Effects of
the Islamic Conquests

The problem of finding an explanation for the phenomenon of
Muslim expansion and its effects on the political and economic
fortunes of the Mediterranean world is complicated by the long
history of hostility between Christian Europe and the Islamic
world. At times, as in the eleventh and twelfth centuries, there
has been fruitful and positive interaction, due to Islam's development of a rich and varied culture, from which western Europe
benefitted enormously; but in the main there has been hostility
and prejudice. Historians of Islam in the nineteenth and early
twentieth centuries were primarily from those European nations
which held colonial possessions in the Middle East, and they
viewed the Arabs as uncivilized. Furthermore, the Islamic religion
itself has had a "bad press" among Westerners. Many of its tenets
are derived from Judaism and Christianity—the strict monotheism, for example, and the insistence on periods of fasting and
giving alms. But the composite whole, although in ethical content
on a par with the latter two religions, is very different from them.
The result is that Islam has often been seen as a distortion and the
Muslims as intolerant religious fanatics, intent on converting the
world.

The truth of the matter is that the desert could support only
a limited number of people, and there was a decided population

growth with its attendant economic hardships in the sixth century, which propelled the rapid expansion of the seventh century. But the Arabs had been moving out of the desert long before Islam, and Arab tribes were inhabiting Byzantine and Persian territories well before the birth of Muhammed. Islam, without question, inspired the loyalty of the Arabs and gave cohesion to their movement, but religious conversion was not its prime motivation. Conversion proceeded, for the most part, with moderation. Christianity and Judaism were tolerated because they were the two other, and earlier, revealed religions and because Muhammed had established a precedent when he made agreements with Jewish and Christian tribes in Arabia which allowed them to maintain their own beliefs. Members of the tolerated religions, called *dhimmis*, paid tribute, but they were given certain freedoms in return. (If they converted, their taxes were reduced, so that one of the chief incentives to conversion was not fear of the uncivilized Arabs, but economic benefit.)

Although the taxes paid by non-Muslims to their Muslim rulers were high, they were not so high as those exacted by the Byzantine government from its subjects. Furthermore, the alienated, heretical provinces of the Eastern Empire were not altogether reluctant to exchange Byzantine rule for the more tolerant Muslim rule, and they did not offer much resistance to the Arab armies. The economic depletion and the exhaustion of manpower shared by Persia and Byzantium after the years of mutual warfare had left them vulnerable to the Muslim attacks. And the Arabs were determined fighters, hardened by the punishing life of the desert; and their use of horses and camels, and the speed with which they could move their armies, were far superior to the resources and strength of their opponents.

The Belgian historian Henri Pirenne wrote a very influential book, *Mohammed and Charlemagne*, published in 1939. In his book Pirenne concluded that the Muslim invasions destroyed the unity of the Mediterranean forever and that these invasions marked the end of the classical period and the beginning of the Middle Ages in Europe. Pirenne saw the Muslim expansion as the cause of an abrupt break with the past and the beginning of a wholly new civilization in Europe. (There is also an Eastern counterpart to the Pirenne thesis, which postulates a similar break in continuity in the Eastern Empire.) Research on the subject over the past decades has shown Pirenne's thesis to be far too cataclysmic. The effect of the Muslim expansion on Byzantium was surely considerable, particularly due to the loss of the Eastern provinces, but the Byzantine navy was rebuilt, and with the aid of "Greek fire" the Byzantines were able to recover some of their trade in the Mediterranean. And Byzantium began a new expansion of its own into Slavic territory in the ninth century, which opened up whole new areas for trade and political control.

The effect of Muslim expansion on Latin Christendom was, in many ways, more indirect than direct. The Arab invasions were yet another stage in the political separation of the Latin West and Byzantine East which, as we have seen, had begun even before the German invasions. The influence of the Muslims on Europe during the centuries following the invasions is, as we shall see, both more complex and more interesting than the idea of an abrupt change. As one turns to study the formation of European civilization from the late fifth to the late eighth century, it becomes clear that the process was evolutionary, not revolutionary; it is the history of the gradual blending of Roman, German, and Christian elements. It is essentially an internal process which was disturbed and influenced by both Byzantium and Islam, but not at any point totally disrupted.

The Evolution of Western Europe in the Early Middle Ages (480–741)

The Germanic element in the evolution of the first European society was contributed primarily by the Franks, whose name applies to a loose confederation of tribes, some of whom crossed the Rhine into Gaul in the fourth century. The difference between the Frankish movement into the Roman Empire and that of the Germanic tribes discussed earlier is that some of the Frankish tribes remained east of the Rhine, so that contact was sustained between those within and those outside the empire. The Franks expanded, rather than migrated, from a German base and they remained tied to their homeland and their heritage. The farther west they extended into Gaul the less Germanized they became, but the easternmost part of their kingdom retained the German language and many Germanic traditions. Thus instead of being absorbed by Roman culture these peoples added a decided Germanic impression to it.

During the fourth century the Franks fought from time to time as allies of the Roman army in Gaul and a Frankish army helped the Romans defeat the Huns in 451. But the real Frankish impact on European history dates from the accession to the kingship of a chieftain of the Salian Franks named Clovis in 481. Clovis was fifteen years old, exceedingly able, ambitious, and entirely ruthless when he became king. Gaul was divided among four main groups, Clovis' own excepted. There was still some purely Roman territory, governed by a Roman patrician, and there were three major German kingdoms—the Burgundian, the Alemannic, and the Visigothic—along with a sprinkling of minor ones. In 486 Clovis defeated the Romans, and between 486 and 511 he conquered the Alemanni (east as well as west of the Rhine), the Burgundians, and the Visigoths in Gaul.[3] At his death he left a kingdom stretching across most of Gaul from the Pyrenees to the Rhine and extending northeast of the Rhine part way to the Elbe River.

The Conversion of Clovis

The most significant event of Clovis' career relative to the future role of the Franks was his conversion to Christianity. In the recorded story of his conversion the king is deliberately compared with Constantine and even called "another Constantine," and there is some reason for the comparison. The other German tribes in Gaul, if they were Christian at all, were Arian, although individual Germans (Clovis' wife among them) converted to Roman

3. From 511 on, the Visigoths were confined to the part of their kingdom which stretched southward across the Pyrenees into Spain.

Scenes from the Life of St. Remy. *The saint's fame rests partly on his miracles and mainly on his alleged baptism of the Frankish king, Clovis. The bottom scene of this ivory triptych, carved in the late ninth century, shows St. Remy baptising the king.* (MUSÉE DE PICARDIE, AMIENS)

85

Christianity. Clovis' people, the Salians, followed the conversion of their king and became the first tribe to convert directly to orthodox Roman Christianity. During the rest of his lifetime Clovis turned many of his wars of conquest into holy wars against the heretics, establishing the Franks as upholders and protectors of the Roman church. From the time of Clovis' conversion onward, the fortunes of the Franks were intertwined with those of the Roman church.

The Franks under Merovingian Rule

The history of the Franks until the end of the sixth century was recorded by a Gallo-Roman bishop, Gregory of Tours (538–594), and since this narrative is the only literary source for that period of Frankish history it is extremely valuable. Gregory's record also reveals a great deal about the "barbarization" of Gaul—the change in the society from the cultivated Roman world of the fourth century to the far more primitive and superstitious world of the sixth. But the central theme of Gregory's history is that the Franks had come as saviors of the Catholic Roman population in Gaul. Given this fact, the state of nearly continuous civil war among the Franks themselves following Clovis' death was intolerable to Gregory.

One of the main causes of these civil wars was the Frankish law of inheritance. The purpose of the law,[4] as originally applied to land, was to keep a family's holdings intact from generation to generation. If, when a landholder died, he left four sons, the estate was divided among them equally for use, but no one son had outright ownership of his portion. This meant that no part of an estate could be sold and that the size and value of the land could not be diminished. The same law was applied in the same way to royal power. The Frankish Kingdom was regarded as a large

---

4. This law is referred to as the "Salic law," from the name of the Salian Franks whose code it was. The Salians were Clovis' native tribe.

estate which could be divided only temporarily for purposes of administration, and this made for conflict in almost every generation of Frankish kings.

The dynasty which Clovis established is called "Merovingian," for Clovis' grandfather Meroveus. With few exceptions (one of whom was a king named Dagobert, who reigned at the beginning of the seventh century), there were not many outstanding Merovingian rulers after Clovis. After Dagobert's death in 639, the Merovingian dynasty rapidly declined. The kings lost control of their financial resources by continually dividing their lands; they were weak personalities who increasingly turned over their authority to the landed nobility with the result that before the close of the seventh century, the real work of administration was being done by the chief official in the kingdom, the Mayor of the Palace. As a Frankish observer was later to describe the situation, "There was nothing left the king to do but to be content with his name of king, his flowing hair, and long beard, to sit on his throne and play the ruler. . . . "[5]

The position of Mayor of the Palace was not originally intended to be hereditary, but by the final decades of the seventh century it had, in practice, become so. (These hereditary mayors who emerged were the ancestors of the great king Charlemagne—in Latin Carolus Magnus—and are therefore called, after him, "Carolingians.") In the early eighth century Charles Martel (714–741), who defeated the Muslims near Tours, was king in all but name. His rise to power and that of other Frankish Mayors of the Palace signals the changes that had taken place in the Frankish Kingdom since the end of the fifth century.

The Merovingians inherited a land that had managed to retain, however tenuously, some of the attributes of Roman administration. Roman law and the Roman system of taxation were still in operation in parts of Gaul, and the country still had gold. It was not that Frankish Gaul, in any absolute sense, had come through

---

5. Einhard, *Life of Charlemagne*, trans. S. E. Turner (Ann Arbor: University of Michigan Press, 1960), p. 23.

the invasions intact; it was rather that, in spite of them, some of the Roman heritage remained.

The blending of German and Roman elements into one society began in the sixth century. At first German and Roman law existed side by side, but the two were soon merged, although the language of law and administration continued to be Latin. There was frequent intermarriage between the Franks and the Romans; and even though, like Gregory of Tours, there were clergy who as late as 600 could trace their ancestry back to the Gallo-Roman aristocracy, by the next century this class had disappeared.

The Carolingian Mayors of the Palace represented a new Frankish aristocracy, a class of warriors, whose wealth was entirely in land. These aristocrats were not, as the Roman aristocrats had been, connected with or centered in cities in any sense. Frankish Gaul, although in fits and starts, had finally become almost de-urbanized, and the critical change was the decline of a money economy. There had been a resumption of trade with the Byzantine Empire at the end of the fifth and through the sixth centuries, but this was on a small scale and did not continue. Using the Roman system, the early Merovingian rulers were able to collect taxes, but only with great difficulty, and by the mid-seventh century practically not at all. Although during these times there never was a total cessation of trade or a total lack of money in the economy, by the eighth century northern European society, more than ever before since the founding of the Roman Empire, depended on the work of the peasant in the field and the protection of the new aristocracy.

Throughout the sixth and into the early seventh century the Gallo-Roman clergy were strong supporters of the Merovingian royal power. However, as the Merovingians declined in ability and authority and as the clerics themselves came to be drawn from the emerging Frankish nobility, a new alliance was gradually formed in the Frankish kingdom. The members of this alliance were the clergy, the Mayors of the Palace (representing the landed nobility), and the papacy. The instrumental role in forging this bond was undertaken by the church—specifically by the monks of the Benedictine order, and by the popes.

The Church in the Early Middle Ages

Medieval Christianity and medieval Christendom were influenced decisively for centuries by two men, both Italians, who lived during the sixth century: St. Benedict of Nursia (480–ca.543) and Pope Gregory the Great (540–604).

St. Benedict and Benedictine Monasticism

St. Benedict is the founder of the form of monasticism which is characteristically associated with the Western church. Before Benedict, monasticism in Europe had been primarily an imitation of the Eastern type with its emphasis on solitary withdrawal from the world, extreme asceticism, and austerity. After more than a century of monasticism in the West, we read of complaints by the ecclesiastical hierarchy about the rootlessness—and even disorderliness—of the monks, who were unregulated and free to come and go as they chose. Abuses seem to have grown up in the monastic movement, but this apart, the individuality of Eastern monasticism was not well-suited to the Roman devotion to law and order. It was Benedict's genius that he found a way to adapt the monastic ideal to the organized church.

We know something of St. Benedict's life from two sources—his own Rule and his biography written by Pope Gregory the Great. Both deal mainly with Benedict's spiritual life, so there are not many details of the early years before he became a hermit. Benedict was born into a wealthy Italian family and was sent to Rome to study. The circumstances that prompted his rejection of family, studies, and the scholarly life are not known. "His sole desire," Pope Gregory tells us, "was to find favor with God, and so he made the religious life his goal. He withdrew then, knowingly ignorant and wisely unlearned."[6] He became a hermit and lived in a cave for three years. His reputation for piety attracted people to him, and he responded to their desire to be instructed

6. *The Dialogues of Gregory the Great, Book Two, St. Benedict*, trans. Myra L. Uhlfelder (New York: Bobbs-Merrill, 1967), p. 3.

by setting up a small community. The latter undertaking seems not to have been a very satisfactory experience, and in 525 Benedict moved to Monte Cassino, south of Rome, and there established a successful community for which he wrote his famous Rule.

The Benedictine Rule was intended solely for Monte Cassino, and Benedict had no conception of the influence it would have on Western monasticism. The Rule, written sometime between 535 and 543, was itself influenced by the Basilian Rule, by a fifth century modified version written for a monastery in Marseilles by a monk named John Cassian, and by an anonymous earlier Italian *Rule of the Master.*

The purpose of the Benedictine life was, and is, the essence of the monastic ideal—a life devoted to God. It is in the patterning of that life that the Benedictine Rule proved so remarkable. The main vows taken by the monks who entered the order were stability, fidelity, and obedience. Obedience in this case meant not only obeying God's commands, but those of the abbot, who had complete control over the monastic community. And this was a community in a fuller sense than had hitherto been organized. Before Benedict, monks had been able to move about freely, which precluded an integrated and smoothly functioning communal life. Under the Benedictine Rule a monk underwent a probationary period of a year, after which, if he continued, he vowed to remain in the same monastery for life.

Since the purpose of the Benedictine order was devotion to God, the day was organized around the offerings of prayers, the recitation of the liturgy, and spiritual readings called the Monastic Office. Every three hours around the clock the monks would be awakened or called from their work to say the Monastic Office. The extreme ascetic practices of Eastern monasticism were done away with and the Rule provided for a more balanced existence. Prayer was balanced by work, the monks grew their own food, and the craftsmen among them provided whatever other necessities were required. The Benedictine monastery therefore became a self-sustaining economic unit, and though no individual could own property, the community itself was able to own the land.

The Benedictine Rule sets down in detail every aspect of the monk's life: the amount of food and drink at mealtime, the periods of fasting, the periods of silence. Its great virtue is that in so organizing the monastic life, the Benedictine Rule brought the Eastern world-rejecting spirit into harmony with the emphasis on law and order of the Roman church. Before his death in the mid-sixth century, Benedict had founded thirteen monastic communities under his Rule. The Rule did not immediately supplant the other forms of monasticism in the West, but it had a genuine appeal due to its intrinsic merits. As it gradually became the predominant form of Western monasticism, the Rule became so widespread and its influence so important that the centuries from the sixth to the tenth have often been referred to as the "Benedictine centuries."

Two additions which were made soon after Benedict's death help to explain the influence of Benedictine monasticism. Neither was envisioned by the founder. According to Benedict, most of his monks should know how to read and write, because it was necessary to read the monastic Office and study the Bible. But those skills had no purpose beyond assisting the devotional life. The conception of the monks' roles as copyists, preservers, and finally, as transmitters of divine and secular learning was grafted onto the Benedictine system. The influences which produced this important function came from outside, from such diverse places as Cassiodorus' monastery at Vivarium and—as we shall see— from monasteries in Ireland and England. Monastic scholarship was also a response which came in time from the recognition of the need to maintain what might be irretrievably lost.

The second addition to Benedictine life was due largely to Pope Gregory the Great, who encouraged the monks to leave their cloisters and become missionaries.

The Papacy of Gregory the Great (590–604)

Pope Gregory I was accorded the title "the Great" in recognition— justly earned—of his position as one of the most significant pontiffs in the history of the church. This mark of elevation did not come until well after Gregory's death, when he was also entitled the fourth Father of the Latin church in company with Jerome, Ambrose, and Augustine. Gregory was in fundamental ways different from the earlier three Fathers. He was not as learned in the classics as they, nor so devoted to classical scholarship. By Gregory's time the study of classical letters had seriously declined, and although his education was good, it was good in a limited context. Nor was he in any event so intellectually or philosphically inclined, although he was a prolific writer and among his more theological works was a commentary on the Book of Job. Basically, Gregory was a different kind of personality, shaped by two seemingly contradictory traditions and inclinations: the Roman aristocratic tradition of civic responsibility and the monastic ideal.

Gregory was born into a Roman aristocratic family, and after finishing his education (which included some legal training) he followed a career in the city administration until he reached the highest post in the civil government, that of prefect. In 574 he gave up his career, turned his vast inheritance in land over to the church, and entered a Benedictine monastery, where he intended to remain for the rest of his life. However, he had so many administrative abilities that he was soon asked to put them to work for the church. He went on several important missions, even traveling to Constantinople as the pope's representative. In 590 the reigning pope died, and by popular demand Gregory was made pope in a city that was being decimated by both a terrible plague and the attacks of enemies. Near the end of his *History of the Franks*, Gregory of Tours described the installation of the new pope, recording also how he resisted the appointment thrust upon him by the Romans. According to this account, Gregory was ready to go into hiding when he was seized by the Romans and forcibly dragged to St. Peter's Church, where he was first made a bishop and then crowned pope.

The most important of Gregory's accomplishments during his short reign (590–604) was to recognize clearly that the church's real mission lay in the role it could assume in the development of a new civilization in the Western world. He seems to have comprehended the church's destiny and to have recognized that its future was linked, not to the Roman imperial past, but to the emerging Christian society of Europe. To help facilitate that future, and also because of the immediate difficulties in Italy, Gregory wanted the support of a power closer to Italy and less troublesome than Byzantium. He therefore began to negotiate with the Franks for help in Italy, and although his attempts were basically unsuccessful he initiated the papal policy that eventually led to the early eighth century alliance which included the Frankish church, the Mayors of the Palace, and the papacy.

Well before Gregory's accession to the papacy two major theories in support of papal supremacy had evolved. The first was the Petrine doctrine—the theory in support of the papacy's claim to supremacy over the universal church. The second—and the more drastic—was the Gelasian doctrine, which was the theory put forth by Pope Gelasius I that spiritual power was not equal to secular power but was greater than it, because the popes alone were directly responsible to God. When Gregory became pope there was little reality to either theory because papal authority over the churches in Europe was practically nonexistent. The churches in the Frankish Kingdom had become independent of Rome, particularly during the sixth century when the Gallo-Roman clergy was supplanted by members of the new Frankish aristocracy with no ties or loyalties to Rome. In Visigothic Spain the church remained Arian until the end of the sixth century, and even after conversion to Roman Christianity its clergy were more closely attached to their king than to the pope. North Africa was under Byzantine control and, in addition, a church had grown up in Ireland which had no formal affiliation or allegiance to Rome whatever. To make matters worse, from Gregory's point of view, this Celtic church was an actively and successfully proselytizing organization.

The problems confronting the pope in Italy alone would have overwhelmed a lesser man than Gregory. In 568 Italy was invaded by the Lombards, the last and most warlike of the German tribes to settle there. Two things mainly saved Italy from falling completely into their hands: the well-fortified, impregnable walls of some Italian towns—Rome among them—and the division of the

Lombards into separate duchies which did not often combine to take united action.

For the most part, the Byzantine strongholds in the south and Ravenna in the north were able to hold out against the invaders, but by 590 the pope was isolated in Rome, sandwiched between the Lombards (who were either Arians or still pagans) in the north, and the Byzantine centers in the south. Gregory's difficulties with Byzantium stemmed largely from the fact that although the Byzantine centers were able to save themselves, their government was simply not in a position to send aid to Rome or the Italians.[7] On the other hand the Byzantine government insisted that Italy was still part of its empire, so that although Gregory actually negotiated peace treaties with the Lombards these were never acceptable to the Byzantine emperor since they recognized Lombard control of imperial territory. All this took place against the background of rivalry between the Pope at Rome and the Patriarch at Constantinople.

Difficult as the immediate circumstances were, Gregory's activities in the defense of Rome and Italy against the Lombards had long-term benefits for the extension of papal power. When the pope's treaty with the Lombards, negotiated in 593, broke down in the following year and the Lombards resumed their attacks, Gregory himself led the defense of Rome, thus clearly establishing the pope as ruler of the city as well as of its church. Gregory also reorganized papal finances, particularly the income from the lands given the church throughout Italy. He took charge of investing this money, made sure that it was collected, and used it to support hospitals, give charity to the poor, ransom captives from the Lombards, and set up schools. In assuming authority over the disposal of these funds, Gregory set a precedent, probably not intentionally, for securing the income that would in the future be the basis for the temporal authority of the papacy.

Gregory intervened in church affairs all over Europe with varying degrees of success, but more importantly he asserted a papal supremacy that was not actively rejected by bishops in the Western

7. This period in Italy coincides exactly with that of intense warfare with Persia, which was soon followed by warfare with the Muslims.

church. Deeply concerned with the pastoral duties of the clergy, his most influential book, the *Pastoral Rule,* dealt with pastoral care. This sympathetic and humane guide teaches the art (as Gregory himself called it) of caring for peoples and souls. It was not only the care of souls, however, within the church that concerned Gregory, but the conversion of those outside it. He began the conversion of the Lombards to Roman Christianity, then moved to the even more important task of converting the Anglo-Saxons in England.

The Missionary Movement to England

There is a story, hallowed at least by repetition, that before he became pope, Gregory witnessed fair-haired, blue-eyed individuals being sold at the slave market in Rome. When he asked who these people were he was told they were Angles. "Not Angles, but Angels," he is said to have replied, and then and there he determined to convert them to Christianity. Early in his papacy he sent a group of Benedictine monks led by St. Augustine (who founded the Church at Canterbury) to convert the Angles and the Saxons in England.

The missionary movement to the English was an important new development in the history of Christianity. It was initiated in accordance with Gregory's desire to extend the boundaries of Western Christendom, and during his pontificate the Benedictine monks became the good right arm of the papacy, directly under papal control. This was the beginning of the long association of the monastic and missionary movements with the papacy, but the missionary role assumed by the monks also had another function—that of spreading Latin civilization. The language, culture, and traditions of the Roman Empire, to the extent that they were preserved and transmitted, were passed to those outside that tradition by the church. This was the answer to the question of how the Germans and any other strangers to Roman culture would be Romanized and drawn into the civilization of Latin Christendom.

The immediate impetus for the conversion of the English, however, was the fact that they were already being converted to Celtic Christianity by Irish missionaries—that is, they were being converted to a church which lay outside the boundaries and control of the Roman See.

Christianity in Ireland

Some of the major currents that flowed into Western Europe during the early Middle Ages began in Ireland, a part of the world that until the fifth century was scarcely touched by either Roman civilization or Christianity. Then, during the fifth century Ireland was Christianized, and at almost the same time it received its first education in classical culture. The two new traditions combined with the ancient Celtic culture, and the result was the release of an extraordinary creative energy.

The Celts had first been pushed into Gaul by the Germans during the sixth and fifth centuries B.C., and from Gaul some of them had migrated to Britain and Ireland. There existed some trade between the Celts in Ireland and the Romans on the continent before the fifth century A.D., but there seems to have been little, if any, cultural contact or influence in either direction; and although the Romans conquered Britain and made it a colony as early as 43 A.D., their armies never crossed the Irish Sea.

When the Germans broke through the Rhine in full force at the beginning of the fifth century, the Romans decided they needed their legions on the continent and withdrew them from Britain. As soon as Britain was left exposed, the Irish began raiding the country and in one of their raids captured a Roman Briton, the future St. Patrick. He escaped from Ireland and made his way to Gaul on a trading ship. After entering a monastery in southern Gaul and studying for several years Patrick returned to Ireland, as he had vowed he would, to convert the Celts to Christianity.

St. Patrick's monastic experience in Gaul took place during the pre-Benedictine period, and he was therefore trained in the highly ascetic and individualistic Eastern monastic tradition. It was this tradition that he transplanted to Ireland, and since his own life was also the epitome of great missionary zeal, Celtic Christianity from the outset was dominated by asceticism and proselytism.

The organization of the Irish church remained monastic for centuries. It did not adopt the episcopal organization of the Roman church, unsuited as it was to the tribal and rural society of Ireland. There *were* bishops in Ireland, to be sure, but they were never as important in the direction of the church as the abbots of the monasteries. The latter were actually built in imitation of the desert caves of the Eastern hermits, and the asceticism of the Irish monks was as rigorous as that of their Eastern prototypes. But rather than escape to the desert, the Irish monks made the most wrenching demand of all upon themselves—they left Ireland to devote their lives to finding solitude and prayer. These "wandering saints" are the most endearing of all the saints of the early Middle Ages because they simply set sail from Ireland, often with no direction whatever, and placed themselves totally in God's hands. Their extraordinary devotion was coupled with missionary zeal and they quite literally seemed to travel all over once they got started. Their missionary activity, which went on in Europe and in Anglo-Saxon England, began in the last half of the sixth century and lasted through the seventh century.

In addition to the religious aspects of Irish monastic life, the monasteries became centers of learning. The exact process of the transmission of classical learning to Ireland is not absolutely certain, but it seems most likely that classical education was brought by Gallo-Roman scholars and teachers who fled to Ireland when the Germans invaded Gaul in the fifth century. There was an affinity between the Gallo-Romans and the Celts because the original "Gauls" were Celts; and the Celts in Ireland were particularly receptive to Roman literature and learning because they had an educational tradition of their own and a respect for education. Roman rhetoric was undoubtedly especially appealing to the Irish, who were known very early for their eloquence and for their poetry.

The fine, beautifully illuminated manuscripts that were produced in the copying rooms of the Irish monasteries are, without doubt, the essence of Celtic creativity. The pre-Christian Celtic

Initial Page (XPI) from the *Book of Kells* (late 8th c. A.D.)   *This famous manuscript, considered the finest of all Irish illuminated manuscripts, incorporates the richness of at least three artistic heritages: Celtic, Germanic and Christian. Notice the way in which the illuminators have integrated human heads, zoomorphic details, vegetable motifs, and the lacery into a harmonious and strikingly beautiful unit.* (THE BOARD OF TRINITY COLLEGE DUBLIN)

tradition in art was put to work decorating the pages of Gospels, prayer books, and books of Christian learning; and these were carried all over the continent and to England by the monks.

Since the Irish embraced classical learning at a time before literature declined on the continent, they were able to copy, preserve, and study the ancient authors. Those works, too, along with an educational system to teach them, were transmitted by the Irish wherever they went. The most prominent Irish monasteries founded on the continent—at Bobbio in northern Italy and St. Gall in Switzerland—became centers of learning with truly great libraries which housed the illuminated manuscripts the Irish had brought with them. These libraries and manuscripts endured throughout the Middle Ages.

Most of the Irish settlements did not last. This was in part due to the fact that the Irish were not organized in any formal way. The missionary groups which went out into the most primitive and pagan parts of rural Germany developed no real organization that could maintain them from generation to generation, and they kept up little or no contact with the mother church in Ireland. Then, in the seventh and eighth centuries the Irish missionaries to the continent were supplanted by those from Anglo-Saxon England. And finally, though it is not least among the reasons, Ireland resisted joining the Roman world. Ireland had not been part of the Roman world during the empire, and although the Irish church eventually accepted the direction of the Roman church it did so only reluctantly. In this resistance to joining the Roman world, Ireland was exactly opposite from England.

Christianity in Anglo-Saxon England

England had been both Romanized and Christianized after it had become part of the empire, but when the Roman legions withdrew, the country was overrun by German invaders, the Angles and the Saxons. As a result, Roman civilization was almost completely destroyed, as was the early Christian church in England. It was in this environment that the first Irish missionary settlement in England was founded in 563. In the few decades before Pope Gregory sent out the Benedictines under St. Augustine to England,

Celtic Christianity had made great inroads there. It was from the Irish that the Anglo-Saxons received their missionary zeal and their classical education, but it was from the Roman church that the English learned the sense of organization and order that characterized their own missionary activities.

The essence of the English flowering seems to lie in the fact that under the direction of the papacy England was brought back into the orbit of the Roman world and rejoined to continental Europe. This was a relatively quick process. The Benedictines established their church at Canterbury and converted the southern part of England, while the Irish continued to convert the northern part. In 664, at a synod of bishops held at Whitby, the decision was made to bring all the churches in England under papal control. By the end of the seventh century the Anglo-Saxon missionaries were "at work in the fields of the Lord" in the Frankish Kingdom. In their efforts to reach into the most primitive parts of Frankish territory, these missionaries solicited the help of the Frankish Mayors of the Palace, and there was a certain amount of cooperation between the Frankish aristocracy and the monks.

Of all the Anglo-Saxon monks, the most important was Winfred, known as St. Boniface (675–754). St. Boniface was first and foremost a missionary; he is often referred to as the "Apostle to the Germans," meaning those Germanic tribes that were still pagan and quite uncivilized. He began his work in the last decade of the seventh century and continued until he died a martyr's death in 754. In the course of his career he became the archbishop of Mainz, the chief prelate of Germany, and he was also appointed papal legate to the Frankish Kingdom. It was Boniface who promoted the alliance between the Frankish Mayors of the Palace and the papacy, and he saw the fruits of his efforts when he crowned a new king of the Franks in 751.

The Crucial Decade (741–751)

The years from 741 to 751 were particularly significant for the future of Europe because it was then that all the important powers

in the West and Byzantium came into a new relationship with one
another.

Papal-Byzantine Relations:
The Iconoclastic Controversy

From the death of Gregory I in 604 until the early eighth century
was a period of renewed Byzantine interference in Italy. Many of
the popes were actually Hellenized Easterners. It appeared, once
again, that the papacy (and the Western church) might not be able
to free itself of Byzantine control. But in 726 a dispute broke out
in the Byzantine Empire which seriously impaired papal-Byzan-
tine relations and gave the papacy an opportunity and an excuse
to find new allies. This theological dispute was known as the
"iconoclastic controversy."

As a religious problem the dispute was internal to the Byzantine
Empire and confined solely to the East. However, because the
issue involved was theologically important, and because the matter
was brought to a head by the emperor, the pope asserted his right
to interfere. The dispute began in 726 when the Eastern emperor
Leo III ordered the destruction of all the icons in the Byzantine
Empire. In the Eastern Orthodox church the images of Christ,
the Virgin Mary, the saints, and the Apostles are called icons. To
appreciate the effect of the destruction of the images (the literal
meaning of iconoclasm) and the wounds which the controversy
caused within the Byzantine empire, it is necessary to understand
that the icons have a central, indeed integral, place in the liturgy
of eastern Orthodoxy. The sacred icons are believed to be the
earthly manifestations of the archetypes of the saints and, above
all, Christ and the Virgin Mary. They are not, in this view, representations, created by an artistic imagination; they are the actual
appearance of the heavenly archetypes, and the paintings must
therefore follow strict rules so that Christ and the saints can be
seen—visually and dogmatically—as the true reflections of heavenly beings. Each icon has its own special place in the church and,

together, they represent for the congregation the vision of the glories of heaven.

The destruction of the icons, ordered by emperor Leo III, led to rioting, bloodshed and a divisiveness so fundamental that the impact of iconoclasm has been compared to the impact of the Protestant Reformation on the Western church, with the important difference that after a hundred years the icons were restored and religious unity was maintained in the Orthodox church.

The use of images had been much discussed in the early church, and by the end of the fourth century some consensus had generally been reached to maintain statues, icons, and paintings of religious figures—always with the clear understanding that it was the spirit and not the representation that was being worshipped. The emperor Leo III's edict forbidding icons was thus in the pope's view a heretical position. The first period of iconoclasm ended in 787 with the restoration of religious images. (There was a second, less bitter, round which opened in 815 and lasted until the final restoration took place in 843.) But long before the issue was resolved in Byzantium, the papacy had secured its alliance with the Frankish Kingdom and was able to assert a substantial measure of independence from the Byzantine emperor.

Papal–Frankish Relations: The Coronation of Pepin III

Until the death of Charles Martel in 741, the Frankish Mayors of the Palace had remained unresponsive to papal requests for help in Italy. Charles was succeeded by his son Pepin III (741–768), who was favorably disposed to helping the papacy, since he hoped for the church's support in deposing the Merovingian dynasty and establishing the Carolingian line on the Frankish throne.

By the time Pepin became Mayor of the Palace, the path to a papal–Frankish alliance had been smoothed by the work of St. Boniface; and the results of these efforts were figuratively and literally crowned in 751, when the Merovingian king was deposed and the Carolingian Mayor of the Palace, Pepin III, became king.

Pepin was anointed and crowned twice: first by St. Boniface, as the pope's representative, and then in 754 by the pope himself. The Carolingians viewed the coronation as a political victory not only over the Merovingians but also over the papacy, since the new rulers believed themselves to have the upper hand in the partnership. The pope, however, had a different view of it. He believed that by anointing the new king he had asserted his leadership over Christian Europe, and that the papacy was well on its way to making a reality the program envisioned by Pope Gregory the Great one hundred and fifty years earlier.

When Pope Stephen II came to Paris to anoint Pepin for the second time (in 754) he brought with him a document known as

A twelfth-century illustration of the alleged "Donation of Constantine." *In this fresco, in the Church of the Quattro Incoronati in Rome, Constantine is shown transferring his temporal authority to Pope Silvester I. Silvester is seated on the Papal throne, while the Emperor, in a submissive position, is seen handing his imperial crown to the Pope—and looking quite sad!* (ALINARI/EDITORIAL PHOTOCOLOR ARCHIVES)

the Donation of Constantine. That this document was a fraud and a forgery was not discovered for many centuries. The essence of the document, purportedly given to the Bishop of Rome by Constantine, was that in gratitude for the bishop curing Constantine of leprosy the emperor transferred the Western part of the empire to the pope. (Constantine, according to this fiction, presumably then took himself off to the Eastern Empire.) The document was accepted as authentic and was confirmed by Pepin, who was made the protector of the Roman See. In this capacity Pepin was soon called on by the pope to defend him against the Lombards, which Pepin duly did. He made two expeditions to Italy, and after his second victory against the Lombards (in 756) he secured and gave to the pope a block of land extending diagonally across Italy from Ravenna to Rome. The papal title to this land was contained in a document called the Donation of Pepin. The land, known as the Papal States, or the Patrimony of St. Peter, remained the pope's possession until the unification of Italy in 1871. This territory was not easily held, but each pope protected it as fiercely as he could, because it carried with it political power in Italy and an income to pursue the goal of papal supremacy in Western Christendom.

Pepin died in 768, and as was still customary among the Franks, his kingdom was at first divided between his two sons. After three years the younger son died, leaving the entire kingdom to his brother Charles, known as Charles the Great, or Charlemagne. It was during Charlemagne's reign (771–814) that the transition from classical to early medieval civilization was completed.

PART TWO ⟡

THE CENTRAL MIDDLE AGES: THE LATE EIGHTH TO THE LATE ELEVENTH CENTURY

The central Middle Ages began with the reign of Charlemagne, who became sole king of the Franks in 771 and then was crowned emperor of Rome in 800. This is the period that saw the first manifestation of the new civilization that was emerging in Europe.

105

In the beginning, the Carolingian era gave the appearance and promise of stability; but Europe plunged almost immediately into more than a century of invasions, internal strife, and economic depression.

Although Europe's recovery was slow, by the mid-tenth century there were clear indications that the conditions were being created under which European society would be able to grow and expand. This central period was not only a time of chaos but also a time of preparation during which Europe began to build its institutions and seek an orderly life. After a long period of suffering, "the world," a contemporary observer wrote, "was shaking itself and throwing off its old rags."

ॐ 3

Order and Disorder: Europe from the Carolingian Era to the Period of the Invasions (771–955)

Until the Middle Ages were very nearly over, no one thought of "Europe" or "European" in a cultural sense. The terms were used only in a geographical sense, yet looking back at the Carolingian era, we can discern the beginnings of a distinctively European civilization. The boundaries of Charlemagne's kingdom did not, even at their greatest extent, include all continental Europe; but the synthesis formed at the heart of the Frankish Kingdom under Charlemagne was the inheritance to which all Christian Europe would finally, and in varying degrees, fall heir.

The Appearance of Stability: The Carolingian Era

During Charlemagne's reign the three elements which formed the basis of European civilization began to be harmonized. These were the traditions, sometimes dimly remembered, of the Roman past, the Germanic way of life, and, of course, Christianity. Charlemagne devoted his life to blending these elements and trying to bring them into a cohesive whole. In doing this as best he could, he secured the foundation on which European civilization would develop. That in fact that should have been the case is quite remarkable. Europe went through an extraordinarily disruptive period that lasted for more than a century after Charlemagne died, and a great deal of his work was undone. The standard he set remained, however, and the legacy of Carolingian rule survived into the tenth century and beyond. What is equally remarkable is that some of the Carolingian aspirations should have permeated Frankish society at all.

Frankish Society in the Late Eighth Century

At the time of Charlemagne, Frankish society was essentially, though not exclusively, rural, its economy based on the labor of peasants. The members of this class (referred to in the terminology of the Middle Ages as "those who worked") provided the material support for the two other classes, the nobility ("those who fought") and the clergy ("those who prayed").

The peasants lived in villages which were grouped in two different patterns. Where the land was very poor and could support

In this detail from the Moutier-Grandval Bible, Adam and Eve are portrayed as a peasant family. *The illuminators were obviously interpreting the Biblical theme in the context of their own society. This Carolingian manuscript was illustrated in the mid-ninth century (834–43) at Tours.* (THE BRITISH LIBRARY)

very few people, the villages were small and were dispersed quite far apart about the countryside. Within these little communities each family had its own small plot of land adjoining the house and also shared with the other villagers a parcel of open land which was worked communally. On the rich and fertile lands of northern Europe—mainly in the areas that are now northern France and western Germany—and in the valleys of the Rhone and Po Rivers, the peasants lived in villages clustered closely together, and they farmed large open fields. Whatever the form of the community, the peasants had only a tenuous hold over the countryside. More than half of northern Europe (the estimates run as high as two-thirds) was covered with forests. The peasants lived in extreme rural isolation, and the forests added considerably to the feelings of isolation because they acted as barriers—frightening and awesome—between communities.

The land was farmed according to two different methods. In the parts of Europe, such as Brittany and western and central France, where the dispersed villages mainly existed, the communal fields were tilled for only a certain number of years and then abandoned. The shortage of manure, which was the only fertilizer known, was a problem endemic to medieval agriculture. In the dispersed settlements, where the soil was poor, the problem was dealt with by simply moving the tillage when the returns on seed planted began to fall. Thus every few years, when the communal land had become infertile, it was given over to grazing and a new communal field was opened up. In the many places where the soil was richer and where clustered villages existed, a more advanced method of farming was followed. To deal with the shortage of manure, the peasants used a two-field system to maintain soil fertility. Rather than abandon arable land, when the yield fell, they divided their land into halves and left one half fallow every year (because fallowing increases the fertility of soil). This two-field or biennial system is the method that had been used by the Romans.

Roman practices were continued, not only in the rotation of crops, but also in the main implement that was used for farming. The Romans used a light plow which scratched the surface of the land (and is therefore sometimes called a scratch-plow). It is very well adapted to farming the fine, light soil around the Mediterranean, and it continued in use in the south throughout the Middle Ages. The scratch-plow was used in northern Europe also, but it was not sufficient for turning over the heavy, clayey, rocky soil in the north.

At some point just before the reign of Charlemagne, an important innovation was made in agricultural technique; this was the invention of the heavy plow, which could cut deep beneath the surface of the soil and which was drawn by a team of six or eight oxen. The oxen were difficult to turn, so the land was farmed in long rows called furrows. This also allowed the moisture to drain off, since the north had the problem of heavy summer rains. Dating the introduction of the heavy plow is a matter of dispute among historians, some placing it considerably later than the early Carolingian era. Close inspection of the documents from Charlemagne's reign reveals that the heavy plow was certainly known by the end of the eighth century, but the difficulty lies in knowing how widely it was being used by then. It seems quite safe to say that its spread was quite restricted and that, as in all rural societies, change came exceedingly slowly. Still, the heavy plow was an innovation of major consequence because, for the first time in history, it now became possible to farm effectively the rich lands of northern Europe.

There had always been villages of free peasants during the Middle Ages, and always some lands (called *allods*) which had been privately held. By the time of Charlemagne, however, most of the peasant villages in the rich northern areas were no longer free. Typically, a village or group of villages was under the control of a lord and was part of a larger agricultural organization called a manor. The manor, which was the characteristic form of agricultural unit during the medieval period, was frequently a very large estate. We know of a few that were as large as eighty thousand acres. The manors were divided into the lord's own lands, the demesne, and those lands leased to peasants. The demesne consisted of arable land, woodlands, pastures, often vineyards, and the villa where the lord lived. The demesne provided the lord's income and was worked by the peasants whose labor was payment for their leaseholds and houses. In addition to labor, peasants were required to hand over to the lord a yearly rent paid not in money but in kind—a certain number of chickens, farm vegetables, eggs, or goods. Women worked on the manor too, weaving, sewing, and laboring in the fields alongside the men. The manor was, or generally attempted to be, a self-sustaining economic unit, and each manor had craftsmen—bakers, brewers, metalworkers—who supplied whatever was needed beyond the agricultural produce.

Within this large mass of workers, most of whom were peasants, there were many gradations from slave to freeman, with some social mobility both upward and downward. All who lived and worked on the manor were in varying degrees subject to the lord's control. The largest group within the manor were the serfs, who were unfree but not slaves. The serf was bound to the land and inherited the attendant obligations in labor and rents, but he also had the security of knowing that he could not legally be removed from his land. There were also slaves, who were owned outright by the lord. Slavery was on the decline during the Middle Ages, and it was possible for a slave to move into serfdom by marrying above him, which happened enough to have been recorded. (It was also economical for lords to allow their slaves to become serfs—this was cheaper than supporting them.) At the other end of the scale, the decline in slavery was offset by the depression of free peasants into serfdom. Some freemen voluntarily surrendered their land to great lords and became their tenants in return for protection and economic survival, or because the lords forced them to become part of the manor. But, in addition, there were artisans and craftsmen who contributed special and necessary skills to the community and in return were granted exemption from servile rents and dues.

On the whole, life was extremely difficult for the peasants, and the general picture, even in the wealthier parts of Europe, is one of poverty and hardship. The diet was poor for everyone, regardless of class, because it was essentially a carbohydrate diet. The basic food was cereal although milk, cheese, and eggs were also included. The main meat was pork, but meat was not eaten in great quantity and there was a scarcity of fruits and vegetables. We know from exhumed skeletons that the peasants in particular were undernourished—in periods of famine to the point of eating grass. Two and three generations lived in one small hut made of straw and mud, or occasionally wood. A hut contained little beyond mats for sleeping and a table and chair or two. The peasants were illiterate, and, though nominally Christian, many had only recently converted and none had had much opportunity to acquire more than a veneer of Christianity. The majority could not understand the Latin in which the mass was recited because they spoke only their own Germanic dialects, or in the western, more Romanized parts of the kingdom, a dialect derived from Latin but vastly different from it.

The great estates were controlled by the wealthiest members of the nobility ("those who fought"). But "nobility," as it applies to the Frankish aristocracy at the end of the eighth century, encompassed none of the attributes usually associated with aristocracy. (The connotation of grace and manners was to come only much later.) The noble class was formed in a variety of ways. The wealthy lords at the top were landowners. They had acquired

112

their land by seizing it or had received it as a reward for service, either at the time of the Frankish invasion into Gaul or later, during the unsettled periods of warfare under the Merovingians in the seventh century. Royal and local officials sometimes became part of this upper stratum of the nobility, but only when they had been able to acquire land. Having acquired land, the lords then set out to protect themselves, their territories, and the peasants who worked for them by building up private armies of retainers, or vassals. The relationship between the lord and his vassal was sealed by a formal and mutual agreement. The vassal swore an oath of homage and fealty according to which he promised to serve his lord and be completely faithful. The lord, for his part, promised to aid and sustain his vassal, which included providing him with food, clothing, shelter, and equipment for battle.

The relationship between lord and vassal had as its background a long and honorable tradition among the Germans: This was the relationship between the chieftain and his warrier, the chieftain giving protection in return for his warrior's loyalty and support. It was an honorable relationship because the vassal, as the warrior in time came to be called, was a freeman. (It was an unequal relationship, of course, because the chieftain was the more important partner.)

As a consequence of a new technique in warfare introduced at the beginning of the eighth century, the warrior class became a more self-conscious and articulated group. The advent of the stirrup in western Europe quickly led to the exclusive use of cavalry— an innovation which was highly effective on the battlefield, but extremely expensive to support. The existence of mounted troops necessitated not only caring for the horses, but providing armor and regular training and physical preparedness for the shock warfare involved. Sometimes a lord chose to give a portion of his land to a vassal, who would then take on the responsibility of providing his own equipment. This was by no means a widespread practice, and when it was done, the land was not given to the vassal *outright* but on condition of service. This was called at first a *beneficium*, derived from the Roman practice of giving land in a conditional manner.

113

Although the Merovingians had on occasion found it necessary to grant benefices to some of their officials in order to keep them loyal, they had not done so often. When Charles Martel was Mayor of the Palace, however, he had built up his own power by giving such grants of land to the vassals who fought for him in his wars. One of the reasons his son Pepin had sufficient support to depose the last Merovingian king without too much fear of being ousted himself was that the Carolingians had also built up a large retinue of knightly vassals whom they supported on their own estates.

The lords had a great deal in common with the peasants. They had a little more variety in their food, and certainly more quantity, but on the whole, not a much more nutritional diet. Their houses were larger and somewhat better furnished, but until the twelfth century a castle was most often made of wood and was cold and drafty in winter, hot in summer, and completely lacking in privacy. The nobility could occasionally indulge in a taste for fancy clothes. On the wealthier estates where an agricultural surplus was produced, there was a little trade, and silks and other fine fabrics were imported from the East.

The members of this noble class were crude and illiterate men who spent their time fighting or preparing to fight. They were subject to the same fears as the peasants, and their religious beliefs, in general, were similar. The natural disasters which occurred so frequently, the plagues and famines over which the population had no control, led to a good deal of superstition. The belief in the miraculous powers of saints and their relics, such as a bone or a piece of clothing, was widespread. The numbers of shrines erected to saints increased all over the countryside, and so much did the worship of relics increase that locating and selling them became a business. The worship of saints and relics, however, seems to have given people some sense of security and community.

The picture of Frankish society is dismal, but not unrelieved. At the upper level of society, particularly among the higher clergy and the monks, there were educated individuals with a sophisticated sense of what Christianity was about, and some understanding of the Roman heritage. Much of the leaven that worked to bring about change in Frankish society came from elsewhere, from Ireland and England, and from Italy where a higher level of Christianity and culture had been maintained than existed north of the Alps. But Charlemagne had a small nucleus of people to work with in his own kingdom, and the remarkable fact about Charlemagne himself is that although he was securely rooted in Frankish society, he was not limited by it. All his achievements stemmed from his grasp—extraordinary for his day and age—of the essential idea of a state. Charlemagne understood the Roman concept—if not the details—of a government that administered a kingdom. His reforms mirror his belief that his own role as king was to improve life within his kingdom.

The Reign of Charlemagne (768–814)

A good deal is known about Charlemagne's kingship because there is an unusually large amount of documentation from his reign. To a great extent, the documents derive directly from Charlemagne himself, a painstakingly thorough monarch concerned with every area of life and government in his kingdom. Charlemagne wrote letters, edicts, laws, and instructions on every matter, large or small, that came to his attention. And it is fortunate that they should have come down to us because immediately after his death his real accomplishments, great enough in their own right, were obscured by the mythology that grew up around them. His exploits, considerably embellished, were celebrated in song and poetry throughout the Middle Ages and he became a legendary figure. There is also, however, a marvelously human biography of Charlemagne, written by one of his secretaries, Einhard, that allows us to see behind the myths and legends.

Charlemagne was capable of great cruelty to his enemies but also of great kindness to his friends. He was well-liked by his intimates, as Einhard's affectionate portrait reveals:

The King was large and strong, and of lofty stature, though not disproportionately tall . . . the upper part of his head was round, his eyes

very large and animated, nose a little long, hair fair, and face laughing
and merry. Thus his appearance was always stately and dignified. . . .
He used to wear the national, that is to say, the Frank, dress—next his
skin a linen shirt and linen breeches, and above these a tunic fringed with
silk; while hose fastened by bands covered his lower limbs, and shoes
his feet, and he protected his shoulders and chest in winter by a close-
fitting coat of otter or marten skins.[1]

The pursuits Charlemagne most enjoyed in his spare time were
hunting and horsebackriding, "accomplishments in which scarcely
any people in the world can equal the Franks."

When Charlemagne came to the throne he began immediately
to implement two policies that had been at least implicit in Clovis'
career at the end of the fifth century. These had hardly been
pursued by the Merovingians, who were at first too involved with
their own civil wars, and later too incompetent to do so. One was
a policy of expansion that had as its goal the inclusion of all the
German-speaking people into a single kingdom. The other was
the policy of Frankish involvement with the church, which had
begun when Clovis converted to Roman Christianity and won
the support of the Gallo-Roman clergy.

An entirely new stage of Frankish involvement with the church
had begun when Charlemagne's father was crowned king and the
Carolingian line was established on the throne. At his coronation,
Pepin was anointed with holy oil and sanctified (first by St. Boniface and then by Pope Stephen II) in a religious ceremony that
transformed him and the subsequent Carolingian rulers into theocratic monarchs. The tradition of theocratic monarchy reached
back to the rulers of Israel, with King David as the prototype of
the divinely chosen monarch. In the books of the Old Testament,
the church leaders had a divinely inspired historical record to
inform them of God's will and an example of how that will should
be carried out. After choosing David to be king, God had sent
Samuel to anoint him. "Then Samuel took the horn of oil, and
anointed him [David] in the midst of his brethren: and the Spirit

1. Einhard, *Life of Charlemagne*, trans. S. E. Turner (Ann Arbor: University of Michigan
Press, Ann Arbor Paperback, 1960).

King David Playing the Harp, from a ninth-century Carolingian Bible. *The artistic portrayals of David were deliberately used to establish historical and political ties between Carolingian and Old Testament kingship. Among the figures that surround the dancing David are the representations of the ideal kingly virtues: Prudence, Justice, Fortitude, and Temperance.* (BIBLIOTHEQUE NATIONALE, PARIS)

117

of the Lord came upon David from that day forward." (1 Sam. 16:13) Christ's own ancestry was traced to King David, and when Pepin became king of the Franks he was anointed in a ceremony that deliberately recalled the anointing of David. Charlemagne was of course anointed in the same manner.

To Charlemagne, the tradition of Frankish expansion and the tradition of theocratic monarchy were inseparable. He was a German warrior who "did not suffer difficulty to deter him or danger to daunt him." He was also a king by divine right, with a large conception of the duties—and privileges—of a ruler whose throne was entrusted to him by God.

Charlemagne's Wars

The reign of Charlemagne was an era of almost continuous warfare. Charlemagne successfully concluded the conquest of all the German-speaking tribes, and as he expanded his kingdom in all directions he also Christianized it. Behind most of these wars was the king's sense of Christian mission—his belief that he was fighting to widen and defend the borders of Western Christendom. After moving eastward to conquer the German tribes living between the Rhine and the Danube, Charlemagne determined to extend his kingdom even further to Saxony, the region between the Rhine and the Elbe Rivers. This was the longest and most difficult of all the conquests. "No war ever undertaken by the Frank nation," Einhard wrote, "was carried on with such persistence and bitterness, or cost so much labor, because the Saxons . . . were a fierce people, given to the worship of devils, and hostile to our religion . . . . "[2] The Saxons fought as strongly against Charlemagne's absolute insistence on their conversion to Christianity as they did against their subjugation to his authority. Their continual revolts against him were treated with extreme cruelties, such as large-scale massacres and deportations of people from their homeland. This war lasted for thirty-three years, and

2. Ibid.

when it finally ended in 804, the Saxons were forced to convert to Christianity and the border of Saxony became the northeastern boundary of the Frankish kingdom. In order to protect the eastern borders of both Saxony and Bavaria, Charlemagne also fought— always successfully—the Danes, the Slavs, and the Avars. Within Gaul itself he consolidated his power over Aquitaine (where there were revolts against him) and subdued the Bretons.

The campaigns that captured the literary imagination of the Middle Ages more than any of the others were the two that Charlemagne undertook against the Muslims in Spain. These are a perfect example of the combination of Charlemagne's desire for expansion and his belief that he was fighting holy wars against the infidel. Returning from the first expedition to Spain, the Frankish army was ambushed in a pass in the Pyrenees called Roncesvalles. In a total disaster the army was decimated, and among the men killed was the governor of the March of Brittany, Roland, who became the hero of the first great epic in French literature, the *Song of Roland*. The second expedition was more successful, and Charlemagne secured a strip of territory south of the Pyrenees, called the Spanish March. The latter was the first Christian outpost against Muslim control of Spain, and it became an important base for subsequent Christian expansion into the peninsula.

Early in his reign Charlemagne was called on by the pope for aid against the Lombards who, despite Pepin's earlier victories, were on the march in Italy again. In 774 Charlemagne defeated the Lombards, and after his victory, he made his first visit to the pope at Rome and underwent the formality of renewing the Donation of Pepin. Charlemagne, however, did not turn any part of Lombardy over to the Pope. He kept the iron crown of Lombardy for himself. Direct Frankish control of northern Italy affected the future of Germany itself over the next several hundred years, with endless ramifications for German relations with the papacy.

Due to the almost incessant warfare during Charlemagne's reign, the demands exacted from his soldiers were extraordinary. In order to allow these warriors the freedom to spend more of their lives in battle, Charlemagne continued the practice, begun by Charles Martel, of giving them land so that they could support and equip themselves. New conquests brought him new lands to offer in return for service, so Charlemagne was able to maintain an army that was extremely devoted to him. The effectiveness of his militia depended on his strict control over his vassals. Charlemagne was able to control the vassals in part because he had land to offer them, in part because of his forceful personality, and in part because he paid strict attention to everything that was going on throughout his kingdom.

The kingdom that Charlemagne ruled was a genuinely impressive creation. Through his conquests he had more than doubled its size since inheriting it from his father. It included all of modern France, Belgium, Holland, Switzerland, almost all of eastern and western Germany, a sizable part of Italy, and a small area in Spain. It is not surprising, then, that the scholars and theologians at the Carolingian court had begun comparing their ruler to the ancient Roman emperors. In his devotion to Christianity, the Frankish king seemed another Constantine; and in his attempt to found a unified kingdom and rule it constructively, Charlemagne was in the best imperial tradition. He controlled more territory than any single ruler since the great days of the ancient Roman Empire. Thus, the general feeling that Charlemagne had become something more than a German chieftain was in the air when he went to Rome in the winter of 800.

The Coronation of Charlemagne

The immediate event that brought the king to Rome in November was the pope's plea for help against his enemies. The pope was Leo III, and the nature of his difficulty was an early example of the problems successive popes were to face with increasing frequency during the next two centuries. The pope's real strength, as contrasted with his theoretical hope for supremacy in Europe, was in Rome and the Papal States. The pontiff ran the affairs of his principality and derived the income from it, and it was the strong conviction of the old Roman noble families that the papal position should "belong" to them. Leo III was not one of them, and indeed, apparently aroused their enmity. The specific charges which were leveled against him are not known, but it is clear that he was a man commanding neither affection nor respect. After being actually physically assaulted by the Romans, Leo finally begged Charlemagne to come to his rescue. The king, in his role as defender of the pope and the church, went to Rome and had Leo exonerated of the charges against him. Then, with the Christmas season approaching, Charlemagne remained in Rome to celebrate the holiday.

On Christmas Day in 800 the king attended mass in St. Peter's, and when he "arose from prayer, Pope Leo placed upon his head a crown and the whole Roman people acclaimed him: 'Life and victory to Charles Augustus, crowned by God, the great and peaceful emperor of the Romans.' "[3] Until that moment no one in the West had received—or even usurped—the imperial title since Romulus Augustulus had been deposed in 476. The coronation of Charlemagne as Roman emperor was the greatest accolade his contemporaries could bestow upon him, their recognition that he was unquestionably the most powerful man in Europe. And yet Einhard reported that Charlemagne was completely surprised by the coronation, that he was very displeased, and that he never would have gone to mass had he expected it.

Charlemagne was certainly aware that he was being regarded as a worthy successor to the Roman emperors; he undoubtedly felt it himself. But it may well be true that the event, when it actually occurred, took the king completely unaware. It is also altogether likely that Charlemagne was not at all pleased to receive his crown from the pope, having made absolutely clear, from the beginning of his reign, his own conception of the relative roles of king and pope: "It is for us [Charlemagne] with the aid of divine piety, to defend by force of arms the Holy Church of Christ everywhere from the attack of pagans and the devastation of infidels . . . . It is for you, holy father, to aid our arms with hands

3. Ibid.

upraised to God like Moses . . . . "[4] Charlemagne remained absolutely consistent in his belief that the pope should limit his activities to prayer and that the king would take care of all other matters, religious as well as secular. Charlemagne had no intention of being absorbed into the Roman church.

The most significant aspect of the coronation, however, was the pope's implicit claim that the imperial crown was his to give—or not to give—as he saw fit. The papacy, in cementing its alliance with the Franks, was winding up exchanging Byzantine control for control closer at hand. But the papacy still clung to the theory behind the forged Donation of Constantine—that Constantine had transferred the Western Empire to the bishop of Rome. In an attempt to assert papal supremacy over a united Christendom, Leo III conferred the imperial title on Charlemagne. Had the Frankish king a real sense of what lay ahead, he might well have stayed home from church, for the coronation proved to be the beginning of several centuries' conflict between the papacy and the newly created Western Empire. The more immediate consequences, however, were difficult for pope and emperor alike, since from the Byzantine point of view, Charlemagne and Leo were traitors. In 800 the Byzantine Empire was ruled by a woman, Irene, and there was talk in Europe of a marriage between this empress and Charlemagne. This was only a passing idea, however, and, in any event, in 802 Irene was deposed. Altogether it took Charlemagne twelve years of diplomacy with three different Byzantine rulers to reconcile the Byzantine emperor to the re-creation of a Roman Empire in the West. And although the Eastern emperor had, finally, no alternative but to accept a Western counterpart, Charlemagne's coronation exacerbated the growing breach between East and West.

Despite this, the coronation of a German king as the new Roman emperor by the pope was a moving event. The large circle of red porphyry embedded in the floor of St. Peter's where Charlemagne knelt at prayer before being acclaimed Augustus still evokes a

---

4. Quoted in K. M. Setton and Henry R. Winkler, *Great Problems in European Civilization*, 2d ed. (Englewood Cliffs, N.J.: Prentice-Hall, 1966), p. 155.

dramatic scene; and whatever the problems for the future, the Christian empire was a symbol of the growing sense of community in Western Christendom.

Although the imperial title gave Charlemagne enormous prestige, it added nothing to the authority or lands that he already possessed. He never intended to make Rome the center of his empire, and in fact he never returned to the city after 800. To the new emperor, the Roman Empire represented a kind of order and effective administration that he attempted to harmonize with Frankish tradition.

Administration and Commercial Policy

Basically, Charlemagne continued and extended the system of administration that had existed under the Merovingians, but with far greater thoroughness and in a much more paternalistic way. The interior of his kingdom was divided into several hundred administrative units, or counties, each run by an official (a count) appointed by Charlemagne. There was nothing new in this. Along the borders, Charlemagne's appointed military governors were called margraves (from *mark* or *march*, meaning "border"). And to ensure that the rather simple system of local government worked efficiently and honestly, Charlemagne sent out messengers (*missi*), always in pairs—one an ecclesiastic, one a lay person—to check on local affairs and report directly back to him. He also sent his sons to oversee the counts and margraves, and he personally traveled all over his kingdom in order to supervise the nobility and keep his subjects loyal. Although the capital was wherever the king and his court happened to be, the place Charlemagne came to prefer and where he eventually spent the most time was Aachen, or Aix-la-Chapelle.

Charlemagne's commercial policy is an even better example of his concern with order, and there the contrast between Charlemagne and the Merovingians is particularly illuminating. The Merovingians had no settled economic policy, and their coinage reflected the weakness and fractiousness of the Merovingians themselves. Money was minted locally by almost anyone who cared to do it, and there was little confidence—beyond the Merovingians themselves—in this currency. Charlemagne centralized the minting of coins and established the Carolingian coinage on a silver standard, and after stabilizing the monetary integrity of the Frankish Kingdom, he actively encouraged the Franks to engage in overseas trade, particularly in the North Sea.

The North Sea had been crossed by the Romans of the early empire in order to trade with England and Ireland, but it was not an active highway compared with the Mediterranean. During the fourth and fifth centuries the turmoil of the German invasions caused this route to be rarely used. Even then, however, it was not completely inactive. (In the fifth century St. Patrick escaped from Ireland on a Roman ship carrying Irish hounds to Gaul.) Toward the close of the sixth and into the seventh century, due in part to the influence and travel of the Celtic and Anglo-Saxon missionaries, there was a revival of trade in the North Sea.

The Franks manufactured swords, pottery, and glassware in northern France and the Rhineland, and these were exported to England, the Scandinavian countries, and the Lowlands (then known as Frisia). Grain was exported to Scandinavia, where the need for agricultural products was very great; and there was other commercial activity in the kingdom as well, although most of it was in the hands of middlemen. The Jews, encouraged by Charlemagne, played a role in the trade between the Franks and the Muslims. In this trade the major export commodity was slaves, bought by the Franks from the Anglo-Saxons who took them to the slave markets in Verdun and Mainz. From there the slaves were carried to the Muslim East by the Jews. At the time of Charlemagne slaves also were brought into Western Europe from the Slavic lands and then shipped to the East, although that link was not yet strong.

Frankish commercial ties with the East were also maintained through some Italian cities, principally Venice. The Venetians, who traded with both Byzantium and Islam, acted as middlemen in the trade between Charlemagne's kingdom and the East. Swords, slaves, and pottery were brought to Venice and then shipped east in exchange for spices and silks. The picture of an essentially agrarian society has therefore to be modified to include trade and travel ties with the world outside the Frankish Kingdom.

The North Sea commerce, which Charlemagne particularly tried to foster, is significant because his efforts there reflect the growing importance in all areas of life of the northern lands that occupied so large a physical part of the Carolingian empire. Charlemagne accomplished the far-reaching change begun early in the eighth century by establishing the prominence of the North and its people in the formation of this early European civilization. The basis of Carolingian personal wealth and power was in the triangle formed by three northern rivers, the Meuse, the Moselle, and the Rhine, and this triangle remained the focal point of Charlemagne's kingdom.

At the same time that he fostered and developed the North, in much of what he did, Charlemagne showed a desire to transplant Roman traditions to German soil. He built a chapel at Aachen, for example, which is a paradigm of what he hoped to do. The chapel was modeled on the Church of St. Vitale, built in Ravenna by Justinian, and Charlemagne's architects actually went to Ravenna and Rome for the marble and the columns used in constructing it.

Although the latter is more massive and its decoration far simpler than that of St. Vitale, the resemblance between the two churches is unmistakable and deliberate, and the octagonal plan which Charlemagne imitated is closely identified with Roman imperial architecture.

The Revival of Learning

Of all Charlemagne's efforts, the most durable and significant was his attempt to raise the level of learning among Frankish clergy, not many of whom were even literate. The pastoral priests usually learned the mass by heart, and off in the countryside, as the years went by, the words became jumbled together and most of the text was forgotten. On the average, the monks were not much

better educated. Even those entrusted with the copying of manuscripts could barely read them. The Merovingian manuscripts
which we have are difficult to translate because the words all run
together, there are many errors in the texts, and the handwriting
is poor. Despite this generally low level of learning, there were
some educated bishops and abbots, and in the monasteries founded
by the Anglo-Saxon missionaries there were literate monks and
the beginnings of some great libraries—at St. Gall, at Fulda, and
at Reichenau, for example. Even so, Charlemagne could not find
a single fully correct text of the Vulgate in his kingdom and had
to send to Rome for one. Nor was there a complete text of the
Benedictine rule, although the Frankish monasteries were presumably run in accordance with it.

Charlemagne's insistence on educating the clergy stemmed from
several motives. At his court he was referred to as "David," and
he took seriously his role as God's anointed protector and defender
of the church. Above all Charlemagne wanted uniformity in the
Frankish church, under his own direction. By the Carolingian era,
the laws by which the church was governed were not at all cohesive or consistent. Many diverse beliefs and local practices had
arisen, the liturgy was not recited and sung in a uniform manner,
and in many parts of Gaul it was different from the Roman liturgy.
All these abuses Charlemagne wished to correct, and in addition,
he wanted an educated clergy to proceed with the conversion of
the newly conquered German tribes, educate the Franks, raise the
general literacy, and serve in the administration of the kingdom.

Charlemagne was personally devoted to learning, and he took
great pains with his own education. He "gave attention," Einhard
tells us, "to the study of foreign [languages], and in particular was
. . . a master of Latin . . . but he could understand Greek better
than he could speak it . . . . The king spent much time and labor
. . . studying rhetoric, dialectics, and especially astronomy . . . .
He also tried to write, and used to keep tablets and blanks in bed
under his pillow, that at leisure hours he might accustom his hand

**An interior view of Charlemagne's chapel at Aachen, constructed between 792 and
805 A.D.** (STOEDTNER/PROTHMAN ASSOCIATES)

to form the letters; however, as he did not begin his efforts in due season, but late in life, they met with ill success."[5] In the context of Frankish society, Charlemagne was extremely well-educated, but it is sobering to realize that he could be considered learned without ever being able to write.

In the last decade of the eighth century Charlemagne sent a directive to the abbot of the monastery at Fulda which initiated the revival of learning in northern Europe. "Be it known . . . that we . . . have deemed it expedient that the bishoprics and monasteries entrusted by Christ's favor to our government, in addition to the observance of monastic discipline and the practice of the religious life, should vouchsafe instruction also in the exercise of letters to those who with God's help are able to learn, each according to his capacity . . . "[6]

The program thus begun under Charlemagne's patronage was designed by only a handful of people, almost none of them Franks. The channel through which learning flowed back into northern Europe is easy to trace. From the monastic schools and libraries in Celtic Ireland, it flowed to Anglo-Saxon England, and from there to Gaul.

The Anglo-Saxon Influence

When Pope Gregory the Great sent the Benedictines to convert the English to Roman Christianity, Celtic schools were already well-established in northern England. After the decision was reached at the Synod of Whitby (664) that the entire English church would affiliate with the Roman church, new monasteries and schools had been founded, run by the Anglo-Saxons and closely tied to Rome. Soon after Whitby, the pope sent an unusual scholar to be archbishop of Canterbury. As his name indicates, Theodore of Tarsus came from the eastern Mediterranean. He had been

5. Einhard, op. cit.
6. Reprinted from M. L. W. Laistner, *Thought and Letters in Western Europe*, A.D. 500 *to 900* (Ithaca: Cornell University Press, 1931), p. 196.

educated in the fine secular schools that flourished in the Byzantine Empire, which meant that his education was grounded in the study of Greek classical literature. It is not clear just how much Greek was transmitted to the Anglo-Saxon schools, or how much existed even at the highest level of scholarship, but at least an appreciation of the Greek past had been added to the three main traditions of learning which met in England: the Celtic, the Roman, and the Anglo-Saxon.

This combination produced many outstanding schools—Canterbury, Jarrow, and York, among others—and many distinguished scholars. The most famous English scholar of the early medieval period—and to this day one of the most frequently read—was Bede (673–735), a monk who taught at Jarrow. Bede thought of himself as a teacher, and from all reports he was an exceptionally good one, but his fame rests on his *History of the English Church and People*. This was the first history of England ever written, and it is a careful and thorough work of historical scholarship on the English church from its beginning to Bede's own time. The *History* is a remarkable book because its author had a gift for telling a story well. Bede's achievements as a historian and his reputation during his lifetime as the most learned man in England are all the more extraordinary because he was essentially self-taught. Jarrow had a good library of manuscripts, and from them Bede learned the sciences, theology, and the arts of reasoning and of writing well. Despite the fact that his own physical world was always bounded by the monastery at Jarrow, which he never left, he had an understanding of the world and of people that overcame the limitations of his own time and place.

The Anglo-Saxon scholar of the greatest reputation in the generation following Bede was Alcuin, who taught at the school at York. Alcuin was born in 730, five years before Bede died, and was educated at York, where there was, as at Jarrow, a rich manuscript collection. Alcuin became director of the school and library and, in his own efforts to add to the library, made several trips to Rome for manuscripts. On one such trip he met Charlemagne in northern Italy. The king persuaded Alcuin to leave York in order to come to Aachen to design a curriculum for the palace school that would set the pattern for the other schools in the kingdom.

Alcuin's program was both clerical and scholarly. Its ultimate purpose was to train the clergy and the monks, but its method of instruction was a modified and simplified version of the Roman educational system and was based on the study of certain classical texts. Alcuin's program was modeled on the division of academic subjects devised during the first quarter of the fifth century by a scholar, Martianus Capella, who wrote an encyclopedia of education which was one of the most influential educational treatises of the Middle Ages. Martianus divided the seven liberal arts into the *trivium* and *quadrivium*—the trivium being composed of grammar, rhetoric, and dialectics, and the quadrivium consisting of geometry, arithmetic, astronomy, and music.

By the time of Alcuin there were very few books, even in Anglo-Saxon England, on which to base the study of the *quadrivium* and, although it was not totally neglected, the revival of the *quadrivium* did not really come about until the eleventh century. Until then only a little arithmetic was taught, and that at a very elementary level, since its study was considerably hampered by the fact that Roman numerals, which are very clumsy to handle, were still being used. Some astronomy was taught, primarily because the church was concerned with the correct computation of dates for religious holidays, such as Easter. Some attention was paid to music and its relationship to numbers and the movement of the planets but, all in all, none of this was of much consequence.

The heart of the academic program was the *trivium*, and even there the study of dialectics, or the art of logical reasoning, was given scant attention for another two hundred years. Education, then, was essentially literary. However, grammar was not a narrowly confined discipline as we think of it today; it encompassed the study of language itself, modes of expression, and meaning. The study of grammar began with the reading of classical authors, such as Vergil, the poets Juvenal, Horace, and Ovid, and the playwright Terence. For rhetoric, the basic texts were Cicero's work, *On the Orator*, and a book written at the end of the first century A.D. by an orator-teacher, Quintilian. The discipline of rhetoric had a larger purpose than speaking well and framing cogent arguments. Ideally, it touched on at least history and philosophy because the perfect orator, as Quintilian defined him, was not only an excellent speaker but had also "every excellence of mind."

In addition to literary works, what was learned was extracted from compilations and encyclopedias of knowledge from the past. One of the most popular of these was the work *Etymologies* by a scholar-bishop of the seventh century, Isidore of Seville. *Etymologies* was an encyclopedia of everything, and it touched on all the arts, sciences, on history, and on theology. This compendium of information—and misinformation—spanned an enormous range of topics. In general, however, the educational emphasis of the time was not on factual information but on Latin. The standard was the Latin of the early Roman authors like Virgil (whose works had become classics by the second century) and the Latin of the church Fathers, particularly St. Jerome and St. Augustine.

From the textbooks that have survived from the Carolingian era, we know that education began—and for most students, remained—at a fairly rudimentary level. For those who "with God's help" were able to go farther, the basic texts were a preparation for the detailed study of the Bible and writings of the great Latin Fathers. There was altogether a distinctly Christian purpose behind this program of learning, but to fulfill that purpose, students gained some familiarity—if only through excerpts—with classical authors.

From the Carolingian era until the rise of the universities in the twelfth century, instruction was given at two kinds of schools. One was the cathedral school for the education of the priesthood, directed by a bishop or a schoolmaster called a *scholarius*. The second was a monastic school, usually directed by an abbot and devoted primarily to the education of monks. Some monasteries had two schools, an inner school exclusively for novices, and an outer one for the training of clerks. Although in theory it was possible for a layman to attend school, this was rare before the eleventh century, except in the royal household.

Many monasteries now instituted *scriptoria*, or writing rooms, where manuscripts were copied; and from the early ninth century onward, the number and variety of manuscripts steadily increased in Europe. These were studied with scholarly care and it was no longer a matter of copying mistakes; it was necessary first to find and establish the correct text to be copied. This researching was a highly specialized skill that required, as it still does, depth and breadth of scholarship and great devotion. The copying itself was also difficult because it took place under terrible conditions. The light from the candles was poor; the monks' hands became stiff with cold in the winter, and now, at Charlemagne's insistence, a handwriting reform was instituted. Unlike the cursive script used during the Merovingian era, the letters of the new script were separately formed and the words themselves were spaced. This script is called the Carolingian miniscule, and even without knowing the Latin, it is eminently readable. The new calligraphy required that all monks try to write exactly alike, and this was hard, hard work.

With the help of a literate clergy and the use of correct texts, Charlemagne tried to standardize the liturgy throughout his kingdom and reform the monastic system. He had every intention of obtaining a full text of the Benedictine Rule from Monte Cassino, but this was not actually accomplished until the reign of his son and successor, Louis the Pious (814–840). Early in Louis's reign, he brought a monk, Benedict of Aniane, from Aquitaine to a monastery near Aachen. Benedict restored the original Benedictine Rule, with some additional religious observances, and in 817 Louis

An example of Carolingian writing from the ninth century. (LEIDEN, UNIVERSITY LIBRARY, MS VOSS. LAT. QU. 79, FOL. 74)

issued a law requiring that all monasteries in the Frankish domain adhere to the Benedictine Rule—another important step in the direction of religious unity in Europe.

All in all, one of the most important consequences of the entire Carolingian program was that it encouraged the spread of uniform religious practices and a uniform culture. This was in keeping with Charlemagne's well-formulated concept of a *respublica Christiana*, or Christian republic, or Christian commonwealth. This idea, with its strong implicit hope for unity, was at once both Roman and Christian. In Charlemagne's view, this Christian society, whose boundaries were to be the boundaries of Latin Christendom, should of course be governed by God's anointed king. Since the popes who were Charlemagne's contemporaries were weak, they had little choice except to do the king's bidding and pray "with arms upraised to God." And actually, Charlemagne's reforms might have brought the Frankish church into close conformity with Rome, had Europe not been thrown into chaos within so few decades of his death.

Charlemagne's efforts to found an educational system had several lasting effects. Standards were established for education and tests devised to measure a cleric's ability to teach, and even if at first these standards were not very high, the principle was accepted. Charlemagne's reforms furthermore established that education was once again a public matter, and Carolingian education ensured that the classical Roman tradition would survive in northern Europe. That the church would actively preserve that tradition now became certain, with the result that some schools managed to survive the darkest days of the ninth century, and when more settled conditions arrived, those monastic and cathedral institutions were ready to implement a larger and better educational system for a new age. The pattern of European education and spiritual life for several successive centuries proceeded from his enlightened programs. Over the long run Charlemagne's wish was fulfilled: He is supposed to have said that what he desired to teach his children—his own and those of his kingdom—was to fight like Franks and to read like Romans.

Charlemagne was regarded as a colossus by his contemporaries, and during his lifetime was showered with praises and gifts—the most famous of which was undoubtedly the elephant sent to him by Haroun-al-Raschid, the caliph of Bagdad. (According to Charlemagne's biographer it was the only elephant the caliph possessed.) But the empire that Charlemagne had created, the very accomplishment for which he was so highly praised, was to last for only one more generation.

Louis the Pious (814–840) and the Division of the Empire

The emperor died in 814 at the age of seventy. He was succeeded by his son Louis the Pious (814–840), but the fact that the Carolingian crown passed to a single ruler and that the empire remained intact was accidental, not deliberate. Charlemagne had intended to continue the Frankish law of inheritance and, since he had three sons, planned early in his reign to divide the kingdom among them. But only Louis outlived him, and so the unity of the empire was for a time accidentally preserved. Charlemagne himself had crowned his son Roman emperor in 813 without benefit of clergy, but Louis held the papacy in higher esteem than his father, and after Charlemagne's death allowed himself to be crowned again by the pope. The pope thus succeeded in confirming the precedent that it was his prerogative to confer the imperial title.

Louis had inherited from Charlemagne the devotion to a unified Christian commonwealth, but his devotion to this ideal went beyond that of his father because Louis intended the empire to remain politically unified. Also, he planned to follow the Roman rather than the Frankish law of inheritance in having the empire pass only to his eldest son. However, Louis's three sons would not agree to his decision and they had the support, naturally enough, of their own vassals for the continuation of the Frankish practice. As a consequence, the civil wars that had been one of the earliest problems in Frankish history reasserted themselves, and Louis's sons fought against their father. When he died in 840 the sons warred against each other for more land.

In 843 the church intervened to end the feuding, and peace was negotiated under the Treaty of Verdun. The Carolingian empire was thereby divided into three territories—a West Frankish Kingdom, an East Frankish Kingdom, and a Middle Kingdom which went to Louis's eldest son. The concession to the Roman tradition was the establishment of the principle that the latter son would inherit the Middle Kingdom and the Roman imperial title as well.

The only overt intention of the framers of the Treaty of Verdun had been to divide the Carolingian inheritance into three roughly equal shares in order to prevent further bloodshed. However, the boundaries of the West and East Frankish Kingdoms conform, in their basic outlines, to the boundaries of modern France and Germany. Although there was no conscious attempt to define these territories as separate political entities, each had a certain internal unity, and they were already very different from one another.

The West Frankish Kingdom was the oldest part of the Frankish lands (except for the original center from which all the Frankish territories expanded). It had been the earliest area to be Christianized. It had also been, and remained, the most Romanized, and the Romance language that developed into modern French had already begun to evolve there. The East Frankish Kingdom included lands, such as Saxony, which had been added only as recently as Charlemagne's reign. The eastern people were the least civilized, their lands the least developed of any territory in Europe, and they retained their Germanic tongue. Apart from whether or not it might have been feasible to do so, there was not sufficient time to consolidate the peoples within Charlemagne's empire in the brief period during which it remained unified.

The Middle Kingdom, unlike the other two, had no internal unity whatever. It was a strip of territory about a thousand miles long that ran from the North Sea to Rome and included the two prerequisites for the imperial title: Aachen, the Carolingian capital, and the control of northern Italy. Yet the Middle Kingdom fell apart almost as soon as it was formed because the Alps created an insuperable physical barrier to unity, because its people were at varying levels of civilization, and because there was no common language.

The entire Carolingian empire was partitioned in various ways during the ninth century, depending on how many sons there were to inherit. But in the end, the East and West Frankish Kingdoms emerged with their lands fairly intact, and they have since fought over and divided up the land that lay between them—the original Middle Kingdom—from the ninth century to the close of World War II.

The Disruption of Order:
The Muslim, Viking, and Magyar Invasions

The internal divisions of the empire were accompanied by civil wars which were damaging and disruptive for all within the Frankish Kingdom. The beginning of these wars during the reign of Louis the Pious (814–840) was indeed *only* the beginning and constituted but one aspect of the general disruption of European life during the ninth century and the first half of the tenth century. Not only the Frankish Kingdom, but Western Christendom in its entirety, was subjected to a series of invasions by three different groups of invaders.

The Muslims

The earliest attacks on continental Europe were launched at the beginning of the ninth century by the Muslims from North Africa. An attack on Sicily in 827 opened the second period of Islamic expansion in the western Mediterranean. Sicily, like much of southern Italy, was still controlled by Byzantium, and as long as the latter could keep its naval bases in Sicily, it could also control shipping in the western Mediterranean. Thus, the Muslim invasion of Sicily logically began with an attack on Byzantine naval supremacy in the West. The fighting between the Byzantines and Muslims over Sicily went on sporadically until 895–896, when the Byzantine government finally acknowledged the loss of Sicily to Islam. In the meantime, the Muslims had also established bases at Bari and Taranto on the southern mainland of Italy and another stronghold on the western coast, south of Rome. From their garrisons on the mainland these Saracens (as they were often called by the Christians) repeatedly attacked northern Italy and Gaul, managing to cut off whatever trade passed overland from northern Italy into Frankish territory.

The Muslims held onto Sicily and southern Italy until the eleventh century, and their very presence created a problem for the Italians—and particularly for the papacy—even when they were not actually harassing Italian towns or demanding tribute from the pope. The Muslims disrupted at least temporarily the flow of goods between Italy and Byzantium, and their pirate ships were everywhere in the western Mediterranean. To have a large and rich Islamic community so close to Rome, the center of Christianity, was a fact of life the popes were not willing to accept any longer than they had to, and the hope of ousting the Muslims greatly influenced papal policy in the eleventh century, as we shall see.

The Vikings

The second group of invaders were the Vikings, or Northmen, from the Scandinavian countries. Of all the attacks suffered by the Europeans during a long and troubled period, the most dramatic and the most feared were the Viking attacks. Though by no means confined to the continent, these attacks were also the ones with the most far-reaching consequences for the future of Europe. One of the more incredible aspects of these invasions is that the Vikings struck everywhere, appearing where and when least expected.

The Northmen came from Denmark, Sweden, and Norway, and as a group they belonged to the same Indo-European parent stock as the Germanic invaders of the fourth and fifth centuries. Their paganism and many of their customs were clearly related to the earlier Germanic tribes, but with many differences. By the eighth century, when the Vikings began their first raids in their long-prowed ships, they had become the most expert and daring seamen the Western world until then had known. They were farmers as well as seafarers, but the geography of Scandinavia, with its rocky, indented coastlines and stony soil, left little room for large-scale agriculture. And so the Scandinavians turned to the sea and became fishermen, and once they developed their ships— enlarged the sails and added the keel—they became adventurers, explorers, and pirates.

It has been difficult to find a reasonable explanation for the extraordinary expansion of the Vikings. One likely theory is that not enough food was being produced to feed an expanding population. The earliest raiders did not plan to settle away from their homeland, but seemed rather to want to collect booty and return, so there must have been sufficient space, if not wealth enough, to support them. The Scandinavians, and particularly the Danes, also wanted more opportunity to be directly involved in the trade that was becoming active in the North Sea. The ease and success of their first forays were an added impetus for further and extended raids.

The three groups of Scandinavians took three different routes along which they raided and eventually founded settlements. The respective routes are not always consistently distinguishable but, by and large, the Danes went to England, northern Gaul, into Gaul along the rivers, and circled the Atlantic coastline to Italy. The Swedes went eastward, crossing the Baltic Sea and carrying their ships overland until they could set sail again in the Dnieper and Volga Rivers. One group of Swedes, the Rus, founded a settlement near the Dnieper at Kiev in what was first called Rus- land, and finally Russia. The Norwegians raided England, but primarily they went to Ireland and Scotland, and by the last decades of the tenth century they had traveled as far as Greenland. It now seems reasonably certain that the Norwegians also reached North America, which they called Vinland, in about 1000.

The earliest Viking raids in the West were made on the coast of England in 787. In that year Viking ships appeared at the port town of Dorchester, massacred much of the population, and made

The head-post of a Viking ship recovered from the River Scheldt (Belgium) in 1936. (REPRODUCED BY COURTESY OF THE TRUSTEES OF THE BRITISH MUSEUM)

off with a great deal of booty. The raids on England continued and, as was to happen elsewhere too, turned into invasions with the purpose of settling. Within a century, by 871, the Danes had conquered nearly all the island, but in that year Alfred, with good reason called "the Great," became ruler of Wessex, a southern kingdom in England, and began a successful counterattack. Before his death in 899, Alfred had pushed the Danes north of the Thames, and for two more generations England was divided into a northern Danish kingdom and a southern Anglo-Saxon kingdom. Gradually thereafter the Danes were conquered and absorbed into a single, united English kingdom. English resistance to the Danes and the Norwegian raiders was long and arduous, but out of it

139

there developed a sense of unity and purpose achieved earlier than by any other peoples on the continent.

For Ireland there were no such benefits. There was no Alfred the Great to unify the country, and the Irish did not prevail over their Viking invaders. The famous round towers which still dot the countryside are symbols of the Irish defeat. These edifices were pagan in origin and first used for religious purposes. Later, during the ninth century, they were fortified to defend the castles and monasteries, but they were unable to withstand the invaders. Now they serve as reminders only, along with the Celtic cross, of the Golden Age of Ireland in the medieval period.

Until 840 the Franks were only minimally troubled by the Vikings. After 840, however, the Viking raids began in earnest and continued until 911 without respite. Although no part of northern Europe was spared, the West Frankish Kingdom bore the main brunt of the Viking attacks. The Danes came from a harsh land, and they committed harsh and brutal acts in the course of their raids. They plundered churches and monasteries, raped women, murdered children, and destroyed entire communities, leaving people homeless to wander over Europe looking for refuge. When the Vikings took land for themselves and settled, as finally they did, they channeled their immense energy into constructive activities. The major Viking settlement in Europe was the region in northwest France from the lower Seine to the coast, which is called Normandy. In 911 the French king, unable to expel the Vikings, was forced to accept the fact that the Norman settlement was permanent. In exchange for recognition of his territorial claims, the Norman leader Duke Rollo became a vassal of the French king; the duchy of Normandy quickly became one of the most powerful in Europe.

The Magyars

No sooner had the Vikings settled down, than another menace threatened Europe. The third group of invaders was the Magyars, or Hungarians, who were Mongolian nomads related to the Huns.

Near the end of the ninth century they took up a position along the lower Danube, and from there, beginning early in the tenth century, they conducted raids into western Europe. The Magyars went as far as northern Italy and western France, but it was the East Frankish Kingdom which suffered the worst of their assaults. The Magyars caused considerable devastation before they were finally turned out of Western Europe, defeated by an East Frankish army at the Battle of Lechfield in 955. After their defeat the invaders withdrew to their original base, which from then on was established as the kingdom of Hungary. Their first Magyar king, St. Stephen, converted to Christianity, and by the close of the tenth century the Hungarians were included within the boundaries of Latin Christendom.

The Consequences of the Invasions:
The Evolution of Feudal Society

The peoples of Europe, the lands they farmed, the towns they inhabited, the churches they prayed in, all suffered incalculable losses during the decades of civil war followed by invasion. Northern Europe, particularly, was poorer, its lands left less developed, and its population more decimated in the late ninth century than in any previous century. The coherence that Charlemagne and the Carolingians had attempted to forge for Western Europe was badly shattered. Governmental authority under Charlemagne had at best not been very well-developed, although Charlemagne had made a fine beginning, and had not, in any event, had time to take root and grow. In the midst of the violence and fragmentation of life in the ninth century people were forced to make their own arrangements for survival.

This began with the kings themselves, who gave away some of their personal lands during the civil wars to try to ensure their own survival. The kings gave land to win or keep allies, and the land thus given was by the ninth century usually called a *fief*, although sometimes the older Roman word *benefice* was used. Through the granting of fiefs the kings expanded the numbers of

141

their great vassals, the dukes and counts, who in turn added to the numbers of their own knightly vassals. At this time the kings did not hesitate to seize church and monastic lands to give as fiefs, or even to make bishops and abbots vassals.

During the invasions the kings were often simply unable—not unwilling—to provide protection for the people living within their borders. This was particularly true when the Viking invaders appeared without warning, moved in quickly to plunder, and just as quickly left. Instead of standing armies the kings had only knightly retinues, which were hardly sufficient to guard a kingdom. When the Vikings attacked, royal vassals were summoned along with their attendant knights—all of which took time. The king's forces then had to reach the area under attack, and more often than not, by the time this was accomplished the Vikings had long since departed.

No peasant village, monastery, church, or large estate could survive without some sort of protection. As a result, the lords undertook the defense of their local areas with, for many of them, very important consequences. Those who owned land enlarged their estates and increased the numbers of tenants who worked on them in return for protection. If he was powerful enough to begin with, a lord was sometimes able to bring an entire village under his control by this means. In many cases the peasants willingly gave over their land and freedom in return for protection, becoming tenants and incurring the obligations of labor and rent. In other cases peasants simply had no choice but to give up their lands because there was no one to protect them from the greed of the land-hungry lords.

Each time a king relinquished his obligation—and duty—to defend his subjects, royal authority was diminished. In addition to the acquisition of lands, as the lords became stronger, they took, or were given, additional governmental rights until gradually they came to have almost complete jurisdiction over their tenants. As the enforcer of justice on his lands, the lord gained great control over the person of his tenant. Throughout the ninth and early tenth centuries, the lords were also becoming politically more powerful as they benefitted from the collapse of royal authority above them. At the same time, they became economically more powerful because they controlled more land and more labor. Out of these changing circumstances, a distinctly new social pattern was formed.

Medieval European society, when it has become organized in such a way that the economic, military, and political powers are largely controlled by the nobility, is described as a feudal society. We can look back to the pre-Carolingian period and see the background from which this feudal system emerged—the personal relationship between the lord and his vassal, the occasional granting of a fief, the growth of the manors. In the ninth and early tenth centuries the pattern of feudal society was really formed when royal authority broke down and the granting of land became an important and permanent part of the feudal relationship.

The fief, in the earlier period, was a temporary grant, a form of payment for specific military and administrative services. By the mid-tenth century the fief, for all practical purposes, had become hereditary in a family, passed on to the eldest son. The triumph of this hereditary principle had several practical effects. The services owed a lord in return for the land were imposed on the land, as well as on the vassal; and every estate had some sort of service allotted to it. In theory the land in a country belonged to the king who, in turn, enfeoffed his great vassals with their huge estates. The higher nobility often parcelled out their holdings to their own vassals by a process called subinfeudation. Thus the hereditary principle transformed all vassals, great or small, into a closed aristocracy of warriors whose economic unit of support was the manor.

The church was initially opposed to the growth of the feudal aristocracy. By the tenth century, however, churchmen had reconciled themselves to a system from which they, too, benefitted. Clerical lands became feudal domains with the same privileges, incomes, and obligations of service as nonclerical lands. Bishops and abbots were able personally to abstain from shedding blood, but there are records of some who chose to go into battle themselves. The higher clergy and abbots assumed their feudal obligations in return for land, wealth, and power of the same secular kind as that exercised by any other feudal lord. It was not only necessary—and the path of least resistance—for ecclesiastics to serve their secular overlords; the practice enriched the churchmen enormously. The conflict, when one existed, between God and Mammon was most often resolved in favor of Mammon. As the small parish churches also began to come under secular control they were called proprietary churches, a legal term meaning that the person on whose property the church stood considered it to be his personal church.

In time, however, the church exerted an important positive influence on the feudal aristocracy. As the system matured, the personal relationship between lord and vassal was bound by a contract, or charter, drawn up by lawyers who structured the nature of the feudal bond. The church introduced an ethical content into the feudal contract that made it more binding and more equitable. And even more important, the church tried to alleviate the violence that was integral to the nature of feudal society. Then, as now, those who spend their lives preparing for war do indeed go to war. The church attempted to impose limits on the violence by enacting a Peace of God (during such periods as harvest time) when all fighting ceased. This effort was no more successful than the attempts during the twentieth century to limit war, but it did, from time to time, lessen the damage done to the crops and the peasant communities.

The feudal pattern was not evenly disseminated throughout Europe at any one time, and even where most pervasive, it did not encompass all individuals or all the land. The most thoroughly feudalized part of Europe, the homeland of feudalism, was northern France. This was where the Vikings wreaked their greatest destruction and where royal power was most decentralized. It was also there, in the West Frankish Kingdom, that the conditions were most hospitable to the growth of feudal institutions. For one thing, the counties which were the centers of local administration had a longer history in the West Frankish Kingdom than anywhere else in northern Europe. Having been occupied by the Merovingians and then having become more efficient under the Carolingians, these counties were ready-made centers of resistance to invasion, and the counts themselves had some experience in governing. It was also in this geographic area that the majority of the peasants had been integrated into the manors. By the time the invasions of the Northmen had ended, the counts had taken over many clerical lands, had forced the clergy to become vassals, and there remained few free peasants anywhere. Royal power had been so thoroughly usurped by the nobility that it can truly be said that although there was a West Frankish king during the mid-tenth century, he did not have a kingdom to rule.

In the East Frankish Kingdom conditions were not nearly so favorable to the growth of feudal institutions. In the easternmost parts, especially in the most recently annexed territories such as Saxony and Bavaria, the county had not been established as an administrative center and agriculture was not organized into manors. And both before and after the invasions the majority of the peasants were free. In the older, western parts of the kingdom Germany more closely resembled France; even so, the organizational framework was quite different from the multiplicity of feudal systems that existed in France.

Germany was divided into five major duchies, four of which originated from the tribes or "nations" that had been united by Charlemagne to make up the eastern part of his kingdom. The four were the duchies of Saxony, Bavaria, Swabia, and Franconia. The fifth duchy of Lorraine, or Lotharingia, had been plotted into existence on the map during one of the many partitions of the Carolingian empire. The dukes who controlled these territories in the tenth century were descendants, not of the tribal leaders, but of generals appointed by the Frankish kings who, during the disruptions of the ninth century, had managed to turn the ducal position into a powerful hereditary office. The power of these dukes prevented the rise of large numbers of other, lesser nobility, and there was, on the whole, far less decentralization in Germany than in France. The Vikings caused less destruction in Germany than in France, and although the Magyar invasions were more devastating in Germany, the army that defeated the Magyars in

955 was led by a German king—a fact that indicates the relatively better condition of royal authority in Germany. This victory further enhanced the kingship.

By the mid-tenth century all Latin Christendom had been restored to a measure of peace and order. In the aftermath of the invasions, political authority everywhere was fragmented, the total economy of Europe had suffered, and the Carolingian religious and cultural accomplishments had been seriously impaired. The picture was gloomy but, as at the beginning of the Carolingian era, it was by no means unrelieved. The consequences of the invasions were inconsistent throughout Europe, so that while France, which had suffered the most devastation, had a long and slow recuperation, Germany and the northern Italian cities were in all respects better off and able to recover more quickly. The feudal communities themselves now became centers of stability at the local level. The mood of fright and despair that had pervaded Europe in the preceding century and a half now gave way to a new optimism. "The world," as a medieval chronicler wrote, began "throwing off its old rags."

4

Towards A New Political and Religious Synthesis

Once the worst shocks of the invasions had receded in the tenth century, and the general condition of European life had become more settled, the arduous task of constructing a new political and religious order could begin.

When the political theorists of the tenth and early eleventh centuries grappled with the problem of how society ought to be governed, they were not in any doubt that the unity of the Carolingian Empire should be restored—that the empire should provide the civil framework and the church the spiritual direction for the society emerging in Europe. But while the theorists could

147

dream of a unified Christian commonwealth, the inescapable fact of political life was that Europe was decentralized and feudalized. There was the memory of the Carolingian empire, but no empire. The empire was divided into separate kingdoms, and even in these small units there was, as we have seen, little central authority. There were kings, and there was the idea of royalty, but not much in the way of royal power. The kings had no machinery of government and no practical way of enforcing their authority over their vassals. And while churchmen could anticipate a Christian way of life and dream of carrying forward the Carolingian spiritual and intellectual goals, the inescapable fact of religious life was that the church itself was in need of reform.

So the organization of society was, in the end, different from the one envisioned at the start. A new synthesis was born out of the Carolingian inheritance, in concert with—and sometimes in conflict with—the ideas and aspirations that emerged during the tenth and eleventh centuries. At the beginning of this period, however, the intention was to create a stable world by following the Carolingian model.

Germany and the Revival of the Empire

The Carolingian tradition of the empire was first revived in Germany, and it was under German leadership that the theorists' dream of a new unity seemed to come true.

The last of Charlemagne's descendants to rule the East Frankish Kingdom died in 911. Thereafter, the decision of whether to retain the monarchy and, if so, whom to elect, resided with the dukes of Saxony, Bavaria, Swabia, Franconia, and Lorraine. That these five nobles chose to elect a king at all in 911 had to do partly with their regard for the divinity of the royal office and partly with their need for military leadership. Germany was still being menaced by the Danes in the north and by the Hungarians in the east. The five dukes first chose as king Conrad of Franconia. It did not take long for the self-interest of the other dukes to assert itself,

An Ottonian emperor holding the orb and scepter. *This ivory situla, probably done about 1000 A.D., is in the Cathedral treasury at Aachen.* (MARBURG/PROTHMANN ASSOCIATES, INC.)

149

however, and Conrad's attempts to strengthen royal power were generally ineffective. They were also short; he died in 918. Although Conrad's weakness allowed the dukes to strengthen the independent power of their duchies, they nevertheless elected a new king in 918, Henry I, duke of Saxony. Henry was a somewhat stronger ruler than his predecessor, but it was his son Otto I who developed an effective monarchy in Germany and revived the Carolingian empire.

The Reign of Otto I (936–973)

The main internal problem that confronted Otto was the difficulty of bringing the five chief nobles under his control. By the time he came to power, the royal estates which, in Germany, were scattered throughout the kingdom, and the lands belonging to the church, had been at least nominally taken over by the dukes. Otto's plan was to use the clergy as a counterweight to the latter. He intended to restore royal power by giving the church large tracts of royal land and by granting the clergy immunity from all local (ducal) control. In return, the bishops and abbots administered the land, dispensed justice, and fulfilled many duties of government—all as agents of the king. Furthermore, the clergy provided men and supplies for the king's armies, and the clerical lands produced a good part of the king's income. This was an alliance with obvious advantages for the king, and the "Ottonian system," as it is called, worked to give the monarchy an efficient administration and to lessen the power of the higher nobility.

The alliance was also advantageous to the clergy. The lavish land grants bestowed by the king made the bishops and abbots wealthy and powerful. Freed from exploitation by the nobility and protected by the king, the church in Germany became a more stable institution than it had been since the time of Charlemagne. Encouraged by royal support, and with its legacy from the Carolingian era not too much diminished, the clergy engaged in an intellectual revival of lasting importance. When Germany expanded eastward, as it did in the tenth and eleventh centuries, the church participated in the movement and established new bishoprics and gained new lands east of the Elbe River.

The Ottonian system, however, held two potential dangers for the king. The first was that the bishops might become independent enough to turn against him. This danger was mitigated, however, by the tight control the king retained over clerical appointments. Once the bishops and abbots were chosen, they were bound to the crown by oaths of personal fealty and homage, and they were even invested by the king with the symbols of their ecclesiastical offices. The second danger was that the papacy would not acquiesce forever in secular control over the church. It was the latter that ultimately rocked the strongest foundation on which the German monarchy was built, but the papal challenge was a long time in coming and the Ottonian system lasted until the second half of the eleventh century. The best testimony to the system's effectiveness and overall success is that the monarchy retained its power in Germany despite military disasters during the short reign of Otto's son, and despite the fact that after his three-year-old grandson Otto III came to the throne, the kingdom was ruled for several years by a regent.

Once the monarchy in Germany had settled onto a secure base, Otto turned his attention to Italy and to the eventual reinstatement of the imperial crown. He went to northern Italy for the first time in 951 to rescue a Lombard queen, Adelaide, whose kingdom was about to be attacked by at least two German dukes. Otto stayed to marry the queen, becoming king of the Lombards in the process. Eleven years were to intervene before Otto's control of northern Italy was secured and his imperial coronation took place, but during that time, in the eyes of his contemporaries, Otto became the greatest man in Europe. In 955 he defeated the Magyars at Lechfield, near Augsburg. This was a resounding victory, and it was generally believed that Otto had saved all Latin Christendom from the menace of the Hungarians. The latter triumph accorded Otto the designation "the Great" and, like Charlemagne, he felt that he now lacked only the imperial title.

The Coronation of Otto I (962)

The immediate background of Otto's coronation was somewhat similar to that of Leo III in 800. Pope John XII had had political and personal difficulties in Rome which Otto had helped resolve, thereby putting the pontiff in his debt. There are documents that prove that Otto requested the crown from the pope.

The assumption of the imperial title by a German monarch had enormous ramifications for the future history of Germany as well as for Italy, the papacy, and the Slavic lands on Germany's eastern border. It is hardly surprising, then, that Otto's imperial motives have been microscopically examined, and that their consequences have been endlessly discussed. The answer to whether these motives and their attendant consequences were good or bad for Germany seems to be that the motives were sound but the consequences were, for the long run, disastrous. It has been argued that the imperial title symbolized Otto's greatness without adding to it, but this does not accord with the facts. Charlemagne's control of northern Italy was recognized, not in his capacity as king of the Franks, but as Roman emperor. And Otto was with good reason concerned lest northern Italy, politically divided and weak, be conquered by one of the German dukes. Had this happened, his policy of suppressing ducal power within Germany would have failed. The imperial title would presumably carry extra weight in Otto's relations with the German clergy and with the papacy; and also, since the West Frankish kings had a reasonable claim to the title, Otto resolved to get there first.

The unfortunate consequence was that the imperial position committed the German monarchy to pursuing an Italian policy that was forever troublesome. Otto, like Charlemagne, renewed the Donation of Pepin and became Protector of the Papal See, for he understood that the imperial title had special religious significance. Once the Carolingian Empire had been reborn German history, for good or (as was more usually the case) for ill, was inextricably linked to the history of the papacy. It was also linked to the history of all the peoples who established themselves in southern Italy—Byzantines, Muslims, and Normans—as well as to the history of the separate northern Italian cities, the Lombards and the Romans. Thus all too often the problems of controlling Italy were solved at the heavy cost of neglecting Germany's internal development.

It was never true that Otto neglected Germany, though he did expend energy in dealing with Italy and in negotiating with the Byzantine government at Constantinople. Otto sent as his ambassador to Constantinople a most remarkable and learned man, Liudprand of Cremona. Liudprand came from a wealthy and educated Lombard family, many of whose members had been traditionally in diplomatic service. The first time Liudprand went to Constantinople was on a mission for a Lombard king (in 949), and he took advantage of the opportunity to learn Greek. Not long afterward, he entered the service of Otto I. His first trip as Otto's representative was a formality; the second (in 968) was a serious embassy to ask for recognition of Otto's title and to arrange a marriage between Otto's son and a Byzantine princess.

The Byzantine emperors had accepted with ill grace the restoration of the empire under Charlemagne, and now the Byzantine emperor Nicephorus Phocas, furious at what he regarded as Otto's illegal assumption of the imperial title, was ready to foment trouble in the Byzantine province in southern Italy. Although Liudprand had been received with honor on his first visit, his embassy in 968 was a nightmare because neither emperor nor ambassador could contain his anger over the main conflict.

"It was our duty and our desire," the emperor Nicephorus told Liudprand, "to give you a courteous and magnificent reception. That, however, has been rendered impossible by the impiety of your master, who in the guise of an hostile invader has laid claim to Rome . . . . " Later, at a dinner, Nicephorus shouted across the room to Liudprand, "Your master's soldiers cannot ride and they do not know how to fight on foot . . . . Their God is their belly, their courage but wind, their bravery drunkness . . . . You are not Romans but Lombards." And Liudprand, fully aroused, retorted, "When we are angry with an enemy we can find nothing more insulting to say than 'You Roman!' For us the word Roman is comprehended with every form of lowliness, timidity, avarice, luxury, falsehood and vice."[1]

Liudprand's mission was a failure, but Nicephorus was deposed the next year and his successor concluded a treaty with Otto and gave him the Byzantine princess Theophano for his son Otto II. Permitting the marriage—which took place in Rome, in 972—was the Eastern emperor's way of accepting, if not altogether approving, the German re-creation of the Western Empire.

The marriage did not erase for all time the political antagonism between East and West; it was always close to the surface and ready to break out again. On the other hand, the interaction between Constantinople and the Western Empire at all levels of society continued and even increased in the late tenth and early eleventh centuries. Germany benefitted from increased trade between the northern Italian cities and Constantinople, and the art and architecture at the Ottonian court were inspired, as we shall see, by a familiarity with Byzantine art.

The imperial ideal was always very seductive for the German kings, although their individual conceptions of what this ideal actually comprised varied greatly. For some, like Charlemagne and Otto the Great, it implied a mandate to extend the boundaries of Latin Christendom for the greater glory of Germany, and it lent a lofty ideal to the desire to expand eastward. Germany's easternmost border was the river Elbe; and the next major river to the east was the Oder, along whose shores new kingdoms had been settled during the ninth and tenth centuries. With the exception of the Magyar kingdom of Hungary, these new kingdoms were Slavic nations—principally Poland, Moravia, and Bohemia. Between Germany and the new nations were other far less civilized groupings of Slavic peoples, and Germany's initial drive was toward that less settled territory in order to conquer the peoples and colonize their lands with Germans. Poland, Bohemia, and Moravia had been Christianized by German missionaries and could not

---

1. *The Works of Liudprand of Cremona*, trans. F. A. Wright (London: George Rutledge and Sons, 1930), pp. 237, 241–242.

therefore be swallowed up quite as easily. They were allowed to remain independent for as long as they accepted Germany's "civilizing mission," which was simply a less straightforward method of influence and control. This "drive to the east" did not proceed at a steady pace, but it became a permanent feature of German ambition and constantly recurred.[2]

The Imperial Dream of Otto III (983–1002)

For other emperors, the yearning to return to the ancient glory of Rome led to a neglect of the necessities of the present. A prime example of this desire to revive the golden age of the past was the design of Otto III and his teacher-adviser, Gerbert of Aurillac, who became Pope Silvester II. Although Otto III was only three years old when his father died in 983, he was accepted as king of Germany, and his kingdom was ruled by his mother and grandmother—an astonishing happenstance in a time when the rule of women was practically unheard of. At the age of fourteen Otto assumed full power and ruled from 994 until his early death in 1002. He spent very little time in Germany because he was devoted to making the city of Rome once again the center of the empire. His plan was encouraged and greatly influenced by Gerbert, one of the most extraordinary intellects of the Middle Ages. When Otto elevated Gerbert of Aurillac to the papacy in 999, the latter took the name Silvester II as a way of recalling the age of Constantine. (The first Silvester had been the pope who, according to legend in the Donation of Constantine, had cured the emperor of leprosy, in return for which the grateful Constantine had turned over to him the western portion of his empire.)

Otto III's empire was to be the political theorists' dream come to life. From the Constantinian age, these theorists, all of whom were churchmen, had viewed the church and the empire as the two focal points of a single Christian commonwealth. Within that

2. The most recent drive met with defeat in World War II.

commonwealth there were "two powers," as Pope Gelasius had written at the end of the fifth century, "the sacred authority of the priesthood and the royal power." Otto's empire was to be that unified entity ruled from Rome, the "two powers" joined together in reality as they had been in theory.

Otto considered himself a Roman emperor—more Roman than the Romans because he was descended from the Eastern imperial family through his Byzantine mother. Theophano had imparted her knowledge of the traditions of the Byzantine court to her son, and the style and etiquette of Otto's court were modeled on those of the Eastern emperor. Even so, Otto never forgot that he was heir also to the Carolingian tradition. In the year 1000 he went to Aachen to visit the tomb of Charlemagne and pay homage to the memory of the first German emperor. Two years later Otto III died; the following year (1003) Silvester II died, and the German attempt to rule Latin Christendom from Rome abruptly ended.

Otto had been so involved in his imperial dream that he had badly neglected Germany, and during the last years of his reign the German nobility had rebelled against him. His successor, Henry II (1002–1024), restored order by concentrating on German affairs, although he, like all subsequent German monarchs, was crowned Roman emperor. Henry was the last of the Saxon line, and when he died the dukes elected the first Salian Frankish king. The Salian monarchs continued the Ottonian system with few variations until they were challenged by the papacy in the late eleventh century.

The Ottonian Cultural Revival

The culture of the Carolingian era persisted in this eastern part of the Carolingian empire which was in this respect, as in all else, not so seriously retarded as the western part. The Ottonian kings continued the Carolingian tradition of supporting learning and the arts, and there was a cultural renewal, commonly called the Ottonian Renaissance. The latter term was intended to imply that the predominant cultural influence was derived from the classical world, and though it is certainly true that the classical ingredient was essential to the revival, it was by no means all of it. The achievements of the late tenth and early eleventh centuries in education and art were of decidedly mixed ancestry—part Roman, part Byzantine, part German, and even part classical Greek.

One of the very important facts about these ingredients is that they came into Europe from different directions and therefore tell us that Europe was becoming a part of the larger world beyond Latin Christendom. The Ottonian court was influenced by Byzantium partly due to the marriage of Otto II to a Byzantine princess, and partly because the emperor controlled northern Italy and the Italians were trading with Byzantium. Byzantine influence is especially noticeable in some of the Ottonian art. At Cologne, for example, there is a wooden crucifix quite different from anything in earlier Western art. The "Gero Crucifix," as it is called, is a humanized, compassionate view of Christ's suffering on the Cross that is akin to the religious sculpture then being crafted in the East. The literary and artistic interests of the age combined to bring about a revival of manuscript illumination, and one of the great masterpieces from the court of Otto III, produced in about 1000, is an illumination from one of the Gospels showing Christ washing the feet of St. Peter. Its stylistic ancestor is Roman wall painting, transmitted to Germany through Byzantine art.

The broadening and deepening of intellectual life that began during the Ottonian period started with the rediscovery of classical authors who had been unknown during the Carolingian age. In particular, this scholarly resurgence started with the rediscovery of scientific works that led to the study of the *quadrivium*—the study of geometry, arithmetic, astronomy, and music. It is only a minute portion of the Greek achievement that was revived, and one man was primarily responsible for it—the scholar Gerbert—who went to Spain and opened another avenue of influence upon the Latin West.

The decline in the study of the sciences, including medicine,

The Gero Crucifix (970 A.D.) *is one of the great works of Ottonian art; it is named after the Archbishop who commissioned it as recorded in a contemporary hagiography. The image of the dying Christ is a mixture of realism and classicism—altogether so moving that it speaks for itself.* (MARBURG/PROTHMANN ASSOCIATES, INC.)

had been part of the general educational decline during the early medieval centuries, but some factors had conspired against the sciences in particular. At the highest intellectual level, it has always been true that only a handful of individuals have really advanced science, and the Romans had never been as interested as the Greeks in the theoretical aspects of scientific investigation. They studied scientific subjects in Greek, or, if they were not actually pursuing a career—in medicine, for example—they studied the surveys of Greek science in handbooks or encyclopedias. A small number of Greek and Roman encyclopedias survived into the Middle Ages and more were compiled, but the information they contained was fragmented to begin with, and by the tenth century had dwindled even more. No medievalist any longer accepts the classification of the period from about 500 to 1000 in Europe as a "dark age," but in terms of the sciences this description is reasonably apt. Scientific information was scanty and it was often inaccurate.

Apart from the little science that had been preserved in translation and the bits and pieces in compilations, the loss of the Greek language in the West, as we have seen, meant the loss of Greek science, philosophy, medicine, and mathematics. These were precisely the subjects which had found refuge in the civilization of Islam. The culture and language of Islam replaced Greek in much of the eastern Mediterranean because the huge deposit of Greek knowledge which the Muslims had found they translated into Arabic to further enrich their own studies. The work of translation went by stages; often the Greek was translated first into an intermediary language, sometimes Syriac, sometimes Hebrew and, finally, into Arabic. These translations, which were then transmitted to the centers of learning that dotted the Arabic-speaking world, first became known to Christian Europe through the texts that reached Muslim Spain. Translations of Greek treatises from Arabic into Latin were made as early as the tenth century at both Islamic and Christian centers in Spain. The great burst of translation activity did not come until the twelfth century, but from the beginning the most remarkable aspect of the work was apparent: It was a shared venture. The difficult task of establishing accurate texts, translating, and annotating them was done by communities of scholars, working together, irrespective of whether they were Muslims, Christians, or Jews.

Gerbert of Aurillac

The first continental European to study the translations of Greek scientific treatises in Spain was Gerbert of Aurillac, mentor of Otto III, and the man who became Pope Silvester II. Gerbert's career marks a watershed in the evolution of European education. His prodigious learning was the quality that most impressed his contemporaries, sometimes unfavorably, for it overawed and frightened many of them. Gerbert was of his age—although his knowledge was in advance of it—because he understood that the sciences and mathematics would never progress beyond their low level until there existed a substantive body of information for study. Gerbert was also much like the ancient Romans and in certain ways more closely akin to Cicero—whom he admired unstintingly—than to anyone in the tenth century. Like Cicero, Gerbert was a contemplative thinker and a philosopher, although not an original one. Again like Cicero, he participated actively in the affairs of the world and believed that training in rhetoric and logic was an indispensable tool for sharpening the mind and effectively shaping events. Above all Gerbert was a great teacher, and it was through his students that his life's work was perpetuated.

His education was begun at a monastery in southern France, at Aurillac, and his lifelong devotion to classical literature was instilled in him by his own teacher. When he had learned all he could at Aurillac, Gerbert went to Spain with the Christian count of Barcelona. There he studied mathematics and astronomy, and after returning to France he went to Rheims (in 972) where he remained for many years, becoming *scholasticus*, or head teacher, at the cathedral school and eventually archbishop. In 998 he became archbishop of Ravenna; in 999, pope.

The curriculum that Gerbert established at Rheims pointed the direction of learning for centuries to come. It restored the study of scientific and other secular subjects and encompassed the new learning available to the Latin West, preparing students to move on to higher scholarship. Gerbert's academic program included the classics and his own research in mathematics and astronomy. He had evidently studied treatises on the abacus and the astrolabe, and he introduced both to Europe, even constructing a sphere with mechanical parts to demonstrate how the constellations moved. He also reintroduced the study of logic, or dialectics, the third part of the *trivium*, which from the age of Boethius had been virtually ignored in European thought. Students in the twentieth century do not ordinarily have a feeling for the attractiveness of logical treatises (although they were popular until the eighteenth century) but, when it was revived by Gerbert, logic filled a serious need. Tenth-century scholars had only a fragmentary knowledge of the world and no principle around which to organize that knowledge, and logic was to give them a method for ordering subjects and a way of investigating and integrating the new information that was soon to flood Europe.

The overall importance of the tenth-century revival is that although it began slowly, it continued without interruption and gained momentum as it passed into the eleventh century, until even the great cathedral schools and libraries could no longer contain its luxuriant growth. The revival that began with only a handful of individuals here and there in Europe was so vigorously pursued by so many scholars, and was enlarged by so many different subjects, that it ultimately necessitated a new foundation— the university system of the thirteenth century.

Gerbert stands at the beginning of it all, and his influence, as we have seen, was incalculable. The cathedral schools, following the example of Gerbert's own school at Rheims, assumed a special prominence. Until the advent of the universities, they attracted the most intellectually gifted men; in the generation following Gerbert's, these were most often his own students. Although Gerbert was part of the German revival, due to his birth in southern France and his association with Rheims he was also directly and indirectly responsible for the revival of other French schools— first and foremost, for example, the cathedral school at Chârtres, and also those at Liege and Laon. He was truly a pioneer of the mind who inspired others to follow him.

Christianity and Movements of Reform in the Tenth and Eleventh Centuries

In the Christian commonwealth as Charlemagne conceived it, the clergy were charged with very particular functions. Charlemagne envisioned bishops and priests not only reciting the mass, baptising infants, and saying prayers for the dead, but he saw the clergy distinctly separate from the rest of the community, praying for the souls of the faithful, educating those who "with God's help [were] able to learn," and helping him administer the kingdom. Charlemagne was therefore, as we have seen, very concerned with ecclesiastical reform and he encouraged uniformity and education. He expected the monks to live in purity and strict obedience to the Benedictine Rule, with even more hours devoted to prayer and religious ritual—additions made early in the ninth century by Benedict of Aniane when he restored the Rule. And the role in which Charlemagne cast himself, with the encouragement of his clerical advisers, was in complete accord with the belief that the king was God's anointed, divinely chosen to rule a Christian republic.

There was not time enough for this program of reform to take effect all over the Carolingian empire before the invasions began, bringing dire consequences for the church. Churches and monasteries were pillaged and destroyed, and bishops and monks were dislocated like everyone else, and in need of protection. Sometimes the clergy and monks took up arms and protected themselves. More often, they were drawn into the feudal organization of society, propelled by the same needs, fear, and greed as everyone else. It is not surprising that once the higher clergy and abbots joined the feudal aristocracy they identified with it, or that counts and kings wanted to put people of their own choosing into clerical positions.

162

That many clerics had secular responsibilities during the late ninth century and the tenth century did not necessarily mean that all were indulging in corrupt practices; but the temptations were great, and there was a proliferation of abuses. Clergy at all levels of the hierarchy married and had families. So much revenue came with the acquisition of church lands that one of the favorite corrupt practices engaged in by the higher clergy was simony, the buying and selling of church offices. But worst of all, perhaps, for most Christians, the rituals of the church were imperfectly performed and sometimes not performed at all. The secularization of the higher clergy detracted from spiritual concerns, and they often neglected flagrantly their religious duties. The parish priests who lived among the peasantry were peasants themselves, had little or no education, and often could not even read the liturgy. The members of the monastic houses were for the most part susceptible to the same charges as those laid against the clergy: violation of celibacy, simony, illiteracy, and corruption.

The church was badly in need of reform, but the pope could hardly undertake its reconstruction, powerless as he was to cope with the immediate problems confronting the See of St. Peter in Rome. The situation foreshadowed by the pontificate of Leo III (in 800) had come to pass. With the exception of Nicholas I (858–867), the popes were weak, and the papal office in the late ninth century and tenth century was the toy of the Roman nobility—the chief prize of their civil wars. It was the privilege of the rich to place their relatives and friends on the papal throne. (At one point the papal crown was worn, in rapid succession, by the son, the grandson, and the lover of a Roman princess.) Competition among the Roman nobility was so bloodthirsty that few popes were allowed to live very long. And the last care of the popes themselves was for their own—or anyone else's—spiritual welfare. With rare exceptions, the men who held the papal office before 1000 nearly managed to wreck permanently the spiritual eminence of the See of St. Peter.

Once again, the picture, though dismal on the surface, is by no means unrelieved. Individuals at all levels of society were genuinely concerned with religion, although their understanding of

Christianity and the way in which their devotion showed itself were not at all sophisticated. For noble and peasant alike life itself was precarious. People lived with violence and in fear of famine and disease. The world was, at best, a harsh and difficult place, and for the majority of people there was precious little beyond hard work and a good deal of suffering. It is small wonder then that whatever ills had befallen the church, the vast majority of Christians clung to a belief in the kingdom of God and lived in the hope of salvation and a peaceful afterlife.

The manifestations of popular piety were everywhere and peoples' lives were quite enmeshed with the lives of the clergy and the monks. Members of the nobility often had a monk or holy man come to live in their households to pray for them and their families, because the support of holy people was "good work" with—presumably—some advantage in heaven. And it was quite customary for a noble to dedicate one of his sons to a monastery at birth or in early childhood. That the nobility gave gifts of land to the church was a mixed blessing for the latter, but the motive was sometimes the hope of heaven and not always secular control. The peasants were also bound to the church, and in contact daily with priests and monks. Many worked on church lands, and their only holidays were literally holy days. Whether peasants worked clerical lands or not, it was becoming the practice to donate the first fruits of a harvest to the parish church.

The numbers of shrines to local saints continued to increase all over Europe, as did the worship of relics and belief in the miraculous powers of holy men and holy places. There were pilgrimages to the Holy See in Rome, the condition of the papacy notwithstanding; and despite the hazards of travel, the expense involved, and the uncertainty of ever returning home, people undertook religious journeys to distant places. There were pilgrimages to the shrine at Compostela in Spain (believed to house the body of St. James the Apostle), and even to the holiest of all cities, Jerusalem.

The secularization of many clerics and monks was thus only an imperfect and partial reflection of the spiritual temper of the age. And as so often has happened in the history of Christianity, the abuses in the church elicited an active insistence on reform.

Monastic Reform

The first reform movement grew out of a resurgence of monasticism that flourished and spread throughout Christendom during the tenth and eleventh centuries. The monastic revival itself was a manifestation of popular religious devotion and developed hand in hand with a longing for spiritual purity and enrichment. It began, however, in a spirit of reform that gave to the new monasticism of the central Middle Ages its special character and role in society.

Within the monastic ideal there had existed, almost from the beginning, a tension between literal rejection of the world (as exemplified by the desert saints) and the organized communal life as outlined in the Rule of St. Benedict. The monastic revival exhibited both of these aspects. Most of the new monasteries were founded by ascetics whose first intention was to retreat from the world and live out their lives as hermits. This anchorite tradition never completely disappeared, as we shall see, but there was also a strong consciousness in the new movement of a pressing need to reform the older, secularized monasteries and then to have them become a model for society of the disciplined monastic life.

The Cluniac Order

One of the earliest and best examples of the way this new monasticism developed can be seen in the successful history of Cluny in French Burgundy. Cluny was founded by St. Berno, who had been an abbot but had left his monastery to live as a hermit. St. Berno quickly attracted followers, and in 910 the duke of Burgundy gave his hunting lodge at Cluny to the monks. The intention of these ascetics was to restore the Benedictine Rule and live in accordance with it, but their abode quickly became an example for other monasteries, and as a result, older monasteries were reformed and new ones established in conformity with the Cluniac ideal. Many of these houses placed themselves under the direction of Cluny, and soon an order had grown up which in 1049 was officially confirmed by the pope.

The reason Cluny was so successful was that, while it was difficult within the original Benedictine organization to correct abuses and enforce discipline since each monastery was autonomous and independent of outside checks or controls, in the Cluniac system each new monastery was tied directly to the mother house and all Cluniac monasteries were governed by the abbot of Cluny. Every monk in the order had had personal contact with Cluny because every novice was admitted into the order at the mother house. The entire order, moreover, was placed under the direction of the papacy, and although in the tenth and early eleventh centuries this meant relatively little in the way of effective direction from Rome, it did mean that the order was exempt from local ecclesiastical and secular control.

Cluniac monasticism placed far more emphasis on reciting the liturgy than had the original Benedictine Rule, and the Cluniacs became known for their elaborate ceremonies and for the beauty of the churches they built for the adoration of God. These monks did not do manual labor, believing that prayers were of greater spiritual value than work. They supported theocratic monarchy, and wherever the order spread the Cluniacs helped encourage secular rulers to undertake the reform of the church. Often, they offered their services as advisers and even administrators, so that their influence reached beyond the cloister. The Cluniacs were particularly widespread in France, though there were houses almost everywhere in Europe. In the great age of Cluniac expansion during the eleventh century, the Cluniacs spread into Spain and built churches for the pilgrims along the road to the shrine of St. James of Compostela. So large did the order become, in fact, that by 1200 there were about fifteen hundred of their monasteries in Europe.

The Other New Orders

Cluny was by no means the only new order at the beginning of the tenth century. There was an equally influential monastic center at Gorze in Lorraine, and most of the German monasteries, as

The Moissac Cloister. *This beautiful cloister is an original part of the important Cluniac abbey of Moissac. The cloister is well known for its Romanesque sculptures and its richly carved capital which reflect the influences of both classical and Byzantine art.* (COURTESY OF THE FRENCH GOVERNMENT TOURIST OFFICE)

they were founded or reformed, were tied to it. St. John of Gorze, its founder, had contact in 933 with the vital monastic revival that was taking place in southern Italy during the tenth century. The Eastern monastic tradition, with its emphasis on extreme asceticism and the eremitic life, was undergoing its own rejuvenation in the Greek provinces. St. John tried to persuade the monks of Lorraine to return with him to southern Italy, and although this never happened, John and those he influenced retained a deep regard for the world-rejecting aspect of Eastern monasticism while simultaneously providing soldiers to fight for the redemption of Christian society. Many Latin monasteries in Italy were even more directly influenced by the Eastern tradition. There were Greek monasteries in Rome itself, and there was one in which both the Greek and Latin rites were observed under the same roof.

The influences that spread from one country and one order to another are not clear-cut, and in many cases the monastic revival was at first completely spontaneous. In Anglo-Saxon England, for example, reform was associated primarily with three saints in the English church—Dunstan, Ethelwold, and Oswald—who began simply enough with their own inner vocation for a life of monastic purity, though the reformed English monasteries quickly received Cluniac influences. By the early eleventh century there were currents of monastic reform flowing throughout Europe. Although each order that was founded claimed to follow the Benedictine Rule, none interpreted it in exactly the same way. All joined in the hope that the monasteries would serve as examples of the best possible Christian life and that they would effect an improvement in Christian society; and some hoped to extend reform to the secular hierarchy of the church. In the long run this is exactly what happened, and three of the great reforming popes in the last half of the eleventh century came from the monasteries. Until then, however, it was by no means certain that the monastic spirit would, or could, extend to the papal court.

The Papal Reform Movement

Another—and different—kind of religious movement seemed more likely to reform the secular clergy and society at the millenium. This reform arose from the conviction that the spiritual well-being of society depended upon a strong, disciplined church that could promote order in a disorderly world. Before his elevation to the papacy in 999, Silvester II had been one of a growing number of northern European churchmen who insisted that to restore Christian society it was necessary first to restore the prestige of Rome and strengthen ecclesiastical discipline. These ecclesiastics further believed that the help needed to accomplish these goals should come—and in the very nature of things would come—from kings and princes. The care of God's flock was, after all, the responsibility of all his ministers, temporal and spiritual. Churchmen used the same terms to discuss theocratic monarchy as they used to discuss ecclesiastical power—kings and emperors, as well as popes, were the vicars of God on earth, for "the [powers] that are, are ordained of God."

The joint rule of the emperor Otto III and Pope Silvester II was a perfect example of the union of the two powers working in harmony to regenerate Christian society. Otto took his religious duties seriously, and his support of Silvester provided a hopeful moment for the cause of institutional reform. The moment passed quickly when both men died, Otto in 1002, Silvester a year later. The ideal was not forgotten, however, and although the papacy once more fell back into the arms of the factions in Rome, the situation came to be no longer tolerable to a growing number of secular rulers. They were frequently dedicated men, conscious that as God's vicars, they had a responsibility for His church. And so it happened that the same class that helped to secularize the church became involved in the movement to free the church from the abuses that attended secularization. The paradox is that from their point of view, it succeeded too well.

In 1046 there were three claimants to the papal see, and at that dismal juncture the current German emperor, Henry III (1039–1056), intervened. Following the Ottonian tradition of royal control over the church, Henry III had a close relationship with the ecclesiastical hierarchy in Germany and, considering the potential for factionalism, a relatively secure kingship. He was also a sincerely religious man who believed it was his obligation, as well as his right, to dominate church affairs if he thought that intervention was

169

necessary. Thus when it happened that papal politics were in such disarray in 1046 that there were three rivals for the See of St. Peter, Henry III took it upon himself to decide the election.

At two synods—one at Sutri, the other at Rome—Henry rejected all three contenders and put into office a man dedicated to reforming the church. Before this, Henry had actually appointed and supported three popes, one after the other, none of whom had lived long. Unquestionably, Henry's most important appointee was Pope Leo IX (1048–1054). Leo, the first in a line of reforming popes, was a German monk from Gorze who brought with him to the papal court a small group of other monks who were also absolutely dedicated to reform. In addition to joining the ranks of the monks to the papacy, Leo also took an important practical step toward strengthening the supremacy of the pontiff over the ecclesiastical hierarchy. He was a very active man and made several trips across the Alps to assert in person the power of the papacy over the bishops throughout Europe.

Leo was a reformer in the traditional mold, and he worked well with Henry III. This pope believed, as did many other theorists of his generation, that reform should be carried out by secular as well as spiritual leaders, and that the bond between the "two powers" was established by God and could not—and should not—be dissolved. During Leo's pontificate, however, a more radical program was being prepared, and within only a few years of his death the reform movement underwent a change of such profound consequences that it became a revolution.

The Background of Radical Reform

Although they are closely intertwined, we can distinguish two distinct currents within the radical reform movement. One had to do with a new—or rather, renewed—religious strain within Christianity that emerged at the very beginning of the eleventh century. In many ways this new religiosity was a conscious effort to return to the anchorite tradition. Eastern monasticism was still strong in Italy, as we have seen, so it is not surprising to find the extreme asceticism that is so much a part of the Eastern tradition first reappearing in Italy.

In the spirit of the desert Fathers, there were many solitary hermits, but there were also two orders founded during the first half of the eleventh century. St. Romuald, who had formerly been the abbot of a Cluniac monastery, led a community of hermits at a monastery called Camaldoli, which gave its name to the Camaldolese order. It was modeled on the strict ascetic practices of the Egyptian Fathers. Not long afterward, an even stricter order was founded, the Vallombrosan order, which insisted on absolute poverty, perpetual silence, and the total enclosure of the monks. Every new monastic movement has within it elements of reform that spring directly from the religious and political conditions of society, and these two orders were not exceptions. Among many monastics there existed a growing feeling of misgiving that the Cluniacs had become too much taken up with ceremonial and that their monasteries and churches were too richly endowed. These new orders were the first signs of a reaction against the Cluniacs which would become stronger by the end of the century.

The Cistercian order, founded in 1096 by Robert of Molesme in Burgundy, was in word and deed critical of the Cluniacs. The Cistercians were extremely ascetic and chose the most isolated places they could find in Europe to establish their houses. Austere, and at first rejecting all worldly goods, they devoted themselves to prayer and work, reducing the hours of the liturgy to allow time for manual labor. The order grew large and influential during the twelfth century, and had among its members the most prominent churchmen in Europe. The other order founded late in the eleventh century, and which was even more austere than the Cistercians, was the Carthusian order. The Carthusian monks lived in cells from which they could emerge only three times a day for prayers and meals. They seldom were allowed to eat together, and when they did, they had to observe strict silence. From France, where they began, the Carthusians spread to Italy and England; although the order obviously grew, it never had great popular appeal due to the severity of its rule. It was, however, the only order, including the Cistercians, that never had to be reformed.

The men who joined these new religious communities were in search of a personal, mystical religious experience which neither the church nor the less strictly ascetic orders could satisfy, and, in much the same way as the early desert saints, they were exceedingly puritanical. These monastics were particularly concerned about the marriage of the clergy and about the wealth of the church. At the papal court, this ascetic tradition was represented in the first decades of the reform movement by Peter Damian (ca. 1007–1072), a cardinal who had once been a hermit and who had studied with, and been greatly influenced by, St. Romuald.

The second current within the reform movement was more actively revolutionary and centered on the social and political aspects of reform, particularly the relationship between the church and temporal power, and the organization of the church and the laws governing it. The groundwork for revolution was prepared by a number of papal theorists, though the inner circle at the papal court was always small. Among these political reformers at the papal court, the two most ardent and extreme were Humbert, cardinal of Silva Candida and the Italian monk Hildebrand, who was to become Pope Gregory VII (1073–1085).

Humbert of Silva Candida was a German monk and perhaps even a Cluniac, although this is uncertain; he was an intellectual and knew Greek well (which was unusual), had been trained in logic, and was a skilled debater. He was also radical. Hildebrand had within him both the fiery radicalism of Humbert and the antisecular spirit of the monastery—the puritanism of Peter Damian. Hildebrand's contemporaries characterized him as either a saint or a thoroughgoing politician, and he seems to have been a mixture of both. He was certainly fully prepared to do battle in the world.

The actual implementation of a radical program began after 1056. In that year emperor Henry III died; his son and heir, Henry IV, was only six years old, and for ten years the empress ruled as regent. The German dukes immediately took advantage of the regency to emancipate themselves from the crown, and the papal reformers took advantage of the fact that no one in the imperial household was in a position to take much interest in the papacy. The leaders of the radical reform therefore seized this opportunity to push forward a practical program of papal independence.

The custom followed for electing popes (and the other bishops as well) before 1059 was that a secular person—usually a member of the local nobility, or a king, or the emperor—who "represented" the populace, nominated a candidate, and the clergy of the diocese confirmed the nomination. The first important step in the reform program was a law enacted in 1059, during the brief reign of Pope Nicholas II (1059–1061), which gave to the cardinals the exclusive right of electing the pope. The cardinals were either bishops or priests with ecclesiastical responsibilities in the churches in Rome. They were also advisers and councillors to the pope. However, they were not a formal group until the law of 1059 formed them, first of all, into an electoral college. The purpose of the law was to make certain that neither the Roman nobility, the emperor, nor any other secular ruler would ever again be able to interfere in papal elections. In this same year Humbert of Silva Candida published his *Three Books Against the Simoniacs*, a statement of the extreme radical position that there ought not be, in any instance whatever, any secular interference in church affairs. It was this principle which Hildebrand carried onto the battlefield soon after he became pope in 1075.

The Papacy of Gregory VII (1075–1083)

Gregory VII was the first revolutionary actually to reach the throne of St. Peter (Humbert had died in 1061), and it was his absolute conviction that secular intervention had destroyed the church's freedom. If, in Gregory's words, the church was to "remain free and chaste and Catholic," then the influence of the laity had at all costs to be removed. Gregory was not content to stop with this, however, but insisted that secular authority was in all matters to be subject to the spiritual authority. He wanted to overturn for good the traditional theories which supported the union between temporal and secular powers and establish the supremacy of the pope.

Gregory's own explanation of his intention is clearer than any restatement of it could be—and far more revealing of his personality:

Who does not remember the words of our Lord and Savior Jesus Christ: 'Thou art Peter and on this rock I will build my church, and the gates of hell shall not prevail against it. And I will give thee the keys of the kingdom of heaven . . . . ' Are kings excepted here? Or are they not of the sheep which the Son of God committed to St. Peter? . . . Furthermore, every Christian king when he approaches his end asks the aid of a priest as a miserable suppliant that he may escape the prison of hell, may pass from darkness into light and may appear at the judgement seat of God freed from the bonds of sin. But who, layman or priest, in his last moments has ever asked the help of any earthly king for the safety of his soul? . . . But since it is our duty to exhort everyone according to his station, it is our care with God's help to furnish emperors, kings, and other princes with the weapons of humility . . . . "[3]

The papal position did not, of course, go unchallenged. There were churchmen not nearly so radical as Gregory who opposed him, and many churchmen wrote in support of theocratic monarchy which, after all, the church itself had formulated. The major opposition, however, came from the empire itself, where the Carolingian tradition of a Christian commonwealth ruled by the emperor had, until Gregory's time, been successfully revived.

The Investiture Controversy

Although the real battle was over the leadership of Christian society, the specific issue over which Gregory and the young emperor Henry IV fought was that of lay investiture of the clergy. The phrase *lay investiture* refers to the practice of secular rulers performing a religious ceremony in which they bestowed upon the

3. Quoted from *The Correspondence of Pope Gregory VII*, trans. E. Emerton (New York: W. W. Norton, 1969), pp. 167, 171–172.

bishops and abbots the symbols of their ecclesiastical offices. This ceremony was itself of course heavily symbolic of the other aspects of secular control, namely appointment to clerical office and a tradition of interference in church policy. Shortly after his own investiture as pope (1075), Gregory banned lay investiture and threatened to excommunicate any ruler who continued the practice. In doing this, Gregory chose a powerful "weapon of humility," and he took deadly aim at the foundations of royal authority, most particularly in the German empire.

The Emperor Henry IV had reestablished his authority in Germany by restoring the Ottonian system—that is, by administering his empire through the church. The renewed success of the Ottonian system was at one and the same time unendurable to Gregory VII and absolutely necessary to Henry IV. Thus, for pope and emperor the stakes in the conflict that began openly in 1075 were exceedingly high. Henry did not stop investing clerics, and actually stepped up imperial interference in the election of a northern Italian bishop. Gregory retaliated by threatening to depose Henry if the emperor did not obey the ban forbidding investiture.

Henry's immediate response was to send an angry letter to Gregory that began "Henry, King not by usurpation but by the pious ordination of God, to Hildebrand, now not Pope, but false monk." The letter went on to defend divinely ordained monarchy: "[Y]ou were emboldened to rise up even against the royal power itself, granted to us by God. You dared to threaten to take the kingship away from us—as though we had received the kingship from you, as though the kingship and empire were in your hand and not in the hand of God . . . . "[4]

Gregory's reply was to carry through his threat formally to depose Henry. He was able to do this because he had the strong support both of the German nobility, who were always ready to undermine royal authority, and of the Normans. The Normans, having settled in Italy early in the eleventh century, were entirely willing to defend the pope in return for papal recognition of their own territorial rights on the peninsula. Since they placed their

4. T. E. Mommsen and K. F. Morrison, *Imperial Lives and Letters of the Eleventh Century* (New York: Columbia University Press, 1962), p. 150.

army at Gregory's disposal, the pope believed he had little to fear from Henry and the imperial militia.

The next incident was the famous encounter between Henry and Gregory at Canossa in northern Italy in 1077. Gregory was on his way to Germany, and to forestall him, Henry hurried to the castle where the pope stopped before he was to cross the Alps. Henry appeared before the pope at Canossa as a penitent asking forgiveness, and Gregory kept him waiting three days for his reply. To add to this drama, Henry stood outside the castle in the snow for the entire time (according to a doubtful tradition, barefoot). As a priest, Gregory had little choice except to forgive the emperor and restore him to his throne; but in return Gregory exacted promises of total imperial obedience, and for a short time this seemed a victory for the papacy. It was in fact a victory for Henry, who had been on the edge of disaster before Canossa, but who then returned to Germany and continued to exert royal authority over the clergy precisely as he had done before. Gregory deposed Henry once more, and in retaliation Henry marched his army into Italy in 1084 and drove the pope from Rome. Gregory went into exile in the Norman Kingdom in southern Italy, where he died in 1085.

The Solution to the Investiture Controversy and Its Aftermath

The conflict between empire and papacy, once joined, did not end with Gregory's death, but the next stages were worked out over the conference table rather than on the battlefield. The solutions adopted were not formulated until early in the twelfth century, so it is necessary to carry the story beyond 1100. The emperor was not the only ruler to undergo the papal ban on lay investiture. However, although the French and English kings were certainly investing their clerics and abbots, the threat to the papacy was neither so immediate nor so great as that which came from the German kings. (It was, after all, only the emperor who claimed the same universal sovereignty as that claimed by the pope.)

English-papal relations were politically complicated in the last decades of the eleventh century and the issues raised by the ban on lay investiture were not really joined until close to the end of the century. In 1107 a compromise was reached according to which the English king recognized that bishops and archbishops had to be elected in conformity with church law, without secular intervention, and invested with the symbols of ecclesiastical office by the church. For their part, the clergy were to do homage to the king for the lands which the church held from the monarch. Within a few years, this same compromise was agreed to by the French king.

The problem of the empire was much more difficult to resolve, from the papal point of view. For Germany, an exceedingly interesting proposal was made by a pope who was really the one other extreme radical to reach the papal throne in the eleventh century. Paschal II (1099–1118) came from the Vallombrosan monastic order, which was completely ascetic and, among other rigors, had insisted upon absolute poverty. (Not even the order as a whole was permitted to own property outright.) Paschal, who was genuinely otherworldly, proposed that the clergy and abbots of the empire give up all their lands and turn everything over to the king, resolving the entire problem by eliminating the reasons for it. This was far too radical a proposal to find favor in any quarter, and it was rejected. It was nonetheless important because the church's worldly possessions would become in the next century a problem of deep concern to other churchmen, as we shall see.

Finally in 1122, during the pontificate of Calixtus II (1119–1124), a compromise was reached between the church and emperor Henry V (1106–1125). The agreement was the Concordat of Worms (so named for the city where it was signed), and its provisions were the same as those of the English and French agreements, with the important difference that the German king was allowed to be present during the elections to clerical office. This meant that the compromise was, after all, just that, and not a total defeat for the king. The German monarchy, however, had been considerably weakened by the investiture controversy. The German king was never again able to exert his former rigorous control over the higher clergy, yet this in itself might not have been so damaging had it not been for the fact that during the many decades of fighting over investitures, the dukes had been able to wrest considerable power and land from the king. The late eleventh and the twelfth centuries produced a decentralization and a proliferation of feudal institutions in Germany which had not been prevalent before the reign of Henry IV, and which caused a serious and prolonged setback for the future centralization and development of royal government.

That the papacy made compromises at the practical level must not obscure the victory it won, nor the significant changes which resulted from the Gregorian program. The popes had challenged the Carolingian ideal of theocratic monarchy on its home ground— the empire—and the papacy had won. Gregory's ambition had also been to overturn the theory of the "two powers" working in harmony, and in terms of the empire his program had succeeded.

The ideal of unity remained, however. In fact, the ideal of a single Christian commonwealth was never again so strong as it became during the twelfth century. But the leadership had by then clearly passed to the papacy. When this was contested—as indeed eventually it was—the motive was not to restore harmony between the "two powers," but to replace papal sovereignty with imperial sovereignty.

The West Frankish Kingdom

The history of the West Frankish Kingdom, including its relations with the church, during the entire period we have been covering is totally different from that of Germany and the empire. France had been severely damaged in all respects by the Viking invasions, and as we have seen, the countryside during the late ninth and tenth centuries had been arranged into several large counties and duchies, along with some smaller principalities—a feudal society under a weakened king.

During the ninth century when the Viking invasions had begun in earnest, one of the Carolingian kings had appointed Robert the Strong to lead the resistance against these invaders in the north. Robert soon was able to take over land for himself, including the areas around Paris, Orleans, Blois, Tours, and more. By the tenth century, his descendents rivalled the Carolingian kings in power and even, for a brief time, became kings themselves. But until 987 there remained direct descendents in the Carolingian line who were able to keep the royal title from slipping away from them completely.

The Problem of Feudal Monarchy and the Early Capetians (987–1108)

The last of the West Frankish Carolingian kings died in 987, and the great counts and dukes were persuaded by the archbishop of Rheims (who had the responsibility for anointing the French rulers) to elect a new king. They chose a descendant of Robert the Strong, Hugh Capet (987–996), whose candidacy was supported by the duke of Normandy. Hugh was, quite unexpectedly, the founder of the Capetian dynasty which was to rule without interruption for over three hundred years.

The country over which Capet in name and theory ruled had no internal cohesion and no definitive boundaries. The king, although assuming the God-given right to rule, did not simultaneously acquire either a divine ability to do so or any practical institutions through which he could implement his power. Throughout the country, the people, encouraged by the clergy, recognized and respected the idea of royalty and the person of the king. The nobility, for its part, accepted the theory of his feudal overlordship, but did not so clearly recognize his actual right to govern. The king's wealth and power was derived from his own personal lands, which were consolidated into an area known as the "Île de France," and which extended roughly from Paris to Orleans. Yet even over this relatively small territory the king's influence was not secure. There were many nobles who simply ignored his authority, and each royal right and privilege—such as that of enforcing justice or of collecting tolls—had to be vigorously and continuously protected.

The lands of the greatest feudal lords in France were often richer and stronger than those of the king. He was surrounded by those counties and duchies which, by the end of the tenth century, were the best organized: the county of Flanders, the duchy of Normandy, the counties of Maine and Anjou, and the lands of the counts of Blois and Troyes, eventually known as the county of Champagne. (The two other large northern territories, Brittany and Burgundy, were not nearly as affluent or well-controlled, and hence not as threatening to the king.) There was a difference between the well-organized feudalism in the north of France, where feudal institutions had begun, and in the south, where they spread later, but with less uniformity. Two of the principal southern territories were the large duchy of Aquitaine, which backed up to the Pyrenees, and the county of Toulouse. The duke of Aquitaine controlled a substantial part of his duchy, but not all of it, and furthermore he consistently had trouble managing his nobles. The counts of Toulouse had divided their inheritance among their sons, with the result that after many generations the family's power was fragmented.

Nevertheless, the king had no effective way of governing his royal vassals. The Capetians had first to secure their authority, virtually by inches, over their private domain. Early in the eleventh century the Capetians actually lost some of their own territory to their powerful neighbors and it was not restored until the century was nearly ended. Although the dynasty thus began with many liabilities, there were also some assets. The first Capetian insisted that the nobles elect his son to rule with him, thus ensuring the continuation of power in the family line. This precedent was followed in every generation until the early thirteenth century when the kings felt sufficiently secure to allow it to lapse. The Capetians were also fortunate because until the early fourteenth century, each king produced a male heir to inherit the throne. Thus despite the fact that the monarchy had been elective in 987, it gradually became transformed into a hereditary dynasty.

As the crown passed from father to son, the nobility became accustomed to the Capetian family as rulers, but the kings who followed Hugh were weak, sorry figures who accomplished little toward enhancing the power of the monarch. During his long reign Philip the Fat (1060–1108) was able to restore some of the royal territory, but he seems not to have been of much account in general, and it was not until well into the twelfth century that the fortunes of the French monarchy really changed substantially for the better.

In France the Carolingian tradition of theocratic monarchy was maintained throughout the Middle Ages and did not undergo the change that came about in Germany as a consequence of the king's struggles with the church. In fact, the greatest asset of the French monarchy was the support of the clergy, especially the abbots of St. Denis (who had been associated with the monarchy since the Merovingian era) and the archbishops of Rheims. The church encouraged belief in the sacrosanct nature of the kings and at the same time put the Capetians in a direct line of spiritual descent from Clovis and Charlemagne. At their coronations the kings were anointed with holy oil, and the clergy promoted the popular belief that this was the same oil with which Clovis had been baptised, miraculously brought to earth by a dove sent from heaven. The clergy also fostered the belief that the Capetians had the gift of healing a dreaded and disfiguring disease called scrofula.

We have a good sense of how effectively the cult of monarchy was taking root in northern France from the *Song of Roland*. In its bare outline, this heroic narrative tells of Charlemagne's retreat from Spain after his first campaign against the Muslims, and it voices all the ideals the Capetians and the clergy hoped to inspire— the divinity of the French monarchy and its descent from Charlemagne, the loyalty of vassals to their lords, and loyalty to the crown and the lands of "sweet France." The story tells of the ambush of Charlemagne's army on the return to France, and of Roland's death, and how, as he was dying, Roland called "Many things to remembrance—all the lands he had won by his valor, and sweet France, and the men of his lineage, and Charles, his liege lord . . . . " The *Song* was popular, in the full sense of the word, and was recited by wandering storytellers who came to the royal court and to the castles of the nobility to entertain. Sometime before the end of the eleventh century, perhaps during the reign of Philip (1060–1108), the *Song of Roland* was written down, but the story had been told long before that.

The relationship between the French kings and their clergy was a good and close one in the eleventh century and, on the whole, remained so through the medieval period. The Capetian kings supported monastic and clerical reform as the Carolingian and Ottonian kings had done, though not with the same degree of control over the church as that exercised by Charlemagne or the German kings before the papal reform movement. In France, the home of Cluny, the abbots were friendly to royal power, and the Cluniac monks championed theocratic monarchy even during the reform. (Two advocates of the moderate position finally adopted in the early twelfth century as the solution to the investiture controversy were French clerics: Ivo of Châtres and Hugh of Fleury.)

In general, the advancement of learning in the West had been a much slower process than in the East, and the Carolingian program of learning had been more seriously retarded in France than in Germany. The early years of Capetian rule coincided with the revival inspired by Gerbert, and although the latter was closely involved with the Ottonian empire and the East Frankish Kingdom, he was a Frenchman and devoted to his cathedral school at Rheims. There Gerbert taught a generation of pupils who then went on to establish or revive schools in other parts of France. After Gerbert's death in 1003, the school at Rheims remained an intellectual center of scholarly importance, giving rise to other institutions where the study of Latin letters and the *quadrivium* and dialectic flourished. Gerbert taught Hugh Capet's son and successor, Robert the Pious (996–1031), who was not, as it turned out, the most enlightened of pupils. There were others, however, who did much better and followed in their teacher's footsteps to continue his work. Fulbert, who became archbishop at Châtres, founded a new school there, and others went on to such places as Tours and Laon. But besides the revival of letters that took

An illustration from the Chronicle of the Cluniac Abbey of St.-Martin-des-Champs showing King Henry I of France granting a Charter of Liberties to the monks (11th C. A.D.). (THE BRITISH LIBRARY)

183

place during Gerbert's lifetime there was another force at work in the cultural life of France, and this was the influence of Cluny.

On the whole, the Cluniac order was anti-intellectual in the spirit of the early monastic movement. Members did not overtly impede the study of letters, but they did not focus their talents in that direction, and did not therefore encourage the intellectual aspect of French cultural life. The monks were well-educated, but the thrust of the Cluniac spirit was the devotion to prayer and the liturgical celebration of God. The spiritual experience was emphasized, in comparison to which the "wisdom of men," though not despised by the Cluniacs, was certainly not their highest value. The Cluniacs turned their energies to adorning God's churches and making them beautiful, and although the time would come when the Cluniacs were to be sharply criticized for this, they made the world richer because of it.

The Cluniac association with the French monarchy was a singular blessing for the king, and the Cluniacs and the clergy gave the Capetian monarchy its religious character. This, as it turned out, was the central gain made by the Capetians in the eleventh century. In practical terms, during this first century of their rule, they accomplished little except survival; their history—as that of most of Europe—was overshadowed by the history of the Capetians' strongest vassals, the dukes of Normandy.

The Duchy of Normandy

In the decades following the recognition of the Norman settlement as a duchy by the Carolingian king in 911, the Norman people underwent an interesting transformation. Rollo, the first duke of Normandy, was baptized a Christian in 912 and within a short time the Normans had become thoroughly Christianized (and even dedicated to Church reform) and most thoroughly "French." They never lost their love of adventure and travel (or, for that matter, their delight in warfare and plunder), but in Normandy itself and wherever they went, the Normans turned their remarkable energies to the construction of efficient and tightly organized states. After Hugh Capet had become king with the help of the Normans, the Capetians, partly in return for that assistance and partly because they had no other choice, left the Norman duchy to its own devices.

During the period from about 980 to 1050 the Normans developed the model of a centralized feudal state. Their rulers faced something of the same problem that confronted the French king, although on a much smaller scale—that is, a landed nobility which resisted the control of the dukes. The Norman solution during the first stages of organization was to develop an extremely loyal clergy on whom to rely for help of all kinds. The dukes took a positive interest in religious concerns: They built churches and monasteries, endowed church lands, were involved in reform, and fostered monastic education. In return, the clergy aided the dukes in the work of administering the duchy. The higher clergy were given lands as feudal holdings, and the knights who were supported on them formed the backbone of the Norman army. The dukes' relations with the church and the practical support they received from the clergy were different from the ideological and theoretical support given by the clergy to the French king because, in Normandy, clerics were ducal vassals with clear-cut feudal obligations. The relationship between the Norman rulers and the church shared many similarities with the relationship between the German kings and their clergy, although there were fundamental differences in the overall organization of the two states.

The ultimate goal of the Norman dukes was to bring all the lands in the duchy under their lordship. By the 1020s they were sufficiently strong to attempt this, and they began to impose vassalage on the entire secular nobility. This did not take long, although it was far from an easy task to force the barons to accept the duties attendant upon the act of homage and fealty. Since baronial castles were in fact and theory holdouts against the encroachment of ducal authority, the nobility were forbidden to build them without express permission. (When this injunction was violated, the dukes destroyed the castles.)

The last phase of feudalization was accomplished by Duke William II (1035–1087), better known as William the Conqueror.

185

William fought the nobles who opposed his control, and when they were either killed or had left Normandy, as some did, he gave their holdings to those landless—or land-hungry—knights who were loyal to him. William became a staunch upholder of a movement called the Peace of God, which had been designed by the church to impose religious restrictions on the local warfare that characterized feudal society. This was a good weapon for William to use against his rebellious barons, because it added religious sanction to the restrictions that for practical reasons he placed on fighting within his duchy. Finally, William became liege lord—the ultimate overlord—of all the knights in Normandy. His prerogatives over the Norman state were now altogether extensive. With the exclusive right—wrested from the barons—to mint coins, he operated a sophisticated financial system which included the collecting of some dues in money rather than in kind. Although justice continued to be administered locally by the barons, William reserved certain areas for himself, among these the judging of certain crimes that had previously been considered the dukes' prerogative to adjudicate. By September of 1066, when William crossed the channel to fight for the crown of England, ducal power in Normandy was secure.

The Norman Expansion in the Eleventh Century

The invasion of England led by the Conqueror was as carefully arranged as it was purposeful, and in this sense it counts as the first *organized* expansion of Norman power during the eleventh century. Norman expansion actually had begun earlier in the century, however, with an initially unplanned conquest in the south of Italy. From a rather haphazard start, Norman expansion in the eleventh century became nearly as spectacular in its way as the Viking expansion had been. The Normans went all over—to southern Italy and Sicily, to Spain (to fight the Muslims), to England, and finally, to the Holy Land on the first crusade. They went as Frenchmen, and wherever they went they carried with them much of the culture of northern France—the feudal institutions, the close association between the rulers and the church, and the French language, which became the language of the upper class wherever the Normans settled. They also implanted the manners, such as these were, of the French aristocracy in much of Europe and in the East. So while the French king stayed home trying to subdue his unruly nobles in the Île de France, the Normans were spreading the civilization of northern France.

In addition to their French attributes, the Normans had their own special qualities, particularly their energy and constructiveness. They were not themselves intellectuals, or at least they have given few names to intellectual history, but they had a very special appreciation for learning and art, and some of the important people associated with the advance of learning (as we shall see) were encouraged and patronized by the Normans.

The Normans in Italy and Sicily

The first Normans entered southern Italy sometime around 1016: A group on a pilgrimage to Jerusalem stopped in Italy on their way home and were asked to remain to help two Christian princes in need of military aid. They never left, and over the next few decades more and more footloose Normans came to form a mercenary army. Southern Italy was at first ideal for plunder and then for settlement.

Until the Muslim invasions of the ninth century, both Sicily and southern Italy had been Byzantine territory. After the Muslims had conquered Sicily, they went on to establish bases in southern Italy, and they raided it (along with the rest of Italy) but never controlled it. By the time the Normans arrived, the region was in political chaos. Byzantine power had been so weakened that only two areas, Calabria and Apulia, still actually recognized Eastern rule. The rest of southern Italy was, *de facto*, independent. This included Salerno, Capua, and Benevento (all of which were Lombard territories) and cities such as Amalfi and Naples, which were doing business independently and becoming important trading centers. A good deal of fighting was going on among the various rulers when the Normans landed, and the Muslims in Sicily were still an active threat. These conditions presented altogether an excellent opportunity for land-hungry and aggressive young knights eager for adventure and plunder.[5] The first Normans who landed in southern Italy sent home for others to join them, and by the 1040s a sizable army had been established, which from 1053 on was led by a man of quite extraordinary abilities, Robert Guiscard. The Normans in Italy were lawless bandits, and they menaced the peninsula as far north as Rome. In 1053 Pope Leo IX tried to expel them from Italy but was unable to do so.

Within the southern Italian Norman-held territory was the abbey of Monte Cassino. Under Desiderius, elected abbot in 1058, Monte Cassino was fast becoming the chief intellectual center of Italy, and Desiderius, who was largely responsible for its pre-eminence, was a man of considerable influence at the papal court, and friendly to the Normans. Through Desiderius' efforts, papal policy towards the Normans was reversed, and in 1059 Pope Nicholas II recognized Robert Guiscard as duke of Calabria and Apulia, both of which now became papal fiefs. Robert then went on to complete the conquest of southern Italy, and in 1071 he captured Bari, the last Byzantine possession in Italy. In this same period his brother Roger began the invasion of Sicily.

In return for papal recognition of their legitimacy in Italy and their right to drive the Muslims from Sicily, the Normans gave military aid to Gregory VII in his wars with Henry IV. They also generally encouraged the work of the reformed papacy, bestowed gifts on the abbey at Monte Cassino, and supported the election of Desiderius to succeed Gregory VII as Pope Victor III (1086–1087). The Normans thus became closely involved with the papacy at an important juncture in the history of the church and remained involved for a long time thereafter, as we shall see.

By 1091 the brother of Robert Guiscard had wrested Sicily from the Muslims, and the Normans then organized a cohesive and

5. In Normandy, the eldest son of a lord inherited the fief, leaving younger sons landless, and although some entered the ducal service, many of these young men went abroad to seek their fortunes.

efficient state. This was a feat of no mean order because the Norman kingdom in the southern Mediterranean contained many diverse economies and cultural elements: trading cities as well as areas of rich farmland, and a population of Greeks, Muslims, Lombards, and Latins. Although the Normans imposed their particular form of highly centralized feudalism on their new kingdom, they also adapted their government to the existing institutions of the Italian city-states.

The Normans in England

The Norman invasion of England was a very different undertaking at the beginning, since it was planned and directed by Duke William, who went to press his claim to the English throne. The event that precipitated the invasion of 1066 was the death that year of the English king, Edward the Confessor, who left no direct heir to his throne.

During the century and a half before 1066 England had been still part of the Scandinavian world and might, indeed, have remained so had it not been for the coming of the Normans. The Anglo-Saxon kings who succeeded Alfred the Great in the early tenth century successfully continued Alfred's offensive against the Danes in northern England. Alfred's original kingdom of Wessex was expanded to include the northern Danish shires. Nonetheless, there remained a large and well-entrenched Danish population, and its ties with Scandinavia were strong. In the last half of the tenth century England enjoyed a period of peace that was disrupted only when a thoroughly incompetent king ascended the throne. Ethelred (979–1016), called "the Redeless" ("the Helpless") because of his most striking characteristic, was far too weak to prevent the outbreak of factional warfare in his kingdom, and this led to a second Danish conquest and the rule of the Danish king, Canute.

This new period of Danish rule in England made no great impact because there were no fundamental changes in administrative policy and no large immigration of Danish settlers. In 1042 the Danish line died out, the English returned to their own ruling family, and Edward the Confessor ascended the throne.

Edward's ancestry was not, however, purely Anglo-Saxon. His father, the hapless Ethelred, had (in 1002) married Emma, the sister of the reigning duke of Normandy. Edward had been raised in Normandy, and when he returned to England as king he was temperamentally more Norman-French than Anglo-Saxon. He brought Norman advisers with him and relied heavily on his Norman friends during his reign, often appointing them to high offices. These Norman affiliations aroused the antagonism of the Anglo-Saxon nobility and when Edward died they chose their own Harold of Wessex to succeed him. William of Normandy, however, asserted his right to the English throne through his kinship to Edward. He also claimed that Edward had promised him the crown and that even Harold had sworn to support him. William furthermore was able to secure the blessing of the pope, whose disfavor Harold had incurred for supporting an unsuitable candidate for the archbishopric of Canterbury.

The war between the two kingly aspirants was decided in a single battle fought near Hastings in the south of England. William led an army which, for its time, was huge. His personal vassals numbered a thousand, and to this contingency of knights he had added mercenaries hired from neighboring territories in France. His army was well-trained, disciplined, and eager. The Anglo-Saxons, wearied before the encounter had even begun (they had had to march across a good part of England to get to the battle site), put up a good fight but were no match for William's army. The Anglo-Saxon forces were defeated, Harold was killed, and on Christmas Day in 1066 Duke William became the first Norman king of England.

The new king immediately set about imposing a highly centralized feudal monarchy on England, and he possessed the following advantages: ownership by conquest of all the land in England, successful governing experience in Normandy, and vast personal ability. William kept a substantial amount of the conquered land, about a sixth, as the king's private domain, but granted the rest as feudal holdings to the barons who had fought with him at Hastings, or to the abbots and bishops whose lands he had first confiscated then returned as ecclesiastical fiefs. As he had done for Normandy, but with an even greater degree of control, William became liege lord of all the knights of England and had at his command a sizable feudal army.

The king also secured a large and steady income from several sources. There had already been some taxation levied by the Anglo-Saxon and Danish kings, and William continued this practice. In addition, his personal lands provided a good income, and he was merciless in extracting from his vassals all feudal dues and rents owed him. In 1086 the king ordered a survey of all the land and all the resources in his kingdom. The results were compiled in the Domesday Book, which was used to ensure that taxes on all lands and goods were paid in full.

The Anglo-Saxons had established administrative institutions of their own, and where these were still viable, William incorporated them into his own program. The kingdom he had won was divided into shires, each of which was directed by a nobleman, usually an earl (the equivalent of the French count). The former, like his counterpart on the continent, was not intended to be a hereditary office holder, but most earls gained their titles more often than not through birth, so the king's interests were actually best represented by an official called a sheriff. The shire was retained by the Normans as the essential unit of local government, and sheriff remained the important link between local government and the king. There were two kinds of local courts, the shire court and the hundred, and to these, which William maintained, he added the inquest, or jury, which had existed in France.

Finally, William kept as strong a hand on the English church as he had done with the Norman one. The reform movement in Normandy had emanated from the monastery at Bec, where the leading reformer and teacher was a monk named Lanfranc who had come originally from northern Italy and was a staunch supporter of the ducal—now royal—family. William now brought Lanfranc to England as the new archbishop of Canterbury, and the two of them together continued the reform of the English church and monasteries, exercising tight control over the higher clergy and the abbots. Most Anglo-Saxons were removed from high church offices and Normans installed instead.

At his death William bequeathed to his son a feudal kingdom unsurpassed for centralization anywhere in Europe. He had furthermore succeeded in turning England away from the Scandinavian world and linking its history once more to that of the continent.

The Development of the Papacy and the Expansion of Latin Christendom: The Crucial Half-Century (1050–1100)

The period from the 1050s to 1100 was crucial for internal religious reform, the growth of papal power, and the expansion of the boundaries of the Western church. These developments all derived from the movement which, in the political sphere, had culminated in the investiture controversy, and they were just as revolutionary—perhaps, for the long run, even more so—in their effect on Latin Christendom.

The radical Christian reformers were implacable in their insistence on clerical celibacy, and some of the first laws promulgated by Gregory VII abolished clerical marriage in the Western church forever. The reformers felt so strongly on this subject that clerics already married when the law went into effect had to give up their wives and families if they wished to remain in the church. The entire issue of celibacy once again became prominent in Christian thought, as it had been in the era of the desert saints in the early church—and carried with it the same negative assumptions about women. Once again, the image of women as the root of all evil which had been quiescent for several centuries came to the fore. And there were ramifications, such as the questions of whether marriage as an institution was worthy enough to be considered a sacrament, and how wide the gates of heaven would open for women, even those with a religious vocation. These were to become important practical and philosophical issues in the twelfth century but, as with so much else, they were presaged in the works of the reform movement of the eleventh.

The papacy's determination both to reform and control the

ecclesiastical hierarchy—two things which really went hand-in-hand—led to the growth of papal government in Rome. Once the college of cardinals had become an electoral body (in 1059), the popes began to expand the number and duties of its members. By the end of the century the cardinals had become the pope's chief councillors and advisers on all important ecclesiastical and political matters, until finally no papal decisions were made without them. And instead of appointing only Romans (as had originally been the case), the popes now also selected cardinals from outside Italy, so that there was much more contact between the pontiff and the leading prelates all over Europe.

In other ways, too, the popes increased their direct and personal control over the higher clergy. When, for instance, an archbishop was elected, he had to go to Rome to receive the *pallium*—the symbol of office—from the pope. (The *pallium* is a band of white wool with four purple crosses on it.) This papal contact with the candidate also provided an opportunity to determine the latter's worthiness to hold the office being bestowed. The popes also increased their use of legates, who were given full power to act on the pope's behalf, and who began to be sent regularly to oversee reform in the churches of Europe and deal with secular rulers. By these and other practical means, the reformed papacy inplemented its sovereignty over Latin Christendom.

In the cause of reform, the papacy thus established its own highly complex machinery of government, eventuating an administration as secular as that of any temporal ruler. (Under Urban II the papal administrative circle that ran the growing bureaucracy even came to be called the "*curia*," the term used to designate the highest level of administrators in the royal courts.) It is the irony of the papal victory that, freed from secular control, the church itself grew into a sovereign power with the pope as its monarch.

The Crusades Against Islam

In the process of securing its control over Western Christendom, the reformed papacy did not overlook the possibilities of expanding the boundaries of the Latin church.

The intransigence of the Eastern Orthodox church and the Byzantine emperors in resisting papal supremacy was irresistible to try to overcome, and as early as 1054 the explosive revolutionary Humbert of Silva Candida went to Constantinople as papal legate to deal with the Eastern church. The Eastern patriarch (the highest-ranking bishop in the Eastern church) was just as explosive as Humbert, and a violent dispute broke out between the two. Instead of bringing the Eastern church under papal control, the papal legate excommunicated the patriarch who, in turn, excommunicated Humbert. At the time no one would have believed that the two churches would not reconcile as they had in the past when there had been other ruptures. The hope of healing the schism and having the Eastern church recognize papal authority was only encouraged by this incident, not cooled, and this proved to be a factor in shaping papal policy for centuries.

During the eleventh century several changes contributed to the possibility of reclaiming Spain from the Muslims and extending papal control over the Christian churches already there. At the beginning of the century two-thirds of Spain was held by the Muslims and governed by the caliphate at Cordova. By 1034 a situation which happened frequently in the Muslim countries was repeated in Spain: The caliphate had broken into several smaller, factious units. Even before this, however, there had been expeditions of French knights—from Normandy and from Burgundy, for example—to fight the Muslims, and expeditions led by the Spanish Christians themselves. (Early in the century the Cluniacs had begun to build the churches for pilgrims going to Compostela, and the shrine of St. James was becoming one of the great pilgrim and tourist attractions in the West.)

The northern Spanish churches which the Christians had retained in spite of the Muslims, and those in the area of the March taken by Charlemagne, followed rites which were different from Roman religious practices. The Cluniacs tried to bring these Spanish churches into conformity with Rome, but with little success. When Gregory VII became pope he insisted that the Spanish church follow the Roman liturgy and practices, and he also encouraged the Christian reconquest of Spain. It is likely that the Christian successes against the Muslims in Spain played a part in

Christ as a Pilgrim. *An eleventh-century relief at the Cluniac monastery of St. Domingo de Silos, in the Province of Burgos, Spain. Although the relief is based on the Biblical story of the pilgrims of Emmaus, Christ is carrying on his shoulder bag the scallop shell which symbolizes the pilgrimage to the shrine of St. James of Compostela. The beautiful cloister of St. Domingo de Silos shows the diffusion of French Romanesque into Spain.* (COURTESY OF PROFESSOR GEORGE ZARNECKI)

Gregory's plan to take the offensive against Islam throughout the eastern Mediterranean.

Gregory was the first pope to conceive of the crusade, or holy war, against the Muslims in the East, and the idea of leading this mission was part of Gregory's vision of the papal role. The participants were to come from all over Christendom, and the pope's leadership would demonstrate that his words had indeed come true: The "Roman pontiff alone was rightly to be called universal."

Practical considerations also influenced Gregory to plan his holy war. A new group of invaders, the Seljuk Turks, had entered the near East from central Asia in the mid-eleventh century and in less than twenty years had overturned the entire political situation in the Levant. Before the advent of the Turks, Muslim power in the Near East had been divided between two antagonistic caliphates, the Abbasids, who ruled from Bagdad, and the Fatimids who ruled from Cairo and who also controlled Jerusalem. Although the Seljuks had converted to Islam, they had no community of interest with either caliphate, and in 1055 they defeated the Abbasids and then continued onwards to conquer Mesopotamia and the Syrian-Palestinian coast. In 1070 they wrested Jerusalem from the Fatimids and in the next year inflicted a disastrous defeat on the Byzantine Empire. At the Battle of Manzikert in Anatolia, the Turks won nearly all the Byzantine province of Asia Minor and came within a hundred miles of Constantinople. At this point the Eastern emperor appealed to Gregory VII for help.

Gregory's response was to plan the first crusade, more help than the Byzantine emperor—who had merely hoped for a mercenary army to help him fight the Turks—had bargained for. Gregory became too quickly and thoroughly involved in the investiture controversy to lead the crusade, however, so that it was not actually preached until 1095 by Pope Urban II (1088–1099).

Between the 1070s and 1095 the balance in much of the Mediterranean world shifted in favor of the Christians. The reconquest of Spain was continuing successfully, and in 1085 the Christians took Toledo from the Muslims, which, besides being an important geographical gain, also gave the Christians control of a major intellectual center. By 1091 the Normans had completed the conquest of Muslim Sicily. The Turks were formidable enemies and, by all reports, exceptionally barbarous as well, "an accursed race, a race utterly alienated from God,"[6] as Urban called them. How-

6. This and all subsequent references to Urban's speech are from *The First Crusade: The Accounts of Eye-Witnesses and Participants*, trans. August C. Krey (Princeton: Princeton University Press, 1921), pp. 30–33.

ever, they had not yet been able to unite the Muslims in the Levant, so the time seemed especially propitious to undertake an aggressive war against them. The Byzantine emperor, Alexius Comnenus, made an appeal to Urban for help again, and Urban did not overlook the possibility that the crusade might afford the papacy the opportunity to heal the schism of 1054 between the Eastern church and Rome. And then there was always the hope of extending papal authority over the orthodox church.

In 1095 Pope Urban therefore went to Clermont in France to appeal to the nobility to deliver the Holy Land from the Muslims and restore Jerusalem to Latin Christendom. "For the Lord," he said to them, "has made you stewards over his family . . . . You will be blessed, indeed, if the Lord shall find you faithful in stewardship." This speech was a moving and effective plea, and when Urban had finished the Frankish lords shouted with one voice, "*Deus vult!*" ("God wills it!") Within a year they had made their preparations and departed for the Holy Land.

Urban's speech initiated a series of holy wars which continued into the fourteenth century. The crusading movement is a dramatic chapter in medieval history, and for that reason it is tempting to overestimate its effects. The crusades grew out of the special circumstances of the late eleventh century: the leadership of a reformed papacy; the emphasis on religious unity (which quickly grew into an insistence on religious uniformity for those outside as well as within the Roman church); the intense popular piety; and the general restlessness of Europeans. In varying degrees, the crusades are related to developments that will be discussed in the next chapters, so that they will be referred to again in the context of an expanding population, agricultural and commercial prosperity, and those intellectual changes that came with the intermingling of so many diverse cultures. But the spirit of the first crusade is the spirit of the late eleventh century, and this was never repeated, although the crusading ideal was to remain dear to the heart of the papacy for a long time to come.

Of all the crusades, only the first was undertaken with tremendous popular enthusiasm, and only the first was successful from a military standpoint. (It resulted in the formation of a Latin kingdom on the Syrian-Palestinian coast and established Western hegemony in the Mediterranean.) The second crusade (during the mid-twelfth century) and the third (at its end) also had some popular support, but never again was there anything like the groundswell of fervor that had greeted Urban's speech.

Urban's appeal to the Frankish nobility was based on many factors, not all of which were religious. He spoke of the atrocities committed by the Turks on Christians in the Holy Land, and of the virtue of fighting "the infidel" rather than turning their aggressions against one another. Furthermore, he held out the possibilities of winning new lands, the opportunity to "lay up . . . treasures on earth" as well as in heaven. The greatest appeal of the first crusade, however, was that it offered an outlet for all the intense religious feelings associated with medieval Christianity at the end of the eleventh century. The same piety which had impelled people to enter monasteries or to go on pilgrimages to Spain or Jerusalem now led them to join the holy wars. "Undertake this journey," Urban told them, "for the remission of your sins, with the assurance of the imperishable glory of the kingdom of heaven."[7] And so they did. To many who went on the first crusade, it was above all else a pilgrimage; those who responded to Urban's entreaty at Clermont by taking the cross and crying "God wills it!" interpreted quite literally the faith to which they gave voice.

The enthusiastic response to his speech was more widespread than Urban had dared hope. The call was answered by the French nobility as he had anticipated, but it was also answered from Scotland, Spain, Scandinavia, Germany, England, from the Italian cities, and from all the Norman territories as well. These crusaders did not all unite into a single army, but instead set out in several groups to march overland through Germany and the Balkans to Constantinople, where they were all to meet. They started for Constantinople in 1096, but before they reached Byzantium, a far different group converged on the Eastern Empire—the so-called Peoples' Crusade led by Peter the Hermit.

7. Ibid.

The Peoples' Crusade

The Peoples' Crusade displayed at once a fascinating and horrifying aspect of medieval religiosity. As the impulse spread, the call to a holy war was taken up by itinerant preachers and evangelists, and the religious ecstasy engendered by the hope of reaching Jerusalem and gaining salvation became uncontrollable. For many peasants and townsmen who flocked to the banners of the evangelical preachers there was little to leave behind, and, caught up in the excitement, they emptied entire towns and villages. Women and children also joined the Peoples' Crusade, coming from France, Flanders, and Germany particularly. The most charismatic preacher was the monk known as Peter the Hermit, who became the chief leader of the movement. As they marched from city to city in Germany, Peter and his followers attacked and slaughtered many thousands of Jews. To Peter's army, the Jews were the infidels close at hand, and the fury that had been whipped up toward the Muslims was unleashed first on them. Jews were massacred in Speyer, in Worms, in Mainz, Regensburg, and Prague, and these pogroms associated with the first crusade ushered in a new era of brutality towards the Jews of Europe.

The massacres of the first crusade were condemned by the clergy and by many secular leaders, but they were "popular" in all the senses of the word. A chronicler of the crusades wrote that "Although they [the people] ought to have traveled the road undertaken for Christ, . . . they turned to madness, and shamefully and wantonly cut down with cruelty the Jewish people in the cities and towns through which their passage lay."[8] It was not long until this virulent anti-Semitism spread through all the layers of Christian society. There had been Christian anti-Semitism for a thousand years, but the persecutions had been sporadic and not a matter of consistent policy. This change at the time of the first crusade is perfectly summarized by a priest in *The Anguish of the*

8. Edward A. Synan, *The Popes and the Jews in the Middle Ages* (New York: Macmillan, 1965), p. 70.

Jews: "During the first half of the second millenium, the history of anti-Semitism and the history of Judaism so converged as almost to coincide."[9]

When Peter the Hermit's band reached Constantinople the Byzantine emperor, Alexius Comnenus, was horrified at the sight of them. They were without discipline and certainly without military experience or arms, but they insisted on fighting and Alexius finally sent them off to Asia Minor, where the Turks massacred them.

Alexius was almost as aghast at the sight of the legitimate crusading army when it arrived at his city. It was larger and far less controllable than he could have hoped. (Although the figures for its size vary, the most reasonably estimates place the cavalry at 4,500 and the infantry at 30,000 men.) Alexius extracted an oath of allegiance from the leaders and the promise that the lands which were once part of his empire would be returned. The crusaders then set off to Asia Minor where they defeated the Turks and actually returned the province to the emperor, keeping the rest of the lands in the Near East for themselves.

After winning Asia Minor the crusaders went to Armenia, where the Christians helped them defeat the Muslims and to cement the alliance, Baldwin of Lorraine left the crusade and married the daughter of the Armenian king. Baldwin carved out the county of Edessa, the first community ruled by a Latin in the East. The remainder of the crusading army moved on to Antioch.

The battle for Antioch lasted the winter of 1097–1098 and was nearly a disaster for the crusaders. At the point at which they almost gave up, they were spurred on to greater efforts, and success, by supposedly finding the Holy Lance, which had been used to stab Christ when he was on the cross. They were also aided, not so miraculously, by the Genoese navy, which brought supplies. After Antioch had been secured, the main leader at the siege, Bohemond, decided to keep it. Bohemond was one of the sons of Robert Guiscard, the Norman overlord of southern Italy and Sicily. There was opposition to his plan to remain in Antioch,

---

9. Edward H. Flannery, *The Anguish of the Jews* (New York: Macmillan, 1965), p. 89.

but in the end he prevailed, so that there was now a further expansion of Norman power. The rest of the crusading army marched down the Syrian-Palestinian coast to Jerusalem, which fell relatively easily into the Christians' hands.

The so-called liberation of Jerusalem (in June 1099) was actually a holocaust. The crusaders sacked and looted the city mercilessly.

For many of the followers the freeing of Jerusalem marked the end of the crusade, and they left for home. Those who remained now had to organize their holdings and prepare to defend them. The solution was to form a feudal kingdom, the Latin Kingdom of Jerusalem, which was organized into four fiefs: the county of Edessa, the county of Tripoli, the principality of Antioch, and Jerusalem itself. The first ruler, Baldwin, was a Frenchman and all the other high-ranking nobility were either French or Norman. The crusaders solved the problem of defense against the Turks partly with the help of the Venetian, Genoese, and Pisan fleets.

A scene from the first crusade; Godfrey of Boulogne with his knights battling the Muslims before the gates of Jerusalem. *This fourteenth-century manuscript shows Peter the Hermit at the very left of the illustration, thus linking the story of the Peoples' Crusade to the first official crusade.* (ALINARI/EDITORIAL PHOTOCOLOR ARCHIVES)

201

The first crusaders had traveled overland, and it was not until the seige of Antioch and the establishment of the Latin Kingdom that the necessity of a navy for transportation, supplies, and defense was recognized. Thereafter, ships were used extensively.

The famous crusaders' castles, many of them large enough to contain small villages, were built for defense. There were, of course, feudal armies in each of the states, though these were always small since the Latin population was considerably smaller than that of the conquered peoples. The need for defense and the need to protect the pilgrims and to care for the Christian sick gave rise to the military orders in the church, and their history in many ways parallels that of the crusading movement itself. The two earliest were the Order of the Temple (known as "the Templars") and the Knights of St. John, more commonly called "the Hospitallers." Both were founded in the Holy Land during the decades following the first crusade and were, at first, famous for their good works, charity, ministrations to the sick, and the protection of pilgrims and crusaders alike. But both orders grew rapidly in size and wealth and, seduced by the riches of the East, entered trade and banking, acquired large amounts of land and began competing with each other, as well as with everyone else. Thus the original purposes of the religious orders had been diverted well before the end of the twelfth century, and the same could be said of the crusaders.

The best defense the crusader states had was that it took the Muslims several decades to unite, but when finally they did they successfully attacked and captured Edessa in 1144. When news of the fall of Edessa reached Europe, a second crusade was launched in 1146, but the lost territory was not recovered. Soon afterward the Muslims found their greatest leader, Saladin, who joined them together and captured Jerusalem in 1187. The third crusade was then preached and financed with a large sum of money raised by a papal tax (the Saladin tithe) levied for the first time on all Christians. The third crusade had, among other leaders, the English king Richard, known as "The Lion-hearted"—by all odds one of the most overrated of medieval heroes. Richard loved fighting, but he was not a leader, preferring individual heroics that would glorify his own reputation. His valorous deeds, such as they were, did not help the crusade and, either because of him or in spite of him, the crusaders did not regain Jerusalem. However, Saladin concluded a peace treaty with the Christians, giving them a small strip of land along the coast and allowing them to visit freely the holy places in Jerusalem. This was an inglorious ending, though nothing in comparison with what was to come.

The fourth crusade, begun in 1202, ended in 1204 with the out-and-out rape of the city of Constantinople. The city—captured for the first time in its history—was plundered by Westerners wearing the Cross on their tunics. The details of the defection of the fourth crusade are tied to the economic history of a later period and will be recounted in that context. It suffices here to point out that it ended with the establishment of a Latin Empire in Constantinople; and although Western rule lasted only until 1261, this was the terrible conclusion to a long history of hostility between the East and West, eclipsing totally any hope the papacy had of reconciling the two churches. The daughter of the Byzantine emperor at the time of the first crusade wrote a history of her father's reign. "And indeed the actual facts," she wrote, telling how her father dreaded the arrival of the Western forces, "were . . . far more terrible than rumor made them." The actual events a century later were even worse than could have been imagined.

The fourth crusade was in a real sense a turning point in the crusading movement in the West. Popular enthusiasm had so dwindled that it had become difficult to get people to go on these missions or to raise money for them. Still, the papacy continued to preach them, and intermittently there would be a burst of religious zeal to recover Jerusalem or a monarch (like St. Louis of France in the late thirteenth century) who was sincerely devoted to the ideal. As we shall see, the papacy in the thirteenth century turned the crusading ideal to its own use and preached holy wars against heretics and political enemies in Europe as well as in the East. Only as it applied to the first crusade was it possible to use the pope's phrase "holy pilgrimage" with truth and authenticity.

The conquest of the Holy Land, the Norman expansion, and the reconquest of Spain were all part of the increasing human

mobility during the eleventh century. It was not only that people were settling in areas that were new to them; they were once again traveling—across their own continent and across the Mediterranean. Pilgrims, monks, kings, scholars, and traders were moving out into the world—tentatively at first, but as the century progressed, more confidently and in increasingly large numbers. This restlessness is one of the characteristics of Europeans in the eleventh century—along with their deep spiritual concerns and their willingness to experiment. And these qualities were all expressed in the new building of churches that began during this period.

The Architecture of Renewal

So many new churches were built all over Latin Christendom that a chronicler wrote that it appeared as if Europe were suddenly covered with a "mantle of churches." These new structures were built in a style called Romanesque, which means Rome-like, or in the Roman manner, although this accounts for only a part of the artistic influence.

During the Merovingian and Carolingian eras, churches were generally quite small and built partly of stone. The roofs were wooden and flat, and there was no sculptural decoration on the outside. The Roman influence in the new churches called for the use of stone throughout the structure and the ornamental sculpture which decorated the churches. These two features, combined with a basic floor plan and the numbers and huge size of the buildings are the features common to Romanesque architecture. There is great variety in the appearance of these churches, however, because each region modified the structures, depending on local influences. The churches designated "Romanesque" in Italy are

An exterior view of the Church of St.-Sernin at Toulouse. *St.-Sernin is a perfect example of the type of Romanesque pilgrimage churches that emerged along the four major roads in France which led to Compostela. In this aerial view, the cruciform plan followed by most Romanesque churches is clearly visible. The huge size of the church, and the several chapels surrounding the apse, allowed for the accomodation of large numbers of pilgrims at one time.* (FRENCH GOVERNMENT TOURIST OFFICE)

205

closer to their Roman antecedents than Norman churches, and the Norman churches, in turn, are different from the pilgrimage churches built by the Cluniacs along the route to Santiago.

From the fourth century on, when the Christians began building churches, they occasionally—as at Charlemagne's chapel at Aachen—imitated the rounded style of Eastern churches, but mainly they followed the rectangular plan of the Roman basilica. Gradually it became customary to build churches in the form of a Latin cross, which required only a small alteration in the basilica plan. The nave (or central aisle) was the same as in the basilica: From the entrance it ran through the church toward the east end, where it terminated in what is called an apse—usually a semicircular niche. To make the cross, a transept perpendicular to the nave was added.

When the architects began to build on a large scale—both in terms of size and numbers—they grappled with the problem of making a stone roof, since the wooden ones were highly inflammable and also because they wanted to vary the design. The first resolution to the roofing problem was to make, in effect, a tunnel of stone, called a barrel vault, that rested on huge stone pillars and covered the nave. This solution was satisfactory for relatively small edifices, but not for larger ones because the pillars could not be made heavy enough to take the full weight of the vaults. The increased size was necessary, and not simply for the sake of impressiveness. The chroniclers have written about the huge crowds of people going to churches to pray and to visit the relics of the saints, and monks even complained of the difficulties of controlling the crowds within the sanctuaries.

Architects experimented with various methods of constructing stone roofs for the larger buildings and discovered that one of the best was to build transverse arches connected to pillars on opposite sides of the nave—in other words to break up the barrel vaults with several sets of arches (called "ribs") which enabled them to use lighter stone to fill in the space between the arches. "Rib-vaulting," as it is called, realized its fullest possibilities in the Norman churches in England during the early twelfth century. In the early Romanesque churches the interiors are dark, and there

The nave and choir of the Church of St.-Sernin.   *In this picture it is possible to see how the barrel vault was divided by transverse arches to increase the height of the nave and allow more light to enter the church.* (ARCH. PHOT. PARIS/S.P.A.D.E.M.)

The Apostle of St.-Sernin (ca. 1090 A.D.). *One of the better known examples of Romanesque sculpture.* (ARCH. PHOT. PARIS/S.P.A.D.E.M.)

is about these structures a kind of massive strength and mystery due to all the heavy stone and the unbroken walls, which were only slightly pierced to let in light. In the later churches, the lightness and space associated with the next style of architecture began to appear.

The addition of monumental stone sculptures to decorate the exteriors of churches began in France in about the mid-eleventh century and afterward spread all over Europe. In these sculptural pieces, restlessness is also a characteristic feature; one can feel in the statuary a sense of tension and movement. In Romanesque art there exists that feeling of things in flux—conveyed through even so intractable a medium as stone. In their art, as in the other aspects of their lives, Europeans were just beginning to overcome the limitations imposed either by their environment, or by the lack of knowledge, or by social and economic conditions. The pioneering spirit which infected Europeans is first seen in the eleventh century, but the great age of expansion was yet to come.

PART THREE ❧

THE LATER MIDDLE AGES: THE LATE ELEVENTH TO THE LATE THIRTEENTH CENTURY

These centuries were a period of astonishing and rapid change and creativity. The period opens with an age of expansion: New lands were being settled and cultivated, economic activities expanded, and the population was growing. The energy that was released was then poured into every area of human endeavor.

211

The twelfth and thirteenth centuries were the culmination point of medieval civilization, and the period from which we draw our largest legacy—truly, as Christopher Dawson wrote, the "root and ground of the culture itself." During this age of amazing growth the boundaries of the states of Europe were stabilized, existing cities were enlarged and new ones founded, and the urban character of European civilization emerged. The universities were begun, and the intellectual traditions which they embodied and which we have inherited were developed. And much more besides.

This was also a period with a character as distinctive and recognizable as the style of any of the great Gothic cathedrals. It was the time of the greatest unity for all Latin Christendom, and the theme underlying the history of this period is the theme of unity, one church, one culture—Rome again, now in its most Christian incarnation. It is also the time of greatest diversity in the medieval experience and, at the close of the period, the time of the greatest balance between unity and diversity: the synthesis of medieval culture.

Medieval Europe Transformed:
A New Pattern in Economy,
Society, and Culture

Sometime soon after the millennium—it is certainly not precisely
clear when—the pattern of devastation of the land and death from
warfare and starvation was replaced by a new pattern of growth.
After the major waves of the invasions receded, agricultural life
began to expand and become prosperous, and the population
began to increase. This growth in agricultural production and
population began slowly, and the changes at first were probably
hardly perceptible; but by the mid-eleventh century they were

213

clearly visible, and during the twelfth century their cumulative effect made substantial alterations in European society. The other aspects of European expansion—the volume of trade, the extensive growth of towns, and the rich intellectual and artistic culture of the urban world of the twelfth and thirteenth centuries—were made possible, and then sustained, by the new agricultural prosperity.

The Expansion of Agricultural Life

The earliest sign of the change in rural life was quantitative: More land was put under cultivation. In the areas that were already settled and where there was room to do so, peasants extended the borders of their fields to increase the amount of arable land. Where forests or swamps surrounded the village communities, peasants joined together to cut down trees and drain the marshlands to prepare new land for cultivation. This effort to bring wasteland under the plow developed into a huge undertaking that gained momentum in the mid-eleventh century and continued until nearly the end of the thirteenth.

Within Europe there were large tracts of wilderness, particularly in northern France, England, and the Low Countries, and these lands were settled by a steady stream of pioneers. Sometimes the land was settled haphazardly by people who simply had the cour-

Peasants mowing for the month of August. *An illustration from a Monk's Calendar, second quarter of the eleventh century.* (THE BRITISH LIBRARY)

age to pick up and move. At other times, land would be granted by charter of the king of England or France to one of the lesser nobility, who founded colonies; often entire peasant villages would come to a new area in order to farm. Some of the hardest labor was done by members of the monastic order, especially by the Cistercians, who provided strong leadership in the movement to clear the land.

The ascetic ideals of the Cistercians required that they reject the world and its goods, and so they sought out the wilderness, or something approaching it. They took literally St. Benedict's statement that "idleness is the enemy of the soul," and, more than most other orders, the Cistercians emphasized labor and did their own work. They settled in the most inaccesible parts of Europe and cleared forests and drained marshlands. It was they who were responsible for reclaiming Holland from the sea. They drained the water, built the dikes, and patiently over years fertilized the land by pasturing animals on it in order to prepare the soil for planting. This was a remarkable undertaking, and at the same time the Cistercians, joined by monks from other orders, did the work of diffusing agricultural information among the peasantry. The Cistercians taught the peasants how to prepare their fields for cultivation and eventually taught them the new methods of improving the yield of the land. The monks performed a function in the expansion of agriculture in twelfth-century Europe very much like that of the rural extension agents in nineteenth-century and twentieth-century America.

Impelled by the need for land, thousands migrated enormous distances during the course of the twelfth and thirteenth centuries. From approximately the mid-twelfth through the mid-thirteenth century the Germans took the lead in settling colonies on the vast tracts that lay between the Elbe and the Dnieper Rivers. The German rulers encouraged a huge eastward migration that included peastants from all over Europe. The usual way a colony was established was for a German noble to send agents through Germany and into other thickly inhabited countries, like Flanders, offering attractive terms to the peasants to come and work the new land. In this way central and eastern Europe, a poor and unexploited part of the world in 1000, gradually became a rich grain-producing area.

The German expansion into the Slavic lands east of the Elbe was the most effective of the colonizing movements within the traditional boundaries of Christian Europe. The pioneers who settled these colonies faced hardships, dangers, and deprivations as great as those braved by their American counterparts—and with as much courage. But they were also offered the promise of greater personal freedom—and ultimately, better living conditions—than they had enjoyed on the manors. The German lords who wanted to secure their expansion into Slavic territory by colonization made attractive offers to the settlers; specifically, they built villages and offered land and houses at low rent.

The crusades to the Near East, the Norman conquest of Sicily, southern Italy, and England, and the Spanish reconquest of Spain were all to some extent motivated by this desire for land (although, as we have seen, other forces were also at work in these movements).

When Pope Urban II addressed the Franks at Clermont, he included in his reasons for the first crusade the possibility of new land. "Let none of your possessions detain you . . . since this land which you inhabit, shut in on all sides by the sea and surrounded by mountain peaks, is too narrow for your large population; nor does it abound in wealth; and it furnishes scarcely food enough for its cultivators." But "Jerusalem," Urban continued, "is the navel of the world; the land is fruitful above others, like another paradise of delights."

All three illustrations are initial pages from a Cistercian manuscript of the twelfth century, *produced at the mother house of Citeaux, showing the monks at their labors. According to legend, the brown habits the monks are wearing were later changed into white habits at the request of the Virgin Mary.* (BIBLIOTHEQUE PUBLIQUE, DIJON, FRANCE)

217

It was evident by the end of the eleventh century, when Urban delivered his speech, that there were many more people living on the land. But if this had been simply a matter of quantity—of more people farming more land—the social and economic alterations which took place during the twelfth century would probably not have occurred. Qualitative changes were also being introduced which released people from the soil to do other work. The major change in agriculture was the spread of the three-field, or triennial, system of crop rotation. Farmers discovered that on the rich, northern lands of Europe they were able to leave less land fallow than in using the two-field system, and consequently in any given year they could use approximately two-thirds of their land. On one-third they planted a winter crop, either wheat or rye; on the other third they planted a spring crop, barley or oats. Compared to the two-field system, which required that half the land be left fallow, the new method of crop rotation permitted cultivators to leave only one-third unplanted each year. This advanced rotational system had in all likelihood been known on a small number of royal and monastic estates at an earlier period, but its spread to the point of making an appreciable overall difference did not take place until sometime during the eleventh century.

The importance of the three-field system and its benefits cannot be overemphasized. The total production of fields cultivated by this method increased dramatically since more land continually produced cereals. Although farmers were plagued by the shortage of manure throughout the Middle Ages, soil fertility was nonetheless improved; and in some limited areas where technology was advanced, it was possible to eliminate fallow land completely by introducing new crops. The most important of these were a variety of legumes which, unlike cereals, add rather than subtract nitrogen from the soil.

The higher yields and steadier food supply which resulted from these agricultural innovations encouraged the increase in the total population of Europe. Although it is difficult to calculate precise demographic statistics for the medieval period, the best recent estimates place the population of Europe at 40 million in 1000, at 48 million in 1100, and at 60 million by 1200. Thus in two hundred years the population increased by a full fifty percent. The greater diversity in the diet of the inhabitants of certain regions may also help to account for this growth. Legumes, for example, are high in protein, so there was not only more food raised but the medieval diet, based in the early centuries largely on carbohydrates, gradually became better-balanced and healthier. During the eleventh century the water-powered mill for grinding grain was introduced and, at the end of the twelfth century, the first windmill appeared in northern France. Besides releasing man-

The Fruit Gatherer. *Sculpture illustrating the month of October, from the West Portal of Amiens Cathedral, early thirteenth century* (MARBURG/PROTHMANN ASSOCIATES, INC.)

219

power, these power-driven mills led to further improvement of the diet. Since bread was now more easily made and therefore more abundant, it began to replace cereal as the staple food.

Due to the improved agricultural techniques, fewer people were needed to work the land. The loss of the labor on the land of a given number of individuals was compensated for by the larger yield. Thus people were freed to enter occupations other than farming with the assurance that because of the greater overall food supply they could be supported. This release of manpower from the land was helped by the replacement of oxen with horses as plow animals. Horses pull at greater speed than oxen (and also there were simply more of them), so that cultivators could devote less time to plowing and more time to other tasks. Horses' hooves, however, are highly susceptible to injury, so they could not be used for working the rocky soils until a method was discovered for making a nailed shoe of heavy metal. The iron horseshoe was invented sometime around the millennium, although, as with all these innovations, its use spread slowly. Also the harness used for oxen was not at all suitable for horses because it pressed on the horse's windpipe and could easily strangle the animal. When a collar was fashioned so that the horse's shoulders rather than its neck took the full weight of the plow, it became possible to utilize horsepower to its fullest advantage. Finally, since horses thrive better on oats than on any other grain, as the supply of oats increased the strain of horses in Europe improved.

The effect of these innovations, as we have said, was that there were more men than were required to farm the land. This occurred at the same time that there developed a demand for skilled labor, so the men who learned, for example, to make horsecollars and harnesses and to shoe the horses began to appear in Europe's villages. This points up the shift that was taking place in rural life. Before the eleventh century, artisans had not been familiar figures in the countryside. Now, in the expanding world of the eleventh and twelfth centuries, village life was becoming less parochial as the division of labor grew more complex. Alongside the peasant there now also worked blacksmiths, masons, and carpenters.

The Feudal Aristocracy

The impact of these agricultural changes came at a time when a change was also taking place within the feudal aristocracy, and the two encouraged one another. The noble class was becoming more complex, and the distinction was more clearly drawn than before between the upper nobility—the counts, dukes, and barons—and the knights. In the course of the twelfth century this upper aristocracy grew wealthier, politically more powerful, more cultivated, and increasingly jealous of its own position.

The great estates, for so long self-contained and self-supporting, were drawn into the market system. The land was now producing a surplus, this surplus could be traded, and it soon became clear that it was more profitable to specialize in the one or two products for which the soil was particularly well-adapted than to continue a wide variety of crops. Thus in southern France, for example, where the conditions are excellent for viticulture, the great lords became wine producers. They shipped their wine to market, sold it, then bought their grain, which most likely had been imported from central Europe.

The element now regularly introduced into the trading transaction was money. Several factors led to the increased circulation of coinage in this later medieval period, among them, as we shall shortly see, a quite extraordinary increase in the volume of trade, as well as the greater availability of metals for coinage and the demand for luxury items. At the markets and regional fairs where agricultural surpluses were traded, there were also fine silks, spices, jewels, lovely glassware, and gold and silver eating utensils—all the things that make life beautiful. And merchants were appearing at the castles of the rich lords, bringing their goods to display and sell.

Profits from the agricultural market were one means by which the nobles acquired the money to buy these luxuries; the other was the occasional conversion of the rents in labor and in kind (owed a noble by his peasants) into rents in coin. The use of coins spread so slowly in the countryside that well into the early modern

The Digger in the Vineyard, Amiens Cathedral. (MARBURG/PROTHMANN ASSOCIATES, INC.)

period peasants were still paying the bulk of their rents in kind. But for the nobility, their commercial relationships and the money to buy and enjoy luxuries supported (and also were symptomatic of) other changes in their lives. Life at home became stabilized, or at least relatively so. And there was a gradual softening of existence in general among the upper aristocracy during the twelfth century. Their values were changing, and this was reflected in the popular literature.

In the castles of the rich nobility the entertainment consisted mainly of songs and stories told in the vernacular by professional reciters and later written down, many of them during the course of the twelfth century. The largest body of vernacular literature, and the one with the greatest influence, was developing in France, where there were two cultural centers, one in the north, in the area of the Île de France, Normandy, and the Loire Valley, and the other in the south, centered in Aquitaine.

The theme of the literature of the north is different from that of the south. In northern France, feudal institutions were firmly rooted and the culture was predominantly clerical, so it is not surprising that the main concern in the songs and stories is with relationships among men. The heroic epics—the *chansons de geste*—exalted the virtue of loyalty and the importance, for the sake of God and man alike, of being faithful under all circumstances to the oaths of fealty and homage. This standard reflected and verbalized a code of behavior which was beginning to modify the self-serving aggressiveness of the early feudal aristocracy.

In the south, where the culture had always remained closer to the Roman past, feudalism was not so deeply embedded in the society, and in the eleventh and twelfth centuries the roads across the Pyrenees to Spain had opened, permitting contact with Islamic culture. These varied influences combined to produce the songs of the troubadours and the romantic epics which emphasized the relationship between men and women. Here a new and feminizing dimension was added to aristocratic life.

It was in the south, at the court of the duke of Aquitaine, that the ideal of courtly love evolved. Essentially, courtly love—an exclusively aristocratic ideal—is the love of a man for a woman who is married to someone else. To win the lady, her erstwhile suitor must undergo many trials—all set by her—to prove his love. (Even then the goal of physical consummation, although definitely part of courtly love, is not assured.)

The literature about courtly love is much more extensive than the original body of literature itself and has engendered much debate, particularly in the wake of the current women's movement.

The romantic ideal is our legacy from the Middle Ages and has been viewed by many women as a decidedly mixed blessing. In the courtly epics, the woman was placed on a pedestal, to be courted and treated with respect and love, and the romantic hero was required to be sensitive to her person and her wishes. Compared to the earlier centuries when women were treated as inferior beings and frequently brutalized, this new idea of love and devotion between the sexes was a vast improvement—at least in theory. The other side of courtly love was that women could now, for new reasons, be cosseted and kept firmly under the protection—and domination—of men. Nevertheless, in upper-class society women and feminine virtues actually did come to be more highly regarded than ever before.

This same period accorded the Virgin Mary a central place in Christian devotion, and the feminine qualities associated with her—maternal love, graciousness and forgiveness—were highly revered. More churches were built in her honor during the twelfth and thirteenth centuries than for any other saint. All the churches named Notre Dame (Our Lady) in Paris, Amiens, Chârtres—the list is quite lengthy—were built to the Mother of God, and many miracles were attributed to her.

During the twelfth century the institution of marriage also came to be more highly regarded, although its value had little to do with the respect accorded women. Marriage was important to the nobility because only children born of a union sanctified by matrimony—and who were therefore legitimate—could legally inherit property. (There are recorded in the medieval courts so many cases of brothers suing to disinherit brothers on the grounds of illegitimacy that this was obviously a problem.) The concern among the aristocracy with regulated marriages coincided with the church's growing interest in what the marriage sacrament was (or should have been), what the rights of the partners were, and under what circumstances divorce was permissible. Unfortunately, although not suprisingly, the information available comes mainly from cases that reached the courts, and since these were all disputes, we have little beyond a literary knowledge of courtly love or of personal relations between men and women. In law and in literature, at least, the lot of women seems to have been bettered.

In every way the amenities of life for the upper aristocracy had now improved considerably. By the late twelfth century castles

A twelfth-century chess set made of walrus ivory, *found in Scotland in the early nineteenth century. The set was probably English or Scandinavian. The chairs in which the royal family and the bishops are seated have been decorated with the intricate abstract designs typical of Germanic and Celtic art.* (REPRODUCED BY COURTESY OF THE TRUSTEES OF THE BRITISH MUSEUM)

were routinely constructed of stone rather than wood; and these comparatively complicated structures were warmed now by fires (which were not so hazardous in a stone building) and even had beautiful tapestries and carpets for decoration and comfort. There is also no question that the nobility was becoming less pugnacious and less mindlessly brutal. The game of chess, an exceedingly popular pastime during this period, is another reliable index of this change. Chess was invented in northwest India in the fifth century, spread to Persia where it was popular among the Muslims, and reached Christian Europe through Spain and North Africa. Although on one level undoubtedly a game of war, it is also a game requiring intelligence, patience, and an ability to focus on a mental problem, and it requires sitting—qualities very different from those associated with the feudal nobility of the tenth century. (The figures in a chess set are interesting in themselves because they represent the entire aristocracy.) During the course of the twelfth century, in the various ways described, the feudal nobility took on the attributes which were to characterize it for centuries to come.

The Peasantry

The extent to which the peasants were positively affected by the new agricultural improvements is a subject much debated by historians. Some believe that the peasants' lives were little changed by the improvements taking place around them; others interpret the period as offering the peasants the greatest possibility for economic and social advancement of any previous century—or, for that matter, any succeeding one until the eighteenth or nineteenth. The latter surmise seems closer to the truth, provided some general facts are kept in mind. The first is that the agricultural changes were of course not universally applied, so that peasants were not universally affected by them. The lives of the majority of peasants were transformed by the new agricultural prosperity only to the extent that everyone benefited from the increased supply of food and from the lessening of the precariousness of physical existence.

The second fact is that the change from rents paid in labor and in kind to rents paid at least partially in currency has been viewed as only a short-term gain for much of the peasantry. At the beginning, the way in which the money rents were established worked in the peasants' favor since lords customarily fixed rent at a permanent amount that did not vary even if prices rose. Thus, in the expanding economy of the twelfth and thirteenth centuries, some peasants were able to accumulate capital. On the other hand, in order to squeeze as much money as possible from their tenants, the lords increased dues on the services provided by their manorial lands (*demesnes*). They charged for the use of waterways which ran through their property, for the use of mills, for crossing bridges and even for the use of roads. The nobles also exacted fines in court for offenses committed within the areas of their jurisdiction. In this way, the new opportunities offered by economic expansion were often offset by the new opportunities seized by the lords. In times of prosperity peasants could afford these exactions, but when prices began to drop they were forced to sell larger portions of their crops in order to meet obligations. When a decline began at the end of the thirteenth century, and the cushion was gone, the peasants' economic status declined rapidly because these dues remained constant.

Those peasants who were positively affected by the new agricultural prosperity, however, had greater opportunities than ever before to alter their lives. The improvement in their status, whenever this happened, came about as the result of the combination of the supply of food and the introduction of money. When rents in labor and in kind were commuted even partially to money rents, some peasants were able to earn money for themselves. The surplus they had once had to turn over as payment in kind could now be kept for sale at market. In this way serfs earned money to buy their freedom and freemen earned money to buy more property. In the former case, particularly, the transaction was agreeable to the lords because they wanted currency to spend and were able to do a good deed in the bargain. The transition from serf to free peasant did not occur all over Europe; nor did it happen all at once. (In England, in fact, the trend went in the reverse direction.) But the legal and practical status of hundreds and thousands of peasants was improved considerably during the course of the twelfth and thirteenth centuries.

For all those peasants able to prosper in this improving economy, there were many who suffered greatly because of it. When lords no longer demanded rent in labor from their tenants, they went out and hired workers, and the condition of the peasant farmer with no leasehold was quite deprived; he was paid a tiny wage and benefited from none of the security of the tenant farmer.

One of the biggest changes for the better was that the options open to the peasant of the twelfth century were greater than ever before. As we have seen, there was now the possibility of colonizing the new areas that were available for cultivation in Europe—and under generally better terms than those offered at home. The new agricultural surplus freed peasants from the soil and enabled numbers of them to learn crafts and enter manufacturing and trade. Many moved to the towns to find work. The rapid growth in the numbers and sizes of towns in Europe was itself caused by this movement of individuals no longer needed to till the land, and by the extraordinary increase in urban commercial activity.

The Expansion of Commercial Life

The commercial leaders were the Italian merchants. Elsewhere in Europe, particularly in Flanders, the stream of commercial activity was also widening and deepening, but the Italians were in a unique position. Due to their location on the Mediterranean, their experience in commerce, and eventually their special role in the crusades, the Italians had virtually always been in a position to take advantage of the immense commercial opportunities in the eastern Mediterranean. During the eleventh century the entire economic balance in the Mediterranean area shifted in favor of the Latin West. Byzantium had lost its last Western possessions with the Norman conquest of southern Italy, and Byzantine shipping had of course been adversely affected by the decline of the Byzantine navy. The commercial advantages which Constantinople had once held so securely began to accrue to Byzantium's ally and trading partner, Venice. And after Venice, the two other Italian seaports which assumed the lead in commerce were Genoa and Pisa.

Historians once considered the crusades responsible for the re-markable expansion of the European economy during the twelfth century. That view has been considerably modified, and we have seen that there had been a revival of trade long before the crusades; but it is true that European military expansion into the Levant was a factor of considerable value to the Italian cities and gave them a significant opportunity which they ably turned to good use. At the time of the first crusade, the Venetian, Genoese, and Pisan navies became essential to the defense of the crusader states as the only available resource for transporting supplies and re-inforcements. In return, the Italian merchants were given their own trading section in those markets and seaports of the Levant which were controlled by the crusaders.

By all accounts nearly every merchant who arrived with the religious warriors and remained in the Near East became rich. "Those who were needy," wrote a contemporary chronicler of the first crusade, "have here [in the Holy Land] been enriched by God . . . . who has ever heard of such a thing? For God wishes to make us all rich . . . . " Above all others, God seems to have wanted to enrich the Italians.

Having established quarters in Constantinople and Alexandria as well as in the crusader states, the Italians quickly gained a substantial share of all Oriental trade passing through the Levant. They made good use of their legacy as they became heirs to By-zantium's markets. The damasks, brocades, and spices carried by caravan from Persia and the silks from China were traded in the Eastern markets and then brought across the Mediterranean to North Africa, Spain, and, of course, to Italy. The demand for these luxury items was continually on the rise in Europe during the twelfth century and the profits were becoming enormous.

The direct result of their prolific trade was that the Italians were able to accumulate large amounts of money to invest for a further profit on the capital itself. As the demand in the West for the luxury goods increased, prices went up, profits rose for the trad-ers, and more currency was put into circulation. Money had never ceased to circulate, but the flow of coinage now became far greater than in the preceding centuries and led to a new attitude toward capital and its uses. The idea that money could—and moreover, should—beget more money took root. (It is almost superfluous to add how well the idea has flourished.)

As Italian business transactions became more complex, merchants and traders developed or accelerated the use of instruments to facilitate carrying out their commercial enterprises. These innovations were partly of Italian invention and partly inspired by the advanced entrepreneurial techniques of the Byzantine and Muslim businessmen. The whole idea of credit—the borrowing of money on the expectation of repayment through future income—was introduced into Europe by the Italians. Letters of credit came into use. These were, in effect, pledges made by an investor who had a good credit rating to back the enterprises of, for instance, a traveling merchant. Another instrument was the bill of exchange, which relieved merchants of the danger and inconvenience of physically transporting gold and silver coinage. The bill of exchange worked very much like traveler's checks—purchasable in the currency of one country and redeemable for a fee in another. The Italians also developed the concept of a backing company in order to minimize the financial liability of the single individual who might gain, but might also as easily lose, a fortune on one cargo. The company was a group of businessmen who would jointly invest in several cargoes traveling in different ships rather than in just one. If one ship was lost, there were still profits to be shared from the others.

One of the principal necessities at the various markets and fairs was the accurate exchange of one currency for another. Many coinages were issued throughout the world; and in Italy alone, most of the commercially advanced cities were, by the twelfth century, issuing their own coinages. The international money-changer was thus a crucial figure in the marketplace, and well-paid for the transactions he concluded. Moneychanging was one of the operations which developed into a regular banking practice. (The word *bank* actually derives from the Italian *banco*, or bench, where the moneychanger did business with his scales and weights.)

Some of the biggest profits and most active business were derived from moneylending. The church was—at least in theory—

steadfastly opposed to usury—or the collecting of interest on loans—and the practice was expressly forbidden to all communicants. The church, however, was opposed only to interest on loans involving no risk for the lender, so the fine line between no risk and risk could be crossed with minimal ingenuity. Although Christians seem regularly to have devised ways to circumvent the injunction against usury and engage in moneylending, it was never considered moral or respectable during the Middle Ages. Since usury was not forbidden within Judaism, the Jews became the chief moneylenders until the appearance of powerful Italian usurers. The Jewish moneylenders performed a necessary function within the economy, but their identification with usury added yet another dimension to the anti-Semitism that had reared its head at the time of the first crusade.

During the last half of the twelfth century the position of Italy in the East became less secure. The Italians had never controlled the sources of the goods which they transported to the West; these were still in the hands of the Byzantines at Constantinople and the Muslims. Then, during the last half of the twelfth century, the crusader kingdom lost territory to the Muslims and was left with only a strip of coastal territory from Tyre to Jaffa—a considerable reduction of the amount of Syrian-Palestinian coast it had once held. Furthermore, after the mid-twelfth century, the defense of the crusader states became a more expensive undertaking for the Italian navies, since the Christians were now clearly on the defensive. In 1202, only a few years after the third crusade (1187–1190), Pope Innocent III preached a fourth crusade to recover the Holy Land, but the crusaders never got that far.

The fourth crusade was fought against the Byzantine Empire, not the Muslims. In 1204, for the first time in its long history, Constantinople was captured and the capital of the Christian East was raped and plundered by Christian Westerners. The question of the responsibility for the deflection of the fourth crusade from Jerusalem to Constantinople has caused much debate, but the Venetians seem on the whole to have been the most directly responsible. The crusaders had contracted with the Venetians for transportation and provisions for the journey, but in 1202 when the crusading armies (mostly French) arrived in Venice they were short of money. After protracted and complicated negotiations, the Venetians transported the crusaders, first across the Adriatic to the Christian city of Zara (which was trying to rival Venice's shipping, and which the crusaders captured) and then to Constantinople. Several factions were behind the crusaders' plan to capture Constantinople, including a claimant to the Byzantine throne. The Byzantine resistance was strong but finally, in 1204, after a siege of many months, the holy warriors captured the richest market in the Mediterranean. They renamed it the Latin Empire of Constantinople. Although the first emperor was French, the lion's share of the spoils went to the Venetians who wanted, and received, the right to choose the Patriarch of Constantinople. The Venetians also took enormous sums of gold from the city's treasury.

The Latin Empire remained under the control of the West until 1261, and for those sixty years the Venetians had complete control of all trade into and out of the Black Sea. In the process of securing trading centers in the ports along this waterway they bankrupted the Byzantine traders. Constantinople was retaken by the Byzantine government only when the emperor won the support of the Genoese, who by the mid-thirteenth century were willing to do almost anything to oust the Venetians from their supremacy.

Although Venice, Genoa, and Pisa were the first cities to profit from the crusades, other western Mediterranean ports, such as Bari, Marseilles, and Barcelona quickly became involved in trade, and the inland cities turned to the production of goods for export. Florence and Milan emerged as the two most prominent—though by no means only—industrial centers. Throughout northern and central Italy, cities were being stimulated to engage in industry, banking, and trade.

The commodities which the Italians imported from the East—and some produced locally as well—were carried from Italy to northern Europe either directly across the Alps or along the Mediterranean coast into southern France. From the valley of the Rhone the Italians took their goods northward to the great fairs held in the county of Champagne, the most important economic clearinghouse in twelfth-century Europe. At the fairs held in different parts of Champagne as often as six times a year, the Italian traders did business at first principally with the Flemish merchants.

The economy of northern Europe had begun a slow but steady revival during the tenth century, and the center of this recovery was Flanders. The Flemish countryside happened to be ideal for raising sheep, and taking advantage of this the Flemings turned their energies to the manufacture of fine woolen cloth. As the demand for Flemish cloth grew, the English were encouraged to

Woman Carding Wool and Women Washing Wool. Chârtres Cathedral, 13th c. A.D.
(MARBURG/PROTHMANN ASSOCIATES, INC.)

233

raise sheep to provide raw wool for export to Flanders. By the twelfth century the wool industry had become the staple of the northern European economy. As it became the most commonly worn of all the textiles, woolen cloth grew to be in such demand that England also entered into its manufacture; but the skill of the Flemish cloth makers was of such caliber and of such long tradition, that Flanders managed to stay ahead of the competitors. Silks and luxury fabrics were worn only by the wealthy (though the number of people who could afford them was increasing) and cotton was seldom worn in Europe. Linen, though manufactured in France, had nowhere near the popularity of wool, and once Flemish wool had begun to be exported to Scandinavia and the eastern Mediterranean the demand for it became nearly universal.

The fuller development and expansion of this northern economy during the twelfth century was due to the increase in the rate and volume of trade with the East. At first northern contact with the Levant was indirect—through the Italians. But the most striking change—and ultimately, the most striking characteristic—of the commercial life in the twelfth century was that it became truly international, with merchants and their goods traveling along many East-West routes.

The principal route from the East to northern Europe extended from the Black Sea to the Dnieper River, and from there to the Baltic and the North Sea. The merchants from Bruges, Antwerp, Bremen, Hamburg, Lübeck, Stettin, and Danzig (among others) became wealthy through their trade with the East, although their wealth was never so great, nor their mercantile activities quite so complex or advanced, as that of the Italian merchants.

The route that linked northern Europe with Constantinople ran through the Russian city of Kiev. When the Scandinavian invaders moved into Slavic territory along the Dnieper in the ninth century, they were encouraged to settle in Novgorod, which was already a trading center. From there they expanded until they controlled a large empire which they ruled from Kiev and Novgorod. (The Scandinavians were absorbed by the large Slavic population, and the language and customs of this empire were Slavic.) Near the end of the tenth century these Russian—or European—Slavs were converted to Orthodox Christianity and were then drawn into Byzantine political and commercial life. The Russians developed the Dnieper as the principal artery between the Black Sea and the Baltic, and throughout the twelfth century maintained continuous commercial relations with western Europe. These contacts with the West were blocked only when the Mongols invaded, and finally conquered, Russia in the thirteenth century; but during the twelfth century Kievan Russia was a principal source of trade for the West.

The Slavs, as the name suggests, were the principal source of slaves during the later Middle Ages. The slave trade was one of the booming businesses of the twelfth century and a major basis of Russia's wealth. Although slavery was declining in Latin Christendom, and this was particularly marked in northern Europe, there remained a slave population and a market for slaves in Italy. The largest market, however, was in the Muslim West, and the route for the slave trade extended from the Black Sea to Venice or to Bari and then on to Spain and North Africa. The other principal commodities which the Russians exported to Byzantium and Europe were furs, honey, wax, and iron. There was also a small but highly profitable trade in Russian caviar.

As commerce expanded, additional trade routes were developed both to and from the East and within Europe itself. A secondary and southerly route which ended in Germany went from Kiev to the Danube region and terminated usually at Regensburg, later the main commercial city on the Danube. Farther north, the Germans were founding settlements to the east and along the Baltic Sea and building new cities to take advantage of the flourishing trade that came into and out of the Baltic. One of the most inspired foundations was Lübeck which, although a brand-new city in the mid-twelfth century, quickly commanded the trade in the Baltic-North Sea region. Once again, as in Roman times, the major European rivers became active trade routes, and cities such as Cologne on the Rhine and Avignon and Lyons on the Rhone grew rapidly to accomodate the economic resurgence.

The several practical obstacles to the easy movement of goods were gradually overcome. The risk of sea voyages lessened as the structure of ships and the art of navigation were constantly improved. Travel overland had its own special problems since roads had been only haphazardly maintained before the eleventh century, and there were heavy and frequent tolls as well as brigandage. The old Roman roads were still surprisingly usable, however, and as time went on were kept in better repair. One of the lasting building enterprises of this period was the construction of bridges to facilitate crossing smaller rivers.

A sampling of the goods that moved along all these routes indicates the variety of industries and natural resources that were being developed during the twelfth and thirteenth centuries. Along with some of the major commodities, such as slaves and textiles, salt was one of the chief articles of trade. It was used to cure meat and fish so that these could be preserved through the winter and carried long distances. Salt was produced (by evaporating sea water) along many coastal areas of Europe, primarily the Atlantic coast of France and the Adriatic coast. Its function in preserving food was a compelling reason for the increased use of spices, since the latter camouflaged saltiness during cooking. The demand for Oriental spices was such that these ought perhaps not be considered a luxury. The spice lists included such imports as almonds, dates, and raisins, along with pepper, ginger, cinnamon, cloves, nutmeg, and cumin, to name only a few. Fish of many varieties were exported from the Black Sea, and herring from the Baltic was in huge demand. Fish made up a sizable volume of the trade and meat less so, although England and Germany exported bacon, one of the mainstays of the European diet.

As much as possible, grain was produced locally, but the major grain-producing areas exported their surpluses in large amounts. These included northern France and several parts of Germany, Poland, and Russia. Butter, heavily salted for preservation, was exported from England, Scandinavia, Holland, and Poland, and English cheese was popular. Leather goods were exported from Spain, glass from Venice, wine from Italy, France, and Gascony, tin from England, copper from northern Germany, and silver from Saxony, Bohemia, and Hungary. The list is virtually inexhaustible.

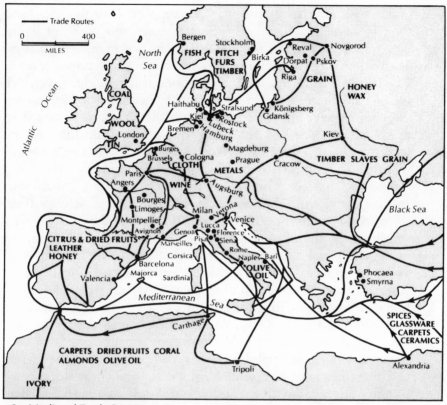

3. Medieval Trade Routes

This expansion of commercial life, supported by the agricultural prosperity and combined with the increase in population, brought a renaissance of urban life unparalleled since the days of the Roman Empire.

The Rise of Towns

In the Roman world life had centered on the city, and although the West was never as commercialized or industrialized as the East, the hub of life was nevertheless in the city. Trade, commerce, and industry were all housed in the cities of the Western Empire, and Roman culture was distinctly urban. Education and intellectual and artistic life were all supported by the cities and took place within them. This was a legacy and mode of living inherited from the Greeks, who believed that man's very nature was such that he had to live in a city to be productive and creative. The Romans had been ambivalent about urban life, however. We read in the poetry and letters of prominent citizens a longing for the countryside; but once away from the city, most wanted to return to the hustle, bustle, and intellectual stimulation of the Roman town. The upper class usually had the best of both worlds—a life in the town and a villa in the country.

Then, in the economic crises that attended the Germanic invasions and the further contractions of commercial activity from the sixth to the ninth centuries, most cities lost their commercial viability and shrank considerably in size, some to the point of being completely abandoned. Many of the towns in Italy and southern France, however, had a continuous existence from Roman times on, although of the ones that did, most—not all—lost their economic functions. Venice is a good, indeed the best, example of a town that maintained trade for all the reasons we have noted, and that was able to outdo its neighbors for a long time. In Venice, the politically powerful people were the traders and merchants, by the tenth century already an aristocracy of wealth. The same is true of other port cities, and here and there some inland towns were engaging in industry by the central Middle Ages.

In other Roman cities in Italy and Gaul, however, there were only the vestiges of town life before the tenth century. Artisans and craftsmen worked to make cloth or bake bread, and small businessmen ran inns—most of them to provide goods and services for the town church or cathedral. So there was a continuity of urban life. And then, in the tenth century, there came the first indications of what was to be a huge and significant change in urban existence.

Though the changes came about in a variety of ways and places, they were all related to the burgeoning economic life of Europe. Old towns in existence since Roman times began to build new walls to accomodate the increased numbers of people who came

A view of the medieval walls of the Castilian town of Avila. *The walls, among the best preserved in all Spain, were built during the eleventh century on Roman foundations as the Christians repopulated the territory between the Duero and the Tajo Rivers. This town was under royal jurisdiction, yet it enjoyed a degree of independence since it had a city council, a charter of liberties, and its own militia.* (ALINARI/EDITORIAL PHOTOCOLOR ARCHIVES)

to trade or find work in the cities. And new towns were founded in northern Europe, slowly during the tenth and eleventh centuries, then at an astonishing rate during the twelfth century. The beginnings of many of the northern towns are quite obscure, and we hear little of them until they were granted charters guaranteeing certain freedoms by the king, by a feudal lord on whose territory a town existed, or by the church. Some of these settlements began as markets which were held sporadically at first; but as the demand for goods increased and the merchants found it profitable to settle, a community would take on permanence. Some towns grew up around the cathedrals and churches which began to cover the countryside; and within these the needs of the cathedral chapter had to be met, as well as the needs of travelers and pilgrims. There were also towns that grew up near castles and fortresses, and still others were agricultural centers which became markets for the exchange of agricultural products. Often a manorial lord would encourage the movement of peasant-artisans to a single location to manufacture armor, cloth, or whatever product he needed. There were also villages of free peasants which gradually became urban centers. Regardless of how these towns came into existence or were enlarged, by the twelfth century most were engaged in trade and industry and were built at locations that offered the best possibilities for participation in these activities. There were, of course, exceptions. Some prominent cities in the later Middle Ages never developed a fully independent economic existence. Rome was one of these, its population being almost completely absorbed in the activities of the church, government, and—as now—tourism. Taken as a whole, the newly founded cities of the twelfth century (and there were literally hundreds of them) were built at locations that offered the best possibilities for trade and industry. Old and new towns alike flourished where there was easy access to highways, waterways, and resources for manufacturing.

It is easy to see how towns attracted people as commerce expanded and the profits from trade and manufacturing became assured. The more difficult question to answer is where the merchants came from in the first place. In a few cities, such as Venice or Marseilles, there was a continuity of trade and therefore a class of people who were continuously engaged in it. But in the north, and in those southern towns which had no important economic functions until the later Middle Ages, the origins of the townspeople are not so clear.

Many of the first merchants were men who started out with packs on their backs trying to sell goods, usually on consignment, at fairs or markets. By a combination of luck and hard work some were able to accumulate a bit of capital to invest. These were the people with nothing to lose, willing to take their chances in the marketplace. Their hardships and successes must have been strikingly similar to those of the immigrant peddler in late nineteenth- and early twentieth-century America. Still others were landowners who invested their surplus capital in business, an experience not unlike that of the robber-baron in nineteenth-century America. The merchant whose initial wealth was in land was usually from Italy or southern France, where the distinction between town and countryside was not so marked as in the north. Other merchants sprang from the numerous craftsmen and shopkeepers in the towns of later medieval Europe.

The most common word for town was *burg,* from the German meaning "a fortified place." In the terminology of the time, the people who lived within the town walls were therefore called "burgers" (or "burghers") and eventually, from the French, *bourgeoisie.* The proverb which says that the "air of a town makes one free" contains a sizable core of truth. It was, for example, the case that if a serf remained within a city for a year and a day he was forever afterward a freeman and therefore a part of the rest of bourgeois population. The town itself was an "island," not necessarily in opposition to the rural area which surrounded it, but always set apart from it. This "island" offered special freedoms, not in an abstract sense, but specific liberties and immunities from the obligations that weighed on most of the population of Europe. The town regulated its own industry and commerce, and even though it was usually located on a noble's property (or a king's or an archbishop's), its inhabitants defended their freedom to carry on their business without outside restrictions or controls, in return for paying taxes or giving political support or help of some other sort.

Within the cities, the most usual form of government was a council whose members were elected by the town burghers. The city officials assessed the collected taxes, administered justice, took charge of civic functions such as repairing walls and maintaining an adequate water supply, and controlled the economic life of the city. This last meant supervising the markets held usually once a week, ensuring the safety of the merchants and guaranteeing their honesty, collecting market tolls, and regulating prices. Since the first group to be most directly affected by the expansion of commerce was the merchants, they were also the first to seek political power in the cities. The wealthiest tradesmen were the ones usually elected to the governing councils. In addition, for their mutual benefit and protection, they organized themselves into associations or guilds.

In their origins the guilds were separate and distinct from the cities and the city governments, but since their functions and purpose in the economic area overlapped, it was not always easy to tell them apart. (Some guilds, in fact, may have predated the formation of city governments.) The merchant guilds were established to promote trade by regulating prices, making it possible for members to buy wholesale, curtailing imports that might be competitive—in short anything that would augment the financial security of the members. These guilds also had social and religious aspects. They were responsible for the care of widows and orphans, celebrated religious festivals and holidays, made contributions to the local churches, and built guild halls that became the centers for social activities in the town. The first guilds were mercantile and included only artisans and shopkeepers, but as industry and manufacturing grew, the craftsmen formed guilds of their own.

By the end of the twelfth century every town had a number of craft guilds. There were guilds of goldsmiths, spinners, weavers, doctors, masons, bankers, butchers, bakers and most of the other skilled crafts and professions. The members of the craft guilds were the masters—those thoroughly skilled individuals responsible for establishing the standards for a craft or industry—who regulated wages, prices, and the conditions of employment. Each craft was taught through a system of apprenticeship: A boy would be apprenticed to a master at age ten or twelve and would begin by performing the most menial tasks and would eventually move through every stage of production. Once the apprentice had learned his craft, he became a journeyman, or dayworker (from the French *journée* meaning "day"), entitled to earn a salary. When he had satisfied the masters that he had become a master crafts-man—not an easy thing to do—he would be admitted to membership in the guild. The craft guilds had the same social and religious functions as their trade counterparts.

Relations between the merchant and craft guilds were often highly competitive. The merchants, whatever their original social origins had been, by the twelfth century had formed a wealthy class with significant power in the cities. The membership of the craft guilds was drawn mainly from the countryside, usually from the peasantry, and the artisans and shopkeepers did not have the same opportunities as the merchants to accumulate vast sums of money. Some craft guilds did become rich and powerful, but these were exceptions, and over time the merchant guilds came to dominate the craft guilds.

All the burghers within a city, however, had in common the desire to gain as much freedom from outside authority as possible. Throughout Europe there was such variation in the degree of independence from outside supervision that no single description fits the varieties of arrangements that existed. Usually a city could gain its independence only by fighting for it. In general, the Italian cities secured the greatest freedom. The northern Italian cities formed the powerful Lombard League which waged several bitter wars in the late twelfth century against the Roman emperor; and by the thirteenth century the towns of Lombardy had become self-determining city-states.

The northern European cities, particularly the towns of Germany and northern France, were subjected to the greatest degree of outside control. In their fight for independence from the nobility they found strong allies among the European monarchs, who for their part needed support and money to help establish strong central government and lessen the power of the feudal lords. More often than not, the alliance between the cities and royalty was thus mutually beneficial, although sometimes the cities discovered they had traded one kind of control for another.

During the early development of commerce and industry in the tenth and early eleventh centuries, the Western merchant, like the town he enclosed with walls, stood apart from the mainstream of European society. Those who engaged in business for profit were looked upon with a considerable suspicion and hostility. The chances for a "rich man to enter heaven" were regarded by the church as fairly slim since he was involved in moneylending and was undoubtedly motivated by avarice. Partly because of this attitude and partly because the Jews had connections with the Levant, the role of the Jews in trade and commerce was deliberately encouraged by Western rulers from the Carolingian era until the first crusade—a fact which, as time went on, was a decidedly mixed blessing.

The European Jews were craftsmen and some owned large estates, but the majority were found in industry and international trade. As trade became a more respected livelihood for Christians, the economic activities of the Jews changed. During the eleventh and twelfth centuries they were superseded, first of all, by the Italians who had by then succeeded in dominating Mediterranean trade. Then the guilds formed during the eleventh and twelfth centuries excluded Jews because the oaths of membership were Christian oaths; and since no exceptions were made, the former were then forced into banking and moneylending, virtually the only businesses left open to them. This decline in economic status was gradual until the eruption of anti-Semitism during the first crusade. After that the economic status of the Jews declined rapidly as they were squeezed out of banking and large-scale moneylending by Christian merchants and usurers who, by the end of the twelfth century, had drawn the bulk of Europe's trade and finance into their own hands. The day of the isolated merchant was over, and the isolation of European Jewry had begun.

Prior to the industrial revolution of the nineteenth century, the twelfth and thirteenth centuries were the period of the most vigorous urbanization in European history. The towns themselves were crowded, busy places and by modern standards, quite small. Few had populations over 10,000, and the ones that did were in every sense exceptional. Constantinople, for example, by the end of the twelfth century had a population estimated at 100,000 and Venice had one of about 64,000. A capital city like Paris, on the other hand, probably did not have more than 30,000 inhabitants.

The average city housed only about 3,000 people within an area usually of less than one square mile. The walls that circumscribed the city were necessary for protection, but they were expensive to build and were rarely higher or stronger than seemed absolutely essential. The result was that as a town's population increased, every available foot of space inside its walls was utilized. Also, particularly in southern European towns, people moved beyond the walls. In the case of Florence, for example, the wealthy built mansions and summer villas outside the walls.

It is easy to picture what a medieval town looked like, since most European cities were founded no later than the twelfth century and their appearances have retained much of the medieval character. The older part of Assisi, for instance, must have looked much the same to St. Francis as it does now. The streets of the towns were exceedingly narrow and usually made of mud, although sometimes the main street and the market square were cobblestoned. Houses were tiny and clustered close together, and when a story was added to a house, it was done in such a way that the second floor projected out over the first, the third over the second, and so on. The result was that houses facing each

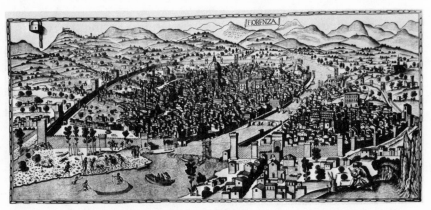

Florence in the fifteenth century: a contemporary view. *The Florentines, unlike the people of Avila, did not have to confine themselves to living within the safety of their defensive walls. As Florence prospered with the revenues derived from manufacture and trade, the population grew and the wealthy Florentines built luxurious mansions and summer houses on the outskirts of the city, beyond the walls.* (ALINARI/EDITORIAL PHOTOCOLOR ARCHIVES)

other on opposite sides of the street nearly met in the middle and the streets became tunnel-like passageways beneath them. The first floor of a building housed an artisan's workroom or a shop, usually both, since craftsmen customarily sold what they made right on the premises. Most houses were made of wood, and these burned to the ground with great frequency. (Fire was one of the worst and most constant dangers in the medieval town.) Some homes of the very wealthy were built of stone, the use of which was mainly confined to the churches, cathedrals, and the town's main civic center. Medieval townspeople lived in fear of violence, and the town gates were locked at dusk to keep out strangers.

With all their physicial inconveniences—and there were many— the cities became, as they had been in Greek and Roman antiquity, centers of a brilliant intellectual life. And within the walls of many a city, dominating the landscape for miles around, stood the most beautiful product of the artistic genius of the twelfth century, the Gothic cathedral.

The Revival of Learning

The explosion of intellectual and artistic activity during the twelfth and thirteenth centuries was both an aspect and a consequence of all the other movements of expansion we have been considering. And having said this, something more must be added to help explain the burgeoning of intellectual life in Europe. There was in this later medieval period a huge upsurge of energy, and a curiosity about the world—and a spirit of daring. One of the immediately striking features of this intellectual ferment is its diversity—the many different texts that were studied, the completely new subjects that were discovered, the new, and often conflicting, ideas being discussed. Many more people were going to school, and most of them for reasons that had little or nothing to do with a religious vocation. There were new careers in law, medicine, and government. In the complex world of business and trade one could no longer remain illiterate. Young men neither rich nor destined for the cloister came to the cities to seek an education that would help them make their way in the world; and in this happy state of affairs, more teachers were needed than ever before.

The world of learning had now become lively and noisy, with many voices clamoring for attention—another way of saying that education had the quality of the city, that it partook of the hustle and bustle of urban life and added to it. One of the most important overall changes, in fact, is that learning in the later medieval period went on in the world, not separated from it as in many previous centuries.

Through most of the Middle Ages the monasteries were the preservers and the transmitters of learning. Influenced by the teaching of Gerbert of Aurillac, some of the cathedral schools (particularly those associated with the episcopates at Rheims, Paris, Chârtres, and Laon) became intellectual centers during the eleventh century. But on balance, the intellectual leadership remained monastic until the end of the century. Then, in the late eleventh century, the monasteries began to draw in on themselves and away from the world. They began closing their external schools and educating only those young men who had chosen the monastic life. Furthermore, the monasteries were located in rural areas quite removed from the lively intellectual give-and-take that was going on in the cities. The slow rhythm of monastic life did not change, and more and more the monastic spirit became identified with the search for an inner, personal, and mystical experience of God. This is not to say that the monasteries did not play a role at all in the intellectual changes of the twelfth and thirteenth centuries. As with so much else, there had been for this new learning a period of preparation, and much of this had taken place within the cloister.

The mainstream of the intellectual life of the later medieval period, however, was urban. It was centered in the city, within the shadow of the cathedrals, and in the cathedral schools themselves. The twelfth century was also the age of the wandering scholars who came to the cities to lecture in their special disciplines, and who attracted droves of students eager for the new learning. Those cities where the schools developed particularly rapidly, such

fanctum fanctam ęcctiam

Schoolroom scene; an illustration from the Canterbury Psalter. *Although the Canterbury Psalter is a twelfth-century manuscript, the illustrations are closely linked to those in the ninth-century Utrecht Psalter.* (THE MASTER AND FELLOWS OF TRIN. COLL. CAMB.)

as Paris and Bologna, seem to have been overflowing with students who, like the clerk in Chaucer's *Canterbury Tales*, "would gladly teach and gladly learn."

Scholars and Scholarship

In the first phase of the new intellectual development, the period roughly from the late eleventh to the mid-twelfth century, we can distinguish three major areas of emphasis. There was a revival of Latin learning and literature, with particular stress on Roman law, letters, and poetry. There was a great spurt in the translation from Greek and Arabic into Latin of scientific, medical, and mathematical texts. And there was the wholehearted embracing of logic and the logical method. It is this last which, more than anything else, gives to the entire period from the late eleventh to the late thirteenth century its most distinctive character.

From St. Augustine in the late fourth century until the eleventh century, the basis—though not the entirety—of education was the *trivium*. Of the three parts of the *trivium*, the two considered essential were grammar and rhetoric—the study of language and the art of persuasion. In terms of a broad education these disciplines meant far more than their names imply. In the hands of a great practitioner, rhetoric could be a high art, but an art with a larger purpose than simply speaking and writing well. Rhetoric and grammar were the tools by which men could penetrate and expound the mysteries of Scripture and the writings of the church Fathers.

The Scriptures were studied assiduously to see how many of their secrets could be unravelled by understanding the words and phrases to find every possible layer of meaning. To do this, a certain amount of knowledge was useful and even necessary. Augustine gave as an example the necessity to learn the exact properties of the olive tree in order to understand why the olive branch should have been used in the Bible as a symbol of peace. He could then explain that olive oil is smooth and little affected by any other liquid, and that the tree is an evergreen. This is a relatively simple illustration, but the principle was the same for all interpretation: A certain range of information was needed to comprehend fully the meaning and contexts of the words. Beyond that, however, as Augustine quoted from the Bible, "Knowledge puffeth up." There was no need to go further, since Scripture held that all knowledge and the final answers were revealed, wanting only a proper understanding. There had been no thought of applying a critical faculty to the study of the Bible until the study of logic, reintroduced into Europe first by Gerbert of Aurillac at the turn of the eleventh century, changed that approach.

The Revival of Logic

The change did not happen all at once. The foundations for the study of logic were a very small number of Aristotle's writings (with an introduction by a Greek scholar, Porphyry) translated into Latin, with commentaries, by Boethius at the end of the fifth century. Compared to the full corpus of Aristotle's writings which would flood into Europe during the twelfth century, these materials were scant; for Europeans in the eleventh century, however, they opened up a new world of possibilities.

Aristotle was the great systematizer of knowledge, and the few early texts that were known in translation presented a new—and previously unimagined—way of organizing and understanding the world. From Aristotle medieval scholars learned a method for observing the objects of the external world and then classifying them according to the characteristics they had in common. They also learned to classify the kinds of statements that can be made about objects, rules for defining terms and analyzing concepts, and the kinds of statements which can be made about ideas. They learned rules for arguing and what makes certain arguments valid and others not. The medieval thinkers had before them for the first time a method for systematizing knowledge and a way of framing questions to test whether their conclusions about any subject were correct. Underlying this method were two assumptions totally different from those on which Europeans had for centuries been nurtured. First, the method of logic (or dialectic) is predicated on the conviction that the world which we perceive is orderly, not chaotic, and therefore capable of being comprehended as long as the rules for arranging what we observe and conclude are understood and followed. The second assumption is that the human mind, unaided, is capable of comprehending the order which exists.

The Aristotelian dialectic could also be used to resolve disputes and reconcile differences and inconsistencies. Conflicting statements about a subject would be presented, and then a question posed which aimed to discover which of the contradictory statements was true, after which a logical argument was offered to arrive at the truth or to harmonize the differences. We will see this method employed in virtually all the emergent disciplines of the twelfth century.

To say that there was, beginning in the late eleventh century, a new importance given to the study of logic does not begin to convey either the excitement of scholars at rediscovering logic or the significance of logical reasoning in the history of Western thought. It is quite simply the case that without the tools and assumptions of logic there would not have been possible that spirit of scientific inquiry which the ancient Greeks pioneered and which, since its revival during the late medieval period, has been an intrinsic and creative part of the development of our culture and civilization.

In the beginning the scholars who familiarized themselves with logic had only the old texts upon which to try the new method; they had the Bible and the writings of the church Fathers—principally the works of Augustine. Until this late medieval period there had never existed a fully reasoned philosophical explanation of the dogmas of Christianity. The appeal to the authority of faith was final *because* it was the authority of faith and also because there was no system of thought with which to question the validity of the "truths" revealed in Scripture. Now there existed such a system, and the application of this critical method to the tenets of Christianity has been called "scholasticism." The word derives from the Latin *scholasticus*, meaning "teacher," but is generally used to apply to something more specific than simply everything taught in the schools which used the dialectical method: Scholasticism is the use of logic to test theological concepts.

The use of logic to plumb the mysteries of faith created many problems—and serious ones—for theologians, but it should always be kept in mind that none of the scholastics set out to attack the dogmas of faith. Logic had freed them from their dependence on authority, but how far from that authority logic would take them—and into what areas and with what results—was not at all clear.

We can trace the initial stages in the application of rational inquiry to the dogmas of Christianity in the careers of a few thinkers who were in the tradition which had begun with Gerbert's school at Rheims. Gerbert's pupil, Fulbert, who taught logic and established the episcopal school at Chârtres, trained the monk Berengar, who went on to teach at the cathedral school at Tours. Berengar's enthusiasm for using logic led him into theological

251

error, and he was branded a heretic by the church because he reached conclusions different from those based on the authority of faith. There followed theologians who debated whether logic should be allowed at all as a subject for study, but for this it was already too late. Although there would always be some who rejected the dialectic as a dangerous tool, even they could not avoid using it as weaponry with which to argue against the very logicians they opposed.

Theologians were now once more confronted with the problem faced by the church Fathers. They had to decide how to reconcile Christianity with a body of classical knowledge. As in the early church, there were those who wished to reject it completely. A reconciliation viewpoint appeared early on, however, under the spokesmanship of St. Anselm (1034–1109), a monk at Bec in Normandy, who ended his career as archbishop of Canterbury.

St. Anselm

Anselm used the logical method to explore and comprehend the truth of Christian beliefs revealed in Scripture. He is most famous for his proofs of the existence of God (which have been debated for centuries), but it is his approach to the subject of the relationship between dialectic and faith that concerns us here. Anselm believed in the authority of the Bible and of Christian dogma; but he did not rest his case on the authority of faith alone. He saw no possible contradiction between the conclusions which could be reached and tested by reason and the truth revealed by faith. Without questioning the ultimate truths of Christianity, Anselm wanted to explore the reasons for them: "I do not seek to understand that I may believe, but I believe that I may understand."

Peter Abelard

In the next generation, in the hands of the gifted, fiery, troubled, and troublesome Peter Abelard (1079–1142), dialectic became a finely honed tool and Abelard was led, through his own intellectual drives and extraordinary curiosity, to a position different from that of Anselm. To Abelard, "nothing could be believed unless it could first be understood," and although he had not intended to go beyond the framework of the church and its teachings, he nevertheless came into conflict with the church. It is hard to escape the conclusion that it was Abelard's life experience that made him so controversial and, by his own admission, his arrogance that made him so provocative, although his teachings pointed up the dangers—from the church's view—inherent in the use of dialectic.

Born in Brittany, the son of a minor nobleman, Abelard from his early youth displayed brilliance and talent for study, and he went off to France in search of teachers. He studied in several places; and as soon as he had learned all he could from one master he moved on (in two cases after publicly refuting what he had been taught). Abelard began to teach and wherever he appeared to lecture he attracted students. His lectures on theology in Paris in 1113 were so well-received that students came from all over, and he became wealthy (since teachers were then paid privately for their lectures). Abelard was so successful and popular that he thought of himself as "the only philosopher remaining in the whole world."

Among Abelard's pupils was a young woman, Héloise, the niece of the canon of the cathedral of Notre Dame. The love affair between Héloise and Abelard is told in Abelard's personal *History of My Calamities* and in the letters the two wrote to one another after they were separated. Héloise became pregnant and had a child, and Abelard wanted to marry her, but Héloise was against the marriage, fearing that it would impede Abelard's career. Although Abelard prevailed and they were married, their union was at first kept secret, and Héloise's uncle, believing his niece to be dishonored, had Abelard castrated. The latter then entered a monastery, and at his insistence, Héloise entered a nunnery, although reluctantly and only out of obedience to her beloved.

Abelard did not stay in one place for long. He quarreled with the monks at his cloister and went to live near Paris, and from there to Brittany for a time, then to Rheims, and then again to Paris. He was always followed by students, and although he was not "the only philosopher remaining in the whole world," he was by all odds the most influential teacher.

Abelard's most famous work was the *Sic et Non* (*Yes and No*), and its title conveys its purpose. Abelard set forth 158 theological propositions and, drawing upon the Bible and the writings of the church Fathers, presented contradictory statements for each proposition. Although, as he made clear, Abelard was not attempting to disprove—or even attack—the beliefs of the church, he did not resolve the contradictions; and it was both because of the method and the lack of resolution in the use of it that Abelard aroused the enmity of some theologians, notably St. Bernard of Clairvaux. (Abelard's vanity and his personal relations with Héloise obviously accounted at least partly for his persecution.) Abelard also wrote a work on the Trinity which was regarded by some theologians as heretical, although little in it was actually seriously heretical. In 1141 at Sens in France, Abelard was condemned at a church council, and the next year he set out from Rome to appeal his case at the papal court. He became ill along the way and died at the monastery at Cluny.

Although in Abelard "knowledge puffeth up," as he himself finally recognized, and although his teaching and the tempestuous nature of his personal life brought him into conflict with church authorities, he did not envision a conflict between faith and reason. He did not want, as he himself said, "to be a follower of Aristotle if that separates me from Christ." His premise, when using logic, however, was far different from that of St. Anselm. The latter, who believed in order as a means of comprehending the mysteries of faith, was in the tradition, still, of St. Augustine for whom without faith and divine grace there could be no understanding. Although he did not set out to do so, Abelard, in effect, threw off the Augustinian shackles. It is a far cry from Augustine and Anselm to the man who taught that it is by "doubting that we are led to inquiry."

St. Bernard of Clairvaux

St. Bernard of Clairvaux (1091–1153), who was chiefly responsible for Abelard's condemnation at the Council of Sens, perceived the dangers to faith in the use of both the Aristotelian method and that of Abelard. Throughout the medieval period, even during the next century when all the works of Aristotle were known, there was no theologian who would "rather have been Aristotle if that separated him from Christ." The difficulty that St. Bernard had with Abelard, and with the use of logic, was twofold: Bernard saw the possibility for preferring to be Aristotle while also believing in an altogether different theological tradition.

Bernard was a complex and highly gifted man. He was the second abbot of the Cistercian order and the most ardent spokesman for its austere world-rejecting ideals. Above all a mystic who sought the love of God through the inner, contemplative life, Bernard was also active in the outside world in the service of the church. He was well-educated, and an eloquent writer and preacher.

There was in St. Bernard the rigorous asceticism of the early desert saints, the harsh and unrelenting belief that the flesh must be mortified in order to purify the soul. He also had a softer nature, and he wrote singularly beautiful and adoring works to the love of the Mother of God. Bernard espoused a very ancient mysticism that now, in the twelfth century, had become once again an important manifestation of the Christian spirit of withdrawal. He spoke out in defense of the anti-intellectual strain in Christianity: "How many men are there who have been saved, being acceptable to God in character and actions, without having been acquainted even with the liberal arts . . . . How many persons does the Apostle enumerate . . . who became dear to God, not by their acquaintance with polite literature, but by a pure conscience and by faith unfeigned!"[1] However, Bernard did not reject all learning out of hand. He knew the value of education, but he attacked those who sought knowledge either for its own sake or out of vanity or commercial greed. He valued those who "wish to know only that they may do good . . . . "—a far different impulse from that of Abelard.

---

1. All quotations from St. Bernard are from J. Mabillon, ed., *Life and Works of St. Bernard*, vol. 4, trans. S. J. Eales (London: John Hodges), 1896.

Peter Lombard

In 1140, two years before Abelard's death, Peter Lombard came to teach at the episcopal school in Paris. Lombard was for a short time a student of Abelard, and he was also a student of St. Bernard, but he does not represent a reconciliation between the two men, because there really could be none. Peter Lombard combined in his person, and therefore in his work, a skill for using the logical method while at the same time preserving a reverence for the authority of faith. He was not so remarkable a personality as either Abelard or Bernard, and perhaps for this very reason he was able to tackle the central issues of Christian dogma with sanity and caution. He seems in all events to have been precisely the kind of teacher—careful, not given to over-confident judgements—whom the church could regard as having shown the way to using the dialectical method to elucidate rather than provoke theological problems. In his most famous work, the *Sentences*, Lombard used the logical method to arrive at definitions of orthodoxy. He wrote on all the major theological subjects—God, the creation, the Trinity, and the sacraments—and his work so clarified the central questions of theology that it became and remained the standard theology textbook down to the sixteenth century. Although Peter Lombard came from northern Italy, his mature years were spent in Paris, first as teacher and then, in 1159, as bishop of the cathedral church of Notre Dame. Thus his influence must be added to that of Abelard in making Paris the center for logic and theology.

The Study of Humane Letters

In the early twelfth century, contemporary with Abelard and St. Bernard, there was at the episcopal school at Chârtres a different approach to the revival of learning, a different kind of emphasis in education. The school at Chârtres became known in the early twelfth century for the emphasis given there to the study of humane letters. Everyone who has written about the school at Chârtres and its traditions, in the Middle Ages and currently, has done so with great affection. This affection derives mainly from two things. First, the school upheld classical education based on the literary texts from the Roman world and on Plato, implying—as indeed was the case—a reflective cast of mind, a leisurely cultural pursuit, and, most important, a value placed on the well-rounded education of the human being. Secondly, there existed a sympathy for the school because it had a sudden decline, went down, as it were, before the more practical and career-oriented education in theology (a subject leading to advancement in the world), law, and medicine. And there is probably a third reason: the fact that Chârtres is, after all, a sublimely beautiful place. Its cathedral is quite literally breathtaking, and there is something heartwarming about seeing prominently enshrined there the representatives of the seven liberal arts—not just logic (also enthroned at Paris), but grammar, rhetoric, music, and all the other parts of the *trivium* and the *quadrivium*. And there were in the twelfth century some great names in scholarship associated with the school. Bernard of Chârtres and John of Salisbury, to name only two, were both steeped in the Roman classics and in what little Plato was then known. In other words, what was continued at Chârtres was the tradition of classical learning which was basically literary.

The scholars at Chârtres valued education for its own sake, and even more because they believed, as the Greeks and Romans did, that education, the best and fullest contact with great minds, beautiful poetry, and noble ideas could make a person a better human being. It is the last motive which is the essence of classical humanism, an ideal that has never completely died out even during periods when it has been less important and less acknowledged. But the humanism at Chârtres was soon to be eclipsed by the newer subjects coming into prominence at Paris and in the schools in Italy.

One of the difficulties with the way the dialectical method had been taken over in the twelfth century was that the enthusiasm for it led to its use, not as a tool, but for its own sake. Coming from a tradition altogether different from St. Bernard's, John of Salisbury pointed to the problem as he saw it. John, who had

257

The Grammar Lesson. *This personification of Grammar is on the West Facade of Chârtres Cathedral. There is humanity and humor in the overall representation. The seriousness of the subject is softened by the mischievousness of one of the little boys.* (HIRMER/PROTHMANN ASSOCIATES, INC.)

studied with the masters of dialectic, had gone back to visit with them and to examine what they were saying,

that we might by mutual comparison measure together our several pro-gresses. I found them as before, and where they were before; nor did they appear to have reached the goal in unravelling the old questions, nor had they added one jot of a proposition . . . . they only had pro-gressed in one point, they had unlearned moderation . . . . And thus experience taught me a manifest conclusion, that whereas dialectic fur-thers other studies, so if it remains by itself it lies bloodless and barren . . . . [2]

2. Quoted in C. H. Haskins, *Renaissance of the Twelfth Century* (Cambridge, Mass.: Harvard University Press, 1927), p. 374.

In part, his criticism is valid. The other side of it is that scholars took over logic with enthusiasm because it was something new and intellectually sharpening. In the mid-twelfth century they still had the old texts to work on, but that would soon change, and there would be new material on which to apply the method.

The Development of Law

While Paris was becoming famous as a center for logical studies and theology, Bologna in northern Italy was emerging as the center for the study of civil and canon (or church) law.

Civil law was based on the revival of Roman law, which had come about with the rediscovery, in the last half of the eleventh century, of the Justinian Code (*Codex Justinianus*). It is not known precisely how and when the great sixth-century compilation of Roman law was reintroduced into northern Italy, but its emergence accords with the general interest in unearthing ancient texts, the renewed interest in the Roman legacy particularly, and the changing social and economic patterns which required something more rational than the hodgepodge of laws resorted to through most of the Middle Ages.

The Justinian Code had, in fact, never been completely unknown, and Roman law had to a limited extent been used in the cities of northern Italy and southern France throughout the Middle Ages. Even so, the law was a mixture of the customary laws of the Germanic peoples along with a smattering of what had survived of Roman law—a mélange that was neither systematized nor relevant any longer to a complex urban society. In Europe as a whole, the laws were a mixture of Germanic and feudal laws based on personal relationships. There had been no systematic codification of the laws, nor had any important changes or modifications been made, due partly to the principle that old law was good law. And the need for uniformity was not felt until the secular governments became more stabilized and were ready to expand the system of justice, or more precisely, to establish a system of justice. The exception was England, where the foundations for a uniform body of laws had been laid before the revival of Roman law. Elsewhere, the Roman inheritance was received wholeheartedly because it presented a rational system and the concept of what law was about. Until the study of the *Codex Justinianus* there was no conception of the difference between public and private welfare, no distinction between civil and criminal law, no legal basis for secular authority, and no rational approach to justice or equity.

However it came about that the full text of the *Corpus Juris Civilis* was found again (and it may have been imported from Constantinople), it was being used and studied in northern Italy by the late eleventh century. Justinian's purpose in having this thousand-year-old Roman tradition and experience in law codified and explained during the sixth century was precisely what appealed to twelfth-century scholars. The emperor's intention had been to review all the laws enacted in Rome, from the founding of the Republic to his own time, in order "to bring . . . [Roman jurisprudence] into one harmonious system, so that it should present no contradiction, no repetition and no approach to repetition."[3] Nothing, then, could better have suited the intellectual temper of the new period—nor was any subject better tailored to practical application in the world.

Sometime soon after 1100, the scholar Irnerius began to teach the Code at Bologna, and he attracted large numbers of students. Irnerius' method was to lecture on a portion of the text and then make commentaries which explained the meaning of the law, the ways in which it could be interpreted, and how it could be applied. The students first would take down the portion of the text that was the day's lesson and then, in the form of marginal notes (or "glosses," as they were called), the instructor's commentaries. Glosses were the essential part of the study of law and soon became the textbooks in the field, the great legal scholars of the twelfth century being known as "glossators." Through Irnerius' reputation and influence Bologna became the chief center for legal studies in Europe, and the students who trained there went on to become the leading teachers and practitioners of the time.

3. Quotations from the Justinian Code are from Brian Tierney, *The Crisis of Church and State* (Englewood Cliffs, N.J.: Prentice-Hall, 1964), pp. 101–102.

260

The twelfth and thirteenth centuries were a great age for law-yers, and a legal career opened possibilities for advancement in every bureaucracy, from the smallest town governments to the royal governments. There was a tremendous amount of work to be done in the study and teaching of law, the development of legal codes, and the implementation of departments of justice. And, in any event, the medieval lawyers soon learned what the Romans had discovered—that law is never perfect, never static, that "the character of human law is to be constantly hurrying on, and no part of it is there which can abide for ever."

The rediscovered Justinian Code provided the basis for the legal systems of all continental Europe and had an important influence on the codification of church law. The impetus for the codification of canon law was the reform movement in the church which began in the mid-eleventh century. In the process of freeing the church from secular intervention, the need to codify and then promulgate laws for an independent institution became very great. And new laws, of course, had to be formulated in accord with ecclesiastical traditions.

In beginning their work, the first canon lawyers were con-fronted with a huge mass of material dating from the early days of Christianity. There were papal edicts, decrees of ecclesiastical councils, Biblical references, the writings of the church Fathers, and an assortment of other pronouncements and documents issued by the papal and episcopal courts. Although the study of canon law had begun independently of civil law, the work of the can-onists was considerably aided and advanced by the reintroduction of Roman law because the objectives of Roman and canon law were much the same. Like the emperor, the papacy wanted a centralized church governed by a single and uniform code of laws. In addition, canon law was the best preparation for the papal office itself as well as for advancement in the papal *curia* and the eccle-siastical courts that developed all over Christendom.

The most important codification of canon law was made by a church scholar, Gratian, who also worked at Bologna and whose influence made Bologna the center for canon law as well as civil law. At its publication in 1140, Gratian's text immediately became the official body of church law and the basis for its future developments. Gratian's method in studying church law was essentially that of the dialecticians. Finding in the welter of legal material many differences of opinion and contradictory laws, Gratian took the opposing opinions on any given subject and used the method of questioning and reasoned argument to try and establish what was authoritative and what was not. His work is entitled *Decretum* but its subtitle, *The Concord of Discordant Canons*, accurately describes the intention and method.

The Translation Centers

Thus far we have considered the revival of subject matter which, although new, stimulating, and provocative, was not foreign to the European scholars. Through nearly the entire medieval period the Latin West was precisely what the name implies—Latin, and fundamentally Roman. Even the small body of Aristotle's logic that Boethius had translated in the fifth century was not outside the general framework of the Roman educational tradition. (It had always been recognized that logic had been once, at least, a part of the *trivium*.) The revival of Roman law, the revival of Boethius—and there were other literary Latin manuscripts from the classical age that were studied now with new interest—all these, once known, became accessible to the Latin scholars in the sense that they added to the stream of knowledge, broadened and deepened it, without diverting it from its course. But from the late eleventh century on, translations were being made of texts that would bring entirely new subjects into the Latin West and make available a body of learning that was foreign, not only in the literal sense, but in the figurative sense as well. The medical, scientific, and philosophical works of the classical Greeks which had been totally lost to the West by the early fifth century—and which were therefore totally unknown—began in this period to make their way back into the Latin World.

These Greek texts did not arrive in Europe unencumbered. After the Muslims had conquered the eastern Mediterranean during the first centuries of their expansion, they set up translation centers (at Baghdad, for example, in the eighth century) where Greek mathematics, science, and philosophy—precisely those disciplines lost to the West—were translated into Arabic. The Muslims then annotated these subjects and, in time, made their own contributions to the learning they had inherited. This additional knowledge was more easily absorbed by the West in some disciplines than in others. In mathematics and in medicine, for example, the Arabic contributions did not challenge fundamental assumptions about the world. In philosophy it was otherwise, however. When the full corpus of Aristotle's writings was trans-

Illustration from an Arabic translation of the Greek medical text, *De Materia Medica* of Dioscordes. *This particular text was translated in Baghdad during the thirteenth century; it is a perfect example of the role played by the Arabs as preservers and transmitters of the medical knowledge of the classical world. The "doctor" is shown preparing a cough medicine from honey.* (THE METROPOLITAN MUSEUM OF ART, ROGERS FUND, 1913)

263

lated, his works challenged many of the cherished assumptions of European scholars, and it took a century for this material to be digested and somehow absorbed. Muslim scholars had also faced this problem with Aristotle, and their own syntheses came into Europe as part of a complex and alien tradition.

The various texts were transmitted into the Latin West through centers where Arab, Greek, Latin, and Jewish scholars worked side by side at the tasks of translation and copying. The main centers were in Spain (Toledo), southern Italy, and Sicily, respectively. Islamic Spain had been one of the richest and liveliest intellectual areas of the Islamic world, and when the Christians conquered Toledo in 1085 they inherited a diversity of new material and found there an established scholarly community. During the first half of the twelfth century a center of translation was begun, and the works of Aristotle, Arabic philosophy, Greek and Arabic science, to name a few—the entire list is very long—were put into Latin. The transmission to the Latin world was not rapid, and the texts arrived by fits and starts over the next hundred years.

The Study of Medicine

The tradition that the medical school at Salerno in southern Italy was founded by a Latin, a Greek, a Muslim, and a Jew is only legend, but it goes far to explain the circumstances of the development of medicine there as a scientific study. When the ancient Greek medical texts had been lost to the West, medical practice quickly became so appallingly crude that it is a wonder anyone survived the ministrations of the practitioners and small wonder that the miracle of healing was so highly esteemed during the Middle Ages. The medicine practiced in the Latin West throughout most of the medieval period was administered by monks and had no theoretical or scientific underpinning. In contrast, Muslim medicine, based on the classical Greek medical texts and expanded by the research of the Muslims, was scientific and highly advanced.

The intermingling of Greeks and Muslims in southern Italy and, to a lesser degree in Sicily, kept alive the study of medicine, and there is evidence that the medical school at Salerno was in existence by the late tenth century. But the elevation of medicine from practice or craft to a scientific study did not really come about until the last half of the eleventh century, when a Muslim physician known as "Constantine the African" came to southern Italy and translated into Latin the Arabic texts of the Greek medical treatises of Galen and Hippocrates.

From the twelfth century onward, medicine became almost as important a field of study as law or theology, and the influence of Salerno radiated out to other schools which developed medical faculties. Although Salerno was granted its charter as a university in 1234 by the Emperor Frederick II, it does not quite fit the pattern of the university system which was emerging in Europe, since it never developed the several other faculties requisite for a university.

The Medieval Universities

Our modern university system is a direct legacy from the Middle Ages. Take away, in imagination, the complex administrative machinery, the buildings, and endowments that help to support our institutions, and the university of today in its essentials is quite similar to its early medieval predecessor. There is no date to mark the beginning of the first universities; they evolved gradually in response to several needs which, in retrospect at least, are clear. The new disciplines required a more coherent and organized course of study than the wandering masters could provide; and the professions of law, medicine, and theology demanded a program and formal certification for a student to be qualified to go out into the world and apply his learning. The age had arrived in which the desire for a *system* was very compelling, as we have seen in the formation of the disciplines themselves. This was also the period when guilds were formed in other crafts, and the impulse toward associations for mutual protection, mutual interest, and established standards was strong.

The word *university* (in Latin, *universitas*) means simply "guild" or "association," without the specific intellectual connotation which it gradually took on and which we still accord it today. The term first applied was *studium generale*, which cannot be translated precisely because it meant a place where one could go to study, a school of some not carefully defined sort, with *generale* referring to the international character of the student body. In two ways, the intellectual life of the twelfth and thirteenth centuries was international and at the same time formed a unity. The language of education was Latin, and so whether a student came from France, Germany, or England, he became part of a community with no linguistic boundaries. And the new learning, as we have seen, came from all parts of the civilized world and was made available through the translation centers that were truly international and cooperative. This sense of community among scholars for whom knowledge was more important than differences in belief, culture, or language was the high ideal which informed the medieval university and which remains the scholarly ideal today.

In their main outlines the universities followed the organization of the guilds. The students were apprentices, and when the period of apprenticeship was completed they became bachelors, which can be equated with journeymen. Then, after satisfying the masters, the bachelors could qualify to be masters themselves, and even go on to a further stage to become truly "learned" or "doctors." Although there were differences among the universities, they also had characteristics in common. The licenses granted to the masters at each university were permits to teach and were recognized universally. Most universities maintained faculties of instruction for all the higher subjects of theology, law, and medicine, as well as an arts faculty which taught the preparatory courses which correspond to our undergraduate schools. As the universities developed as independent and privileged institutions, there grew to be differences within the general framework, and the two oldest universities—one at Bologna and the other at Paris—are prototypes of the two systems that emerged.

The university, or guild, at Bologna was organized by the students—a fact which undergraduates have always found appealing.

The students hired the teachers, terminated an instructor's appointment if he was unsatisfactory, and did everything except regulate the curriculum and award licenses and degrees. The students at Bologna were grouped into four "nations" roughly according to the countries they came from. The two largest were the non-Bolognese Italians and the Bolognese. Each "nation" elected a rector, and it was the rectors who basically ran the university. Since the university at Bologna emerged from the law schools, its law faculty was always the most important and prestigious, although other faculties were developed as well. Then, as now, a university generally had a reputation for excellence in certain special fields. Bologna was also secular, in contrast to the northern university founded at Paris; this was because like most of the northern Italian cities, Bologna had a tradition of secular schools. In general, the universities of southern Europe followed the Bolognese model.

The university at Paris was founded by its masters, which was more in keeping with the guild system. The masters regulated all matters pertaining to faculty—salaries, firing and hiring, and of course the curriculum. The university had grown out of the cathedral schools, and so its masters were clerics who were licensed by the bishops. The university was given a charter by King Philip II of France in 1200, but its statutes were confirmed by Pope Innocent III in 1215, and there always remained a close connection between the university and the church. At Paris, theology and philosophy were the two major areas of excellence—not surprising, since the school's reputation as a center of learning had begun with a clerical caste and had attracted the foremost theologians of the twelfth century. Paris had faculties of medicine and the arts, and a law faculty which in the thirteenth century nearly rivaled that of Bologna.

By far the greatest of numbers of students who attended the universities studied law. The full course of study, beginning with the arts and advancing to law, medicine, or—most difficult of all—theology, was long and arduous. The students were not rich for the most part, since they came from the lesser nobility and from the bourgeoisie, who had little money and saw education as a way to better themselves and provide opportunities for new careers (all of which was true). All living and eating accommodations were "off campus," to use the modern phrase, and the townspeople charged high prices for room and board, giving as little as possible in return. The only weapon the students and professors had was to go on strike, or to riot, or simply to leave (as they did at Oxford, going on from there to found a new university at Cambridge). The origin of our undergraduate system lies in the solution to that problem, the founding of "colleges" which at first were places for students to live and have meals, given by a wealthy benefactor.

One other problem of university life led to a new script, the Gothic, and a new method for producing books. By now the beautiful but slow copying done by the monks could hardly satisfy the demands of students for texts, and at Paris and Bologna, and spreading from those centers to other places as the need grew, a new system came into use. Under the university's supervision, nearby booksellers and stationers were supplied with unbound manuscripts of the texts used by students, and pages for copying were then farmed out to a number of different scribes. The result was an increased number of books and a faster rate of production, but the texts were small (virtually pocket-sized) and the copying was done by a number of different hands in the new script, which was small enough to fit on a tiny sheet.

The intellectual world of the university during the thirteenth century was dominated by the recovery of Aristotle and the Muslim commentaries on his work. Aristotle's writings on natural history (or the workings of the world) and on politics, ethics, and philosophy presented a great challenge to the Christian view of the world—that is, to the tenets of faith. The full corpus of Aristotle's scientific writings propounds a world that can be rationally comprehended, beginning with the observations derived from our sense impressions of the world. Aristotle presented rational causes for the world and everything in it, starting with creation and including the nature of man and his role on earth.

The Muslims had to confront the challenge of Aristotelian

science, and the work of Averroes, the Muslim commentator on Aristotle, was the first major commentary introduced to Europe on the subject of Aristotle's rationality versus faith. What Averroes said, in essence, was that there is a "double truth"—the truth of faith and the truth arrived at by rational, or scientific, means. The two may be completely different and independent of one another, yet each is valid in its own sphere. Averroes' conclusion was accepted by a number of scholastics, and the issues were debated among those who agreed with this theory of a "double truth," those who wanted to retain the old Augustinian view unchanged, and those who wanted even to forbid Aristotle. (The church, in fact, condemned Aristotle's writings several times during the course of the thirteenth century, and tried to prohibit the universities from teaching his work—which of course produced results precisely contrary to those desired.)

St. Thomas Aquinas

It was the great Thomas Aquinas (1225–1274) (known as the "angelic doctor" due to his excellent disposition and his equanimity in debate) who succeeded in Christianizing Aristotle. Far from having his work immediately acclaimed throughout the church, Aquinas was sharply criticized, and it took many generations before he was fully appreciated. As a thinker, Aquinas prescribed for himself a task of overwhelming magnitude by attempting to prove by rational and logical means that the truth of science and the truth of theology are the same. He set out to show that there is no "double truth," but instead, two paths leading to the *same* truth. St. Thomas' two great works are the *Summa Contra Gentiles* and the *Summa Theologica*. In these he sought to prove—and for many of his followers, did prove satisfactorily— that the truth of science and the truth of revelation are in harmony with one another. Some truths of revelation, Thomas believed, are such that unaided human reason cannot comprehend. (The Trinity is one of these, because it is the highest level of truth and therefore not susceptible to scientific testing.) But that is a further point along the one path to the one ultimate truth. Aquinas brought science and revelation together in a construct which, whether one accepts its premise or not, was beautifully reasoned from beginning to end.

St. Thomas' achievement was a stage—for the medieval world, a final and crowning one—in a process that had been going on since the early centuries of Christianity. Thomas undertook to reconcile the new body of classical thought—new, that is, to western Europe—to Christianity. Whether one could effect such a reconciliation using the works of Aristotle had been debated from the time Aristotle was introduced. Almost immediately following St. Thomas' death in 1277, Aristotle was again condemned by the church, along with Averroes and St. Thomas himself. However, Aquinas' essential contribution—the synthesis of reason and revelation—was the intellectual part of the thrust of medieval civilization in the twelfth century and for most of the thirteenth. His work was the intellectual expression of the goal of unity for all Christendom, and every effort of will was concentrated in making that goal a reality. We will see this in political life and in the papacy's desire for religious unity. Intellectual unity was to be achieved through the universities, where the new knowledge would be absorbed into the Christian framework. The *Summa Theologica* is the highest expression of intellectual optimism. That the synthesis of faith and reason did not endure is part of the history of the dissolution of medieval culture.

Now, as then, it is easy enough to find critics of the medieval university, of scholasticism, and of St. Thomas. One general criticism is true—a criticism that John of Salisbury in a sense predicted. The universities took over dialectic at the expense of humane letters and the values of classical education. Yet they also brought another, different, value: the value placed on knowledge for its own sake. This, as much as anything else, led to the downfall of the unity of scholastic thought—the "doubting which leads to inquiry" and the "inquiry which leads to truth," as Peter Abelard had said more than a century earlier.

270

The Architecture of Religious Unity:
The Gothic Cathedral

The beginning of *Gothic*, the new style in architecture, can be precisely dated. The first Gothic structure was the abbey church of St. Denis near Paris, and its rebuilding, traditionally associated with the kings of France, was begun by Abbot Suger in 1137 and completed in 1144. Even before the latter date the style had begun to spread, first throughout the Île de France, and then, within the next hundred years, to every part of Europe and eastward with the crusaders to the Latin Kingdom of Jerusalem.

Few terms are more difficult to define than *Gothic*, because architecturally, the style—and this is one of its secrets—is far more than the sum of its parts, complex and beautiful though these may be. The harmony of elements was the first aim which Suger wanted to achieve in his new church at St. Denis. The other goal was light, and this is the overwhelming impression of most Gothic cathedrals, whatever the variations of style. Not simply ordinary daylight, but a radiance that is filtered through stained-glass windows, gives the interiors of these buildings a mystical and otherworldly quality—again, precisely that heavenly illumination which Suger had hoped to capture.

Structurally, the Gothic style is distinguished by the use of three architectural elements: the cross-ribbed vault (known to the Norman architects and used in the last stages of their Romanesque churches); the pointed arch; and the flying buttress. The latter two technical innovations were particularly important and they were accomplished with a confident mastery that is remarkable, but it is the combination of the three elements that produces the incredible impression of delicacy, or lack of weight, in the Gothic cathedral.

The pointed Gothic arch, in contrast to the rounded arch of the Romanesque churches, could be made to soar very high and could be modulated in ways the rounded arch could not. The pointed arch is also both graceful and flexible, neither of which is a quality of the Romanesque church. But as the Gothic arch rose higher,

and as the architects were able to raise the vaults higher, the problem of support demanded yet another response. The solution was to support, or buttress, the weight of the vaulting on the outside, rather than the inside, of the church. Heavy stone piers were therefore constructed externally to take the weight of the inner structures. Once this idea had been conceived, the buttresses at wall level were a relatively simple matter, but the great technical innovation was the "flying buttress," which could take the weight of the roof at the point where weight was transmitted from roof to pillars. Since the retaining walls no longer had to bear the weight as they had in the Romanesque churches, and since the pillars no longer had to be so thick, the interior of the cathedral consequently became less heavy and cumbersome. Walls were replaced by windows, until there seemed to be almost no sides to the interior of the Gothic church. And as the pillars became airy networks, the entire structure seemed composed of thin shafts and ribs intricately woven together.

The builders of the Romanesque churches had been wrestling with stone, and the Romanesque interiors were painted and decorated with murals in part, at least, to cover the structural deficiencies that could not be completely overcome. Not so in Gothic churches, where the mastery of form and technique was complete and sure. There has been endless debate, in fact, over whether the Gothic style emerged from sheer technical virtuosity, or from the idea of the building and what is was intended to convey.

Everything in the Gothic cathedral is subordinated to the structure itself: Sculpture, the windows, and the decorations which cover the entire church inside and out are all elements integrated for their total effect upon the eye and mind. This total effect is meant to be a mirror of the universe, of the heavenly Jerusalem, and of the world which God created; the churches indeed evoke another existence that is beautiful, mystical, and mysterious. Every line in the church carries the eye upward, and where the Romanesque churches with their "restless" sculpture are massive,

←——————————————————————————————

A Gothic facade; the Cathedral of Amiens. (COURTESY OF THE FRENCH GOVERNMENT TOURIST OFFICE)

rounded, and firmly planted on the ground, the Gothic churches are light, with arches reaching skyward, everything linear, and the sculpture lifelike but at the same time serene and secure within the order of things.

Although Abbot Suger's monastery at St. Denis was the beginning, Gothic is associated with cities, and there were few medieval towns that did not come to be dominated by their cathedrals in the new style. Although Gothic continued until the early fifteenth century, the first hundred years, from the mid-twelfth to the mid-thirteenth century, were its golden age—a time of perfect synthesis of the artistry of the medieval mason and the spirituality of the most intensely religious period of the Middle Ages.

← ───

An interior view of a Gothic cathedral. *The Cathedral of Amiens is the largest Gothic building in France. It was constructed from 1220 to 1269.* (COURTESY OF THE FRENCH GOVERNMENT TOURIST OFFICE)

ᴄᴀᴍᴏ 6

Unity and Diversity: Political and Religious Life from the Early Twelfth to the Late Thirteenth Century

During this extraordinary period of expansion in the twelfth and thirteenth centuries, political and religious life were affected no less than any of the other areas we have considered in the preceding chapter. There was altogether a remarkable increase in political and religious activity that, over time, resulted in substantial changes in kind as well as in degree. In following the changes, the theme that emerges most clearly is the tension, often outright conflict, between unity and diversity. This tension greets us everywhere.

Within England, France, and Germany there was the opposition of royal ambition and feudal diversity. Although many different factors influenced the outcome of the efforts of kings to advance royal authority, the common thread connecting the histories of the three countries is the fact that the success of the monarchy depended to a great extent on weighing down in the balance the power of the nobility. The conflict within each country was played out differently, and with different results, but that the struggle was genuine there is no doubt. Nor were the royal efforts all self-serving: The desire to centralize authority was, in fact, forward-looking. The extension of kingly power offered the possibilities for curbing internal dissensions and bringing, not just more government, but better government.

Within the Church of Rome there was the tension between papal insistence on uniformity and the growing diversity and complexity in actual religious life. By the end of the twelfth century, and particularly during the pontificate of Innocent III (1198–1216), the unity of the church was more fully realized than ever before; yet the church was now confronted by a new wave of reform movements, attacked by heretics, and criticized by dissenters. Thus there was a precarious balance, even at the height of papal power under Innocent, between the unity expressed in the church's laws and the diverse activities of its members.

Overall, there was the belief in the *unity* of Christendom—that it was in the natural order that there should be a universal Christian church and a universal Christian empire. Papal leadership of Christendom was challenged when the secular empire was revived during the mid-twelfth century, and for a hundred years thereafter popes and emperors were locked in their last major struggle for supremacy. This conflict was not a threat to the concept of unity, however. The real challenge to the belief in a universal Christian society came at the end of the thirteenth century, as the medieval period drew to its close; and it came from the "kings of particular regions," as a Roman emperor called them. For during the twelfth and thirteenth centuries, even as the theory of unity was enunciated, the real growth was in diverse and smaller political units.

The Growth of Monarchy
in England until 1272

From the moment William, duke of Normandy (who was vassal to the French king) conquered England, the fortunes of England and France were closely intertwined. At the beginning of the twelfth century the stronger monarchy by far, as we have seen, was the Norman monarchy in England. In the work of consolidating their realm the English rulers had three distinct advantages. They had won their island kingdom by conquest, and they could—and did—enforce their rights as conquerers. They inherited and then made good use of the Anglo-Saxon institutions they

The Norman armies invading Anglo-Saxon England; a scene from the Bayeux Tapestry, the most famous visual testimony of the Norman conquest. *The tapestry was most likely commissioned by the Earl of Kent and the Bishop of Bayeux soon after the conquest to celebrate the Norman victory.* (FRENCH GOVERNMENT TOURIST OFFICE)

found in England. And they came with the experience of having already created a strong centralized government in Normandy. Except for the highly centralized Norman Kingdom in Sicily, the government which William I passed on to his son was the best-organized in Europe. And throughout the twelfth century the English kings continued to build on the foundations laid by William I, developing those institutions through which they could assert royal authority. There was not, however, a single ruler in this period who did not have to face revolts by the barons. Although we will follow the steady progression of royal authority, it should be kept in mind that kingly advances were not easily accepted by the nobility and that royal power was threatened by civil wars during every reign.

England under the Normans (1087–1154)

WILLIAM II (1087–1100)

When William the Conqueror died in 1087 his eldest son Robert became duke of Normandy, and his middle son William Rufus inherited the English throne as William II.

William II was extremely unpopular, and there indeed seems to have been little to commend him for. He found ways of exacting extraordinary dues and taxes from the English barons, who heartily disliked him for his abuse of power. There were revolts against William by the barons and by his brother Robert, who felt that he should have inherited the English throne in addition to the duchy of Normandy. Robert went off on the first crusade, however, which effectively stilled his opposition for a time. (He even had to borrow a great deal of money from William—to the point of almost selling Normandy to the king—in order to go to the Holy Land.) William was unpopular also with the clergy because he taxed the church heavily, and it was during his reign that the investiture controversy first touched England.

William the Conqueror had, as we have seen, continued in England the close relationship between ruler and clergy that had worked so well to administer the duchy of Normandy. When William came to England he brought with him to be archbishop of Canterbury Lanfranc of Bec, who had helped reform the Norman church and was a staunch supporter of the Norman monarchy. In 1089, two years after William Rufus inherited the throne, Lanfranc died and Anselm of Bec was made archbishop. Anselm was receptive to the principles of the Gregorian reform program and began his struggle with the king over the issues surrounding lay investiture. He went to the papal court to ask for help in implementing what after all were papal policies. However, Pope Urban II was more concerned with keeping the good will of the Norman rulers and offered no support; and there the matter lay until the next English king came to power.

HENRY I (1100–1135)

In 1100 William was killed accidentally by a nobleman. William's younger brother, Henry, then seized the royal treasury at Winchester castle and took over the crown.

At the beginning of his reign Henry faced several problems, not the least of which was that the monarchy had become thoroughly unpopular during his brother's reign. Both the clergy and the nobility felt themselves to have been excessively taxed. In addition, Henry's accession to the throne was quickly challenged by Robert, duke of Normandy, whose claim to English kingship was at least as good, if not better, than that of his brother. Early in his reign Henry had to face revolts by his barons—which Robert supported. These were suppressed, and Henry finally invaded Normandy and imprisoned his brother. He therefore learned early that he could not entirely rely on the feudal nobility.

The new king also had to deal with the problem of the church and the investiture controversy. This was renewed when the elderly Archbishop Anselm (who had been forced into exile before Henry's accession) returned to England. In 1107, however, an agreement was reached between king and pope, and the Concordat of London was signed: Henry accepted the principle that he did not have the right to continue the lay investing of the clergy, but the clergy was still to render homage to the king for lands held from the crown. The Concordat, although not threatening to the king's effective control of the church, was the first sign that the close association between Norman rulers and their clergy might be weakened. And from this lesson Henry learned to rely less on monks and higher clergy in his administration than his two predecessors had done.

In spite of these early difficulties, Henry's reign was a period of great constructiveness in the development of royal institutions. One of the first things he did was to issue a charter curtailing the abuses of William's reign against the clergy and the barons and guaranteeing that he would rule in accordance with law. Much has sometimes been made of the liberties expressed in the charter, but the fact is that Henry then immediately proceeded to do as he pleased. And what he pleased to do was to give to the royal government and the English people some of the institutions that were to prove effective in unifying the kingdom under the monarchy.

Until the reign of Henry I the *curia regis*, or king's court, had been extremely informal in the sense that the functions performed by the nobles who participated in the king's household were neither specialized nor regularized. Some individuals were obviously better equipped to deal, for example, with money matters than others, but in general the system was loosely organized. Under Henry, two departments were separated from the court to become specialized governmental institutions. The more fully realized of these was the department of finance, known as the exchequer. The other, which was to be more thoroughly organized and expanded in the last half of the century during the reign of Henry II (1154–1189), was the department which administered royal justice.

The lands and revenues of the English kings were widely scattered throughout England, and the main function of the exchequer was to audit the accounts of the local sheriffs, who had to appear twice a year with the accounting (and, of course, with the money). The term "exchequer" derives from the checkerboard table used for the accounting: pennies in one column, shillings in another, and so on. The records of what was owed the king and what was paid were meticulously kept on parchments called "pipe-rolls." One of these from the time of Henry I still exists; and beginning with the reign of Henry II, there is a complete series of them, down to the nineteenth century.

A start had been made during the reigns of William I and William II to bring the administration of justice in England under the jurisdiction of the crown. The two Williams had insisted that the most serious offenses brought before the local courts be heard before representatives of the crown—either by the local sheriffs empowered to represent the king, or itinerant, specifically dispatched, justices. Henry regularized this system of sending out royal justices, with an important modification. He routinely appointed nobles of lower rank than the barons, who were therefore dependent solely upon the king. (At the level of the *curia regis* itself, however, the cases were still heard by a court composed of the great feudal barons.)

In the ways described, Henry implemented the king's control over the government of his realm. This by no means eclipsed the power of the feudal barons, but the impersonal institutions of government that were formed circumvented the feudal lords, since they were administered by men appointed by and solely responsible to the monarch. As these institutions became permanent, they provided continuity in governing the realm even, as it happened, in the absence of a strong ruler.

Until Henry's death, the English monarchy had succeeded in controlling the decentralizing tendencies of the barons and containing some of the friction caused by Normandy and England having two different rulers. Henry had married an Englishwoman, a descendant of Alfred the Great, and that marriage, as well as simply the passage of time, had begun to lessen the distinctions between the Norman ruling class and the indigenous Anglo-Saxon population. But all Henry's gains were sorely tested when he died in 1135, leaving no male heir to succeed him. His one surviving legitimate child (he had many illegitimate children) was a daughter, Matilda, married to Geoffrey Plantagenet, count of Anjou. Henry had managed to have the barons accept Matilda as heir apparent, but she was not a likable woman and, in any event, the barons took the opportunity to assert their power over the monarchy and elected instead Henry's nephew Stephen, count of Blois.

STEPHEN OF BLOIS (1135–1154) AND THE CIVIL WARS

Stephen (1135–1154) was king, but he ruled hardly at all, since most of his reign was concerned with conciliating the barons and the clergy and trying to keep them from changing sides and supporting Matilda. The work of the Conqueror and Henry I was to a large extent undone because the barons repossessed many of the powers that had accrued to the crown. They took over, in particular, the right to enforce justice; and they built heavily fortified castles, which had been outlawed by William I, but which Stephen was powerless to prohibit. More than a thousand castles were built within a few years of Stephen's becoming king. Furthermore, Stephen was forced to make formal concessions to the clergy which, in effect, undid the Norman-clerical alliance.

Matilda did not give up her claim to the crown, and her husband Geoffrey invaded Normandy while she journeyed to England to try to win back the baronial support. Civil wars raged during most of Stephen's reign, and both Matilda and Stephen had to make promises to the feudal nobility which continually undermined royal power. Finally, an agreement was reached between the opposing forces: that Stephen would rule until his death, and that the crown would then pass to Matilda's young son Henry. Thus when Stephen died in 1154, Henry Plantagenet became king.

England under the Angevins (1154–1272)

HENRY II PLANTAGENET (1154–1189)

The power and wealth of Henry II before he became king of England were enormous, and although he was only twenty-one when he was crowned, Henry had already had several years' experience in warfare and in governing his vast continental possessions. His father had succeeded in conquering Normandy, and

Henry had become duke in 1149. At his father's death, Henry had inherited the counties of Anjou, Maine, and Touraine. And two years before he became king of England, Henry had married Eleanor, heiress to the duchy of Aquitaine. This union was a singular stroke of good fortune both for Henry and for the house of Anjou, and an equally singular misfortune for Louis VII (1137–1180), who was then king of France. Louis had been married to Eleanor, and for several years the duchy of Aquitaine had thus been part of the domain of the Capetian kings. But Louis divorced Eleanor, and she immediately married Henry Plantagenet, bringing Aquitaine as her dowry to her new husband. The French king was faced with a vassal who possessed nearly all western and southwestern France, from the Norman coast on the English Channel down to the Pyrenees. Then, in 1154, Henry became the first Angevin king of England.

Henry Plantagenet was one of the towering personalities of the twelfth century. Forceful, commanding, and eloquent, he was capable of being exceedingly courteous and charming. He also had a terrible temper and was quickly aroused to anger. All the contemporary accounts of the king comment on his enormous energy, which wearied everyone around him. He was continuously on the move, fighting, hunting, working tirelessly, and he paid ceaseless attention to every detail in his vast empire. Once he made his mind up about something he wished to do, he let nothing stop him, "preferring rather," as a contemporary historian expressed it, "to forfeit his promise than depart from his purpose."[1]

As soon as he became king of England Plantagenet began to reassert the rights of the crown that had been taken over by the feudal nobility during the reign of Stephen. This he did with his characteristic swiftness, destroying the castles built by the barons, re-establishing the institutions that William I and Henry I had developed, and much more. Henry's work was eased by the fact that the nobility had by now tired of the warfare which had pre-

---

1. All quotations in this chapter referring to Henry II are from *The Historical Works of Giraldus Cambrensis*, trans. Thomas Forester (London: H. G. Bohn, 1863).

ceded his reign. And Henry's resources on the continent provided him with the funds to pay officials to manage the institutions which he reinstated and expanded, to hire mercenary soldiers, and to build royal castles to secure royal holdings. Although he is always described as—and indeed, was—one of the great architects of the English government, Henry's main strength derived from his continental lands. He devoted much more time to his European possessions than to England, where he spent only about a third of his reign. His absences, however, encouraged him to centralize the governing institutions of England, and to organize them so that they were not dependent on his presence.

Henry restored the exchequer to smooth working order and found ways to increase revenues to the crown and extend his authority as overlord of the English nobles at the same time. For example, he expanded the policy, begun by William I, of converting the service owed by knights into money payments, and he demanded large fees from the barons when (as he insisted they do) they requested his permission to marry off their sons and daughters. His most impressive gains, however, were in the extension of the royal system of justice.

Henry's intention was to have as many cases as possible throughout England heard by royal justices. In the process of doing this he increased the revenue to the crown, since a person found guilty of a serious crime ordinarily had his property taken over by the king. Even more important, this extension of royal jurisprudence provided a more equitable justice for all Englishmen and gradually spread throughout the country a common law. Until Henry Plantagenet's reign the only way a criminal could be brought to trial was if the victim or a friend or relative of the victim brought an accusation to the court. Under Henry, it became the business of the government to see that criminal cases did not go untried. Henry made it a law that in each division of the county, called a *hundred*, a jury of men first came together to testify as to whether or not a certain crime had been committed in their area. Then a person suspected or accused of that crime was brought before the king's justice and subjected to trial by water to decide his innocence or guilt. The use of a jury to determine whether a person should be brought to trial is the beginning of our grand jury.

Since most cases of property disputes were between feudal lords or between vassals of the lords, these had heretofore customarily been tried in the local feudal courts; and customarily the trial was by battle between the litigants or their vassals. Under Henry, it became possible for a person to request from the beginning that such a case be changed to the royal court. This could be done by obtaining a *writ* (an order issued in the king's name) asking that a *jury* (or inquest) be gathered to hear the case before the king's justice. This right to be heard in the royal court was extended during Henry's reign to freemen involved in most types of land disputes or problems.

It was only freemen, however, who gained from this right to have their cases transferred to royal jurisdiction. The nobility were not eager to give up their power, and they began to enforce even greater judicial control over their serfs and unfree tenants, who were unable to remove themselves from baronial jurisdiction. Nevertheless, the effects of Henry's laws were beneficial for a large part of the population, with perquisites that were gradually pervasive throughout the country. For one thing, the nobility became more careful of the way in which it judged disputes, since if it was arbitrary or seemed too punitive, the defendant might take the case away from the feudal court. And the tendency grew in the feudal courts to bring feudal, customary law (which was very varied) into some conformity with the common (or king's) law. Finally, more cases were now able to be brought before the *curia regis* itself, and there was the beginning of a more specialized branch of the *curia*, where cases were heard by men experienced and knowledgeable in the law.

Although Henry's relations with the higher clergy were good and he was generally supported by them, the king's rights with regard to investiture had been restricted by the Concordat of London (1107), and Henry wanted to strengthen his control over the church, as well as to extend royal justice into areas once the exclusive privilege of the ecclesiastical courts. It was over the latter issue that Henry had his famous quarrel with Thomas à Becket.

Becket was both a fascinating and a puzzling man. From a Norman merchant family settled in London, he had as a young man been sent to France to study. When he returned to England Becket had worked for a time in business, but he soon was taken into the household of the archbishop of Canterbury and became the archbishop's secretary. When Henry became king, Becket's unusual abilities led the archbishop to recommend the young man to the new monarch, and Becket was appointed the royal chancellor. He also grew to be the king's good personal friend. In return for loyal service, Becket received many gifts from the king, and he became extremely wealthy. He and Henry hunted together, shared and liked the good life, and sustained a bond of genuine mutual affection. When the archbishop of Canterbury died in 1162, the king offered Becket the highest religious office in the land. Becket, however, was reluctant to assume the office, even warning Henry that his acceptance would lead to dissension between them. Henry insisted, and Becket was installed.

Once he became archbishop, Becket went through a complete change: He became very ascetic, renounced all his former pleasures and wealth, and devoted himself to the church; and as predicted, this soon brought him into open conflict with the king. What compelled Becket is difficult to explain, but he became a good deal holier than the pope, and he was determined to maintain the independence of the church at all costs. This not only made him unpopular with Henry, but with the other English bishops as well. The quarrel flared up in 1164 when Henry brought the higher clergy together for the signing of the Constitutions of Clarendon.

The Constitutions essentially restated and regularized powers which Henry I had exercised over the church. These included, for example, the requirement that the English bishops were to do homage to the king before being installed in their ecclesiastical offices, and that they could not appeal to the pope unless first given permission by the king. All the bishops present at Clarendon were willing to sign the Constitutions—except for Becket, who refused to budge on the issue of legal jurisdiction, and specifically on Henry's insistence that clergy accused of crimes be tried in royal rather than ecclesiastical courts. Becket has often been referred to as an anachronism left over from the era of Gregorian reform. Even if so, he received no support from his fellow clerics, and he was forced into exile by the king. Becket fled to France and tried to win help from the pope, but he would not intervene on Thomas's behalf. (The pope was then embroiled in a conflict with the German emperor Frederick I and had no inclination to lose more friends among the kings in Europe.)

It is difficult not to subscribe to the theory, recounted in a twelfth-century *Life* of Becket, that the archbishop deliberately sought martyrdom. He returned to England in 1170 and further alienated the bishops by excommunicating some among those who had most strongly disagreed with him. And he remained obdurate in his quarrel with the king—to the point that Henry finally became so upset that he flew into a rage and declared in the presence of his court that he wished he could be rid of Becket. Four knights took those words to heart and went off to Canterbury to murder the archbishop. According to the account in the *Life of St. Thomas*, the monks at Canterbury tried to persuade the archbishop to enter the church for refuge, since traditionally churches provided sanctuary. But "he who had long since yearned for martyrdom, now saw that the occasion to embrace it had seemingly arrived, and dreaded lest it should be deferred or even altogether lost, if he took refuge in the church."[2] The monks forcibly transported Becket into the cathedral, where he waited for his executioners. The knights tried to pull the archbishop outside to avoid committing murder in the church, but Thomas would not be budged. Finally his assassins descended on him, and Becket "understood that the hour was approaching that should release him from the miseries of this mortal life."

In the aftermath of Becket's martyrdom in 1170, Henry was excommunicated by the pope for his indirect—and probably unintentional—role in the murder. The king ultimately submitted to a papal legate in 1172 and was forced to make concessions regarding royal jurisdiction over ecclesiastics. The two points

2. Quotations from *The Life of St. Thomas* are from D. C. Douglas and G. W. Greenaway, *English Historical Documents* (New York: Oxford University Press, 1953), pp. 764–768.

The Death of St. Thomas à Becket. *A thirteenth-century version of the murder of the Archbishop in his own Cathedral. An illustration from a Psalter from the Carrow Abbey in England.* (THE WALTERS ART GALLERY, BALTIMORE)

particularly insisted upon by the pope were that clerics accused of crimes be tried in ecclesiastical courts and that the English clergy be allowed to appeal freely clerical disputes in the papal court. Thus Henry's intention to absorb some of the authority of the ecclesiastical courts (as he had successfully done in the secular courts) failed. On the other hand, his actual control over the

289

English clergy remained in all other respects much the same as before.

For the most part, the remainder of Henry's reign was tumultuous. Becket's martyrdom was the signal for a baronial revolt, which Henry successfully put down. His real troubles, however, centered on the Angevin holdings in France and on the rebelliousness of his sons, who wanted more power and independence than Henry had ever allowed them. The dissension between the king and his sons (who were backed by their mother Eleanor) was the Capetian king's one opportunity to weaken Henry's power, and Philip Augustus, who came to the French throne in 1180, stirred up as much trouble as he could for Henry by supporting whichever of the latter's sons happened to be currently in rebellion against his father. In the last years of Henry's life, "such was the exquisite malice of fortune against this king, that where he should have received comfort he met with opposition."

When Henry died in 1189 he was, despite his many difficulties, still one of the most respected monarchs in Europe; and there was finally peace in all the Angevin possessions. Had Henry really obeyed God, his biographer claimed, "such were his natural endowments that he would have been, beyond all comparison, the noblest of all the princes of the earth in his times."

RICHARD I (1189–1199) AND JOHN (1199–1216)

Henry Plantagenet had succeeded in doing as he had planned when he came to the English throne: He had built a royal government sufficiently strong and well-organized to administer the kingdom even in the absence of its ruler. The test came in Henry's own reign, during his long absences from England, and again during the reigns of the two sons who succeeded him, Richard I (1189–1199), known as the Lionhearted, and John (1199–1216).

Richard was hardly present in England, and when he went there, he did so mainly to raise taxes to support his wars. He nevertheless was popular with the feudal nobility, due largely to his reputation for chivalry and valor (and also because he spent so much time out of England). Much of his reputation Richard earned for his participation in the third crusade (1189–1192), although his leadership did not succeed in winning Jerusalem from the Muslims. After returning to Europe from the Holy Land, Richard spent most of his remaining years in France doing battle against Philip Augustus. The French king's aim was the annexation of the Angevin lands, and he pursued it with single-minded determination—if unsuccessfully—throughout Richard's kingship. When Richard died and was succeeded by his younger brother John, the situation changed completely—and to the advantage of the French crown.

John, called with reason, "Lackland," was a moody, temperamental, and disagreeable man, with some of his father's administrative abilities but none of his—or his brother Richard's—likable personal attributes. John had severe depressions, which rendered him incapable of taking action at crucial periods. He also had little of Richard's love for fighting, and certainly none of Richard's chivalry. He pursued women with no regard for the commitments of betrothal, and it was this characteristic which finally provided Philip Augustus with the occasion and excuse to resume the offensive against him.

In 1200 John married Isabella of Angoulême, who was at the time engaged to a vassal of John's, the French count Hugh de La Marche. The latter was away when the marriage took place, and as soon as he returned he appealed to King Philip Augustus for aid. The appeal was in accordance with feudal law since the French king was John's overlord for Angevin lands on the continent. Philip summoned John to appear at the French court, and when John failed to respond Philip declared (in 1202) that he had forfeited his French holdings and prepared to invade Normandy and Anjou. John did nothing to defend his possessions, and by the end of 1204 the French king had succeeded in taking Normandy and Anjou. Before the first phase in the hostilities had ended in 1206, Philip had won nearly all the Angevin lands in northern and western France except for Poitou and Gascony. John's barons were furious with him, particularly, of course, those who lost the continental lands they held in fief from John.

Almost immediately following this disaster, John entered into a long conflict with the pope. The archbishop of Canterbury had died in 1205, and the canons of the cathedral had elected a successor not favored by the king, who insisted on the election of his own candidate. The dispute was then brought before Pope Innocent III, who responded by appointing his own choice, Stephen Langton. The king refused to recognize Langton, and for several years John and the pope contended the appointment, until in 1208 Innocent placed England under an interdict forbidding English priests to perform their liturgical functions. When this failed to bring John to terms, Innocent excommunicated him and in 1209 deposed him. The pope then offered the English crown to the French king, and Philip Augustus prepared to invade England. This threat succeeded, and in 1213 John finally gave in to the pope. Innocent declared England a papal fief, and John became a papal vassal. Stephen Langton became archbishop.

In the years following the French capture of the Angevin lands, John built up alliances with the intention of recapturing his French fiefs. But the French king was also busy soliciting support, since both rulers fully expected another war. John's main ally was Otto of Brunswick, a contender for the German throne, while Philip Augustus' main ally was Frederick II, an opponent of Otto. The decisive battle in the war between John and Philip Augustus was fought in northern France at Bouvines in 1214, and it had an international character and international repercussions. John's allies were disastrously defeated by Philip's French troops, but beyond that Bouvines was a turning point in the fortunes of every leader and country involved. We will soon see this effect on the French and Germans, but for the English king and many of his barons, Bouvines ended all hope of recapturing the French fiefs. (For more than a hundred years the English acquiesced in the outcome of Bouvines.)

John's disaster also provided his barons with the opportunity to rebel against him. In 1215 the nobles presented him with the document which, in its final form, is known as the Magna Carta. Although Magna Carta, or Great Charter, has been viewed as the most significant early stage in the development of English constitutionalism, it is in itself, in fact, a feudal charter. The real intent

292

of the barons was to limit the arbitrary exercise of power by the king in terms of *feudal obligations* exacted. Magna Carta was not intended to be a charter of liberties for all Englishmen. Rather, it asserted the principle—extremely significant in itself—that the king was subject to—not above—the law. In its many specific provisions it defined the royal power and restricted it from going beyond feudal custom without the consent of the royal vassals. Magna Carta also asserted the rights of the barons to resist any unjust use of power, and although this represented for John the supreme humiliation, the barons were not thereby attempting to do away with monarchy. (They had no desire to dispense with the considerable benefits of royal authority, particularly the exercise of justice.) It is significant, however, that the barons acted as a group rather than as competitors, as they might have a hundred years earlier. Although it is too early in 1215 to speak of a national self-consciousness among the English, that is certainly one of the eventual effects of the loss of the continental possessions and the new interest among the feudal nobility in the affairs of England.

John had barely signed Magna Carta when he repudiated it with the full support of Pope Innocent III, who wanted no limitations placed on the power of his royal vassal. So once again there was a baronial revolt. John died in 1216 before it was suppressed, and his son Henry III, then a minor, came to the throne in the midst of the conflict.

HENRY III (1216–1272)

Henry was fortunate in having as regent an Englishman, William Marshal, who was loyal to the monarchy and interested in preventing the division of the realm. Marshal reissued Magna Carta and was able to suppress the barons' revolt, partly by force and partly by assuring the insurgents that the rights they had won were still secure.

Henry III, unfortunately, grew up to be a weak and ineffectual ruler who was easily led. He allowed his court to be run by his friends and relatives, who were mostly foreigners; and since Henry was also a religious man, he was subservient to the pope. Moreover, the king was a spendthrift and was seduced into several foreign ventures which required a good deal of money. Henry allowed the papal legates in England to tax the clergy heavily to help pay for papal projects in Italy, and he became embroiled in a papal plan to take control of the crown of Sicily. All these activities turned his barons against him.

Henry was by no means a wicked or immoral man. It is significant in terms of the developments in England during his reign that some of the animosity he aroused was due to his involvement in affairs outside England which were no longer of real concern. His relations with the papacy were extremely good, but this meant that he allowed the English clergy to be excessively taxed and permitted foreign appointments to the English church. Obviously, this went against the growing feeling among the barons that their own country was more important than the pope's schemes and ambitions. The barons resented the foreigners at Henry's court, particularly since the king invariably asked them for the money with which to finance his foreign enterprises (all of which were unsuccessful).

Near the beginning of his reign, in 1224, Henry lost Poitou to the French king, further diminishing what little remained of the Angevin holdings in France. For the rest of the century, all that was left was a strip along the coast of Gascony and Guienne, and that, too, might have been lost had it not been for the fact that Louis IX, king of France later in Henry's reign, decided not to try to wrest from England this last bit of territory.

Henry repeatedly had to summon the great council of his barons to ask for financial help and, though early in his reign they gave it to him, they became more and more critical of his policies and finally refused him aid. Henry's conflicts with the barons came to a head in 1258, when he had to ask for money to pay off his considerable debts and to contribute to supporting a papal war in Italy. The barons insisted that Henry appoint a committee to take in hand the reform of the government. Henry had no choice, and the committee issued the Provisions of Oxford, a document giving the barons effective control of the government. Though this most surely represented a revolt against the king (which led to the battle against Henry which ended in his defeat and imprisonment in 1264), it was not a revolt against central government. Or at least this was not the case at the beginning: The barons simply wanted better government, and they wanted what they had come to regard as their right to participate in governmental decisions.

There was no solidarity among the barons, however, and once in power, many of them lost interest in the business of governing or found ways to increase their own power. On the other hand, the leader of the group, Simon de Montfort (who was the king's brother-in-law), and many of his followers were determined to maintain the centralized government. To win support, Simon in 1265 called a meeting of the great council which was augmented to include representatives of other groups in the country besides the feudal nobility. De Montfort summoned to this council, or parliament, two knights from each shire and two burgesses from each town. Although the two latter groups were not consulted on matters of policy and were mainly included to broaden the base of Simon's support, their presence indicates the further changes that had taken place in England. It was no longer possible, as it had been even during the reign of King John, for the barons to be the only spokesmen for the realm. The lesser landholders, whom the knights represented, and the townspeople, whom the burgesses represented, now considered themselves—and were at last considered by the upper nobility—to be a part of the kingdom.

In 1265 Henry's son, Prince Edward, led an army against—and defeated—Simon de Montfort. Further, Edward rescued the king, who was then restored to the throne. Henry was a chastened man, and for the remainder of his reign he ruled well over a peaceful England. Henry had learned from the baronial revolt against him and from the example of Simon's parliament, and he too, called representatives of the shires and towns to the meeting of his great council.

The very fact that some of the barons had recognized the need to call on knights and burgesses indicates that feudal control over the smaller landholders was lessening and that the towns and townspeople were growing stronger. The civil war against Henry had therefore a different outcome from that of the previous civil wars: England's internal conflicts were resolved in favor of royal government, but with limitations on the king's autonomy. And although during the reign of King John it would not have been appropriate to speak of "national self-consciousness," the phrase accurately describes the feeling of several classes in England by the end of Henry's rule. In spite of the civil wars (and more likely because of them), England was more unified at the end of Henry's reign than it had been at the beginning. It was also more efficiently governed than any other country in Europe. On the other hand, England was no longer so powerful as before in the larger arena of European politics. Until the reign of King John (in 1199) it had not seemed possible that the French monarchy could overtake the English in power and importance, yet despite the humble beginnings of the Capetian kings in the twelfth century, and the strength of the English institutions, that is precisely what happened.

The Rise of the Capetian Monarchy in France (1100–1272)

The history of the Capetian ascendency during the twelfth century is easily told since so many of the important royal gains were those made in the wars against the Angevins. And the fact that Angevin territory was so crucial to the expansion of Capetian authority underlines one of the main themes of this period in French history. We have seen that although the only land to which the French king could lay direct claim was the small area of the Île de France, the Capetians nonetheless had some advantages that would prove greatly beneficial during the course of the twelfth century and afterward. The Capetians had a continuous succession to the throne, an unbroken line of heirs, thereby avoiding the dynastic problems which confronted the English and German kings. They had also the strong and loyal support of the French clergy and the Cluniac monks, who encouraged the general view of the Capetians as devoted sons of the Church (as indeed some among them were). Together, the clergy and kings carefully and assiduously fostered the cult of monarchy and loyalty to "sweet France."

Throughout the twelfth century, however, there was no such thing as "sweet France." The country was instead a patchwork of duchies and counties, each with its own customs and laws. Furthermore, there was the division between the north and the south. Even the language had developed differently, so there was none of the internal coherence in France that so benefited the Norman rulers in England. This disunity was due not only to resistance by the nobility to any advance of royal political authority; it reflected also a more deep-seated particularism stemming from the cultural and social differences that we have mentioned.

In securing the advantages that came with conquest and developing the institutions through which to rule, the Capetians were a hundred years behind the English monarchy. While the Norman rulers were establishing governmental institutions, the Capetians were still having difficulty enforcing their authority over the vassals of their own personal domain and, although overlords in name, they had no effective control of their vassals in the rest of France. The Capetian kings therefore had to struggle first with the problem of securing their power within the Île de France; then, with some resources, they could attempt to enforce control over the vassals beyond the royal domain. In the process, there was always the hope that the crown could absorb new lands directly. In summary, the Capetian struggle for ascendancy was the model of the way a feudal king, working within the framework of a feudal society, could advance his power.

LOUIS VI (1108–1137)

The first stage in advancing royal power to gain control of the royal domain was accomplished by Louis VI. In spite of his weight, which earned him the nickname "the Fat," Louis was an extremely active man, and he traveled the Île de France constantly to make certain that every tax owed him was paid and that every service rightfully owed by his immediate vassals was performed.

At first, the only way he could enforce his rights was to appear in person. Gradually, however, he gained sufficient authority to be able to summon vassals to appear at the royal court. The king was quick to punish recalcitrant vassals, and he began to earn their respect and finally their loyalty. Louis then took the unprecedented step of intervening in problems that arose in territories beyond the Île de France. Once, for example, he appeared in Aquitaine to aid the bishop of Clermont who was being besieged by the count of Clermont. The king's appearance so surprised everyone that the count withdrew from the siege. On other occasions Louis was less successful, but he had one notable success that serves as an indication of the advances he had made. In 1124 the German emperor Henry V assembled his army to invade France, and Louis called on his nobles to bring their armies to Rheims. Only the duke of Normandy did not obey the summons. The others all came, and the threat of a strong French army caused the emperor to abandon his plans.

Near the close of Louis's reign, William, duke of Aquitaine, died leaving no male heir to succeed him. His only child, Eleanor, was left in the king's care. Louis then arranged for the marriage of his own heir Louis VII to Eleanor, thus adding Aquitaine directly to the crown lands. The acquisition of this large territory, in terms of its size and the wealth of various regions within it, was a not unmixed benefit for the crown. The dukes of Aquitaine had never succeeded in controlling all their vassals, and in many places in the south feudal institutions had never taken hold. Thus the duchy was difficult to administer except through constant vigilance and attendance. Nevertheless, it was an important—if troublesome—gain. (Ultimately, the problems of Eleanor and the duchy were to take on much more serious dimensions.)

Louis had to spend so much of his time moving about his realm that he left much of the actual work of administration to the most talented cleric in France, Suger, abbot of the royal monastery at St. Denis. Suger's considerable gifts included making the plans and directing the building of an abbey church, the first in the new Gothic style. For the king, Suger's services were equally as constructive and lasting. He gave Louis valuable assistance in defining

298

the goals of the royal government and then recruiting and directing a staff of officials to work toward organizing the finances and administration of the royal lands. For these positions Suger chose clerics, members of the lower nobility, and, in some instances, members of the rising urban class—all individuals with no dynastic aspirations, and loyal to the crown.

Suger wrote a biography of Louis, and his assessment of the king's achievements forms a fitting epitaph: "He provided for the needs of the church, and strove to secure peace of those who pray, for those who work, and for the poor. And no one had done this for a long time." Louis altogether laid an excellent foundation on which the next Capetians could build.

LOUIS VII (1137–1180)

One of the most valuable legacies Louis VI passed on to his son was the abbot Suger, who served the new Louis as chief minister and then, in the king's absence during the second crusade, as regent. Thus the work of administering the royal lands and centralizing royal authority was able to continue despite the setbacks which Louis suffered or brought upon himself. When the king went on the crusade in 1147, Eleanor insisted on accompanying him. The queen was altogether a fascinating and intelligent woman; she was extremely independent and had been raised in the south of France where there was a romantic tradition in song and literature, a freedom and aliveness in the culture. Eleanor and her women companions enjoyed themselves enormously in the East, while Louis and the crusading armies had to suffer hardships and finally the humiliation of defeat and withdrawal. There was a good deal of scandal surrounding Eleanor's behavior in the East. True or not, the rumors were that she had at least two affairs, one with her uncle, the ruler of Antioch. Louis considered divorcing his queen, but was persuaded against it by Suger (who did not want France to lose Aquitaine) and by the pope, whom Louis and Eleanor visited on their way home from the East.

The royal reconciliation was brief, however. In the case of Louis and Eleanor, opposites most decidedly did not attract. Eleanor is supposed to have said, with some disgust, that she discovered that she married a monk. Louis, for his part, was unhappy over Eleanor's scandalous behavior and undoubtedly also because she had produced only daughters. Suger died in 1151, and once his restraint was removed, Eleanor and Louis divorced. The loss of Aquitaine represented a serious reduction in the crown lands and then became a major problem for the French king when Eleanor remarried (as she did within only a short time after the divorce). Eleanor's new husband, Henry Plantagenet, was already the wealthiest feudal lord in France. Louis tried to prevent the marriage and, when that failed, spent two years trying to prevent—and unsuccessfully—Henry from taking possession of Aquitaine. In 1154 Henry became king of England.

Some French historians have castigated Louis for the loss of Aquitaine, yet he was in several ways a constructive ruler the remainder of whose reign brought some gains for French royal power. Louis continued to cement the alliance between the Capetians and the clergy, and he protected, whenever possible, bishops and abbots in different parts of the realm from the encroachments of the local nobility. Louis's insistence on settling quarrels and local rivalries among the nobility by adjudication at the royal court won him the respect of the nobility and clergy alike (since everyone basically wanted peace). Gradually, the king's court came to be acknowledged as a forum of appeals for settling disputes that arose beyond the Île de France. Out of practical considerations rather than a particular affection for the bourgeoisie, the king granted royal charters and protection to the towns that were emerging. In this way he increased the revenue to the crown, since he could tax the towns; and the resulting monies gave him the opportunity to free himself from total dependence on the royal vassals when he needed to raise an army.

After his divorce from Eleanor, Louis married twice more, and his third wife gave him the desired son and heir, the future Philip Augustus, who would ascend the throne at Louis's death in 1180.

PHILIP II AUGUSTUS (1180–1223)

Philip's reign was a turning point in the fortunes of the Capetian monarchy, since he successfully waged most of the wars that brought the lands of "sweet France" to the crown. Philip's father, Louis, had been known for his piety and for his moral scruples, but Philip was cut from an entirely different mold. He was hard-headed, often unscrupulous, clever, highly political, and absolutely unswerving in his determination to annex the Angevin lands to France.

During the early years of Philip's reign, Henry II was still king of England, and Philip's policy was to support everyone opposed to Henry. (We have seen how he even supported the latter's sons in rebellion against their father.) This policy accomplished little for Philip other than to fuel hostilities. Both Henry's successor Richard (1189–1199) and Philip went off on the third crusade (1189–1192), so there was peace for a time; but Philip left the crusade in 1191, before it ended, hoping to conquer Normandy before Richard's return from the Holy Land. Richard came back in 1194, and there ensued a bloody war between the two which ended only when the pope (then Innocent III) imposed peace in 1199.

Although nothing was accomplished in the fight against England in these early years of his rule, Philip did begin to expand northward in the direction of the county of Flanders and the English Channel, and he formulated the first of his plans to invade England. The initial northern expansion of Capetian power came as a result of the death of Philip's first wife whose inheritance was Artois, which Philip then claimed for himself. The plan to invade England led to his second marriage, in 1193, to Ingeborg, daughter of the king of Denmark. Since the Danes had once ruled England, Philip believed—or chose to believe—that his marriage gave him a claim to the English throne and the use of the Danish fleet for his planned invasion. But Philip's scheme came to nothing, and since he took an instant dislike to Ingeborg, he had the French clergy annul their marriage.

In 1200 the opportunity finally arrived for a war against the English. In 1200 John of England married Isabelle of Angoulême and then refused to answer Philip's summons to appear at the French court when Isabelle's fiancé complained to Philip. Philip staged his successful invasions of the Angevin holdings in

1204–1206, after which he resumed his plan to invade England when John refused to surrender to Pope Innocent III in the matter of the archbishop of Canterbury. Innocent offered the English crown to Philip, but the invasion was called off when John capitulated and Innocent restored England to him as a papal fief.

Within a few years, however, Philip won his stunning victory over England at the battle of Bouvines (in 1214), and his policies came to fruition. The Angevin power was now broken, and the king of France augmented his realm by bringing directly under French royal control Normandy, Maine, Anjou, Touraine, and, through his first wife's inheritance, Artois. The French royal domain was thus nearly quadrupled and the royal income multiplied by even more. Normandy alone was at least three times richer than the original Capetian holdings, and Artois had within it several wealthy wool-weaving towns. In a complete reversal of fortune—surely unpredictable half a century before—the Capetian monarchy had now become one of the most formidable in Christendom.

During the years of Philip's wars against the Angevins, a battle of a different sort was being waged in the south of France. This was a crusade preached by Pope Innocent III against a heretical group called the Cathars or Albigensians. The heresy and crusade will be discussed in connection with the religious movements before and during the pontificate of Innocent III (1198–1216), but for now it is important to note that, although Philip himself did not take an active part in the crusade, he gave his consent to it, and this was the beginning of the extension of royal control over southern France. The crusade continued into the next generation and the disposition of the territory conquered by the nobility who participated in it was not settled until Louis VIII's reign (1223–1226). The onset of the war in the south, which ended by destroying the unique culture and the independence of the Provençal region, was instigated by the papacy, and so the expansion of royal authority southward was, in a sense, an ecclesiastical gift in exchange for the French monarchy's support of papal policies. And this alliance with the papacy was one which was to benefit the French monarchy throughout the thirteenth century.

In his last, peaceful years Philip dealt with the problem of governing the new and diverse provinces he had brought under royal control. Philip had now acquired a large kingdom over which to rule, with personal wealth greater than that of the English king. Each French province had a distinctive character, with its own particular customs, laws, and society. (These have not been completely eradicated to this day.) Whereas in England the barons had a sense of their own community and the interests of the realm, in France there was no such sense of community among the higher feudal nobility, whose interests and loyalties were to their own duchies and counties. Thus the opposition to the extension of royal power in France took on a different character, as one might expect. In France there was resistance to the king's interference within the provinces, and there would surely have been resistance to the spread of a common law. Philip, however, was a gifted administrator who did not try to eliminate local custom and law within the provinces. He tried instead to link the local administration to the crown, and to make certain that nothing was done at the local level that went counter to the king's interests. He also set about to protect the lower nobility, the clergy, and the townsmen within the provinces from unjust feudal demands.

Philip had already elaborated a better system of governing the royal domain, which he now extended to the provinces by sending out agents of the crown to each of the districts in France. In the northern regions these governors were called *baillis* and in the south *seneschals*. They collected taxes, administered justice, curtailed the power of the local nobility, and generally protected the rights of the crown. These agents were mainly drawn from the middle class, though occasionally they might be clerics. Uniformly, they were individuals whose advancement depended on their loyalty to the king. They were appointed to a district for a limited period and, if proven honest and efficient, could be appointed repeatedly, though not to the same district. This devoted bureaucracy notwithstanding, the king's own court was still a quite personal affair, and primitive in comparison to that of England.

With his system of deputies Philip gave France the first institutions that could be considered governmental in the real sense. Philip also encouraged the trade and industry that were developing so well in the north, and he promoted the growth of Paris as the true heart and center of his realm. Although early in his reign he had had little to do with the emerging university at Paris he now took an interest in it; and he also took an interest in adorning the city and its surrounding areas. (Both the cathedral of Notre Dame and Chârtres were finished with his support.) When Philip died in 1223, he left to his son Louis VIII a country which in large measure he had created.

LOUIS VIII (1223–1226)

Louis VIII followed his father on the throne, and in spite of a short reign he made important advances. He participated in the crusade in southern France and negotiated the surrender of the county of Toulouse to the crown (although this did not officially take place until after he died). Louis also worked out a solution to the problem of providing for the younger sons of the royal family. This had not been a particularly vexing issue since most of the Capetians had had few sons and not so much land. Louis, however, had four sons and a vast kingdom; and he solved the problem of how to provide for them and allow them some independence by dividing the royal domain into four fiefs. The eldest son, of course, inherited the crown; each of the others controlled one of the royal fiefs, which were called *appanages*. The land thus remained within the royal family and was ruled, presumably, by loyal relatives. This seemed an excellent solution at the time, although in later centuries this division of the crown lands would prove a danger to the king and his authority.

LOUIS IX (1226–1270)

When Louis VIII died his eldest son, Louis IX, was too young to succeed his father, so the Queen Mother, Blanche of Castile, ruled as regent until the heir apparent came of age. The early years of the regency were troubled by feudal revolts against the royal power, since this seemed a good opportunity to reverse the Capetian conquests, especially in southern France. The revolts—all of which were quelled fairly easily—also reflected the dislike of many of the nobility for Blanche, a strong, devout woman with a will of steel. (Her influence on her eldest son was manifest throughout Louis' life.)

Louis' reign is interesting, not for what he accomplished, (though he accomplished a good deal), but because he achieved what he did largely through force of character. He was the essence of what a medieval king was supposed to be: pious, just, paternal, upright. He believed that the king was God's appointed, and that he was responsible for the care of the souls entrusted to him. The allegiance Louis inspired in his subjects was the culmination of the

St. Louis Washing the Feet of a Leper, from the Book of Hours of Jeanne d'Evreux, Queen of France, 14th century. *It is extraordinary that such high artistic quality could be attained in so tiny a book. Louis' biographer, Joinville, is seen standing next to the king.* (THE METROPOLITAN MUSEUM OF ART, THE CLOISTERS COLLECTION, 1954)

305

Capetian-clerical intention to bind the people to "sweet France" by instilling in them a love and respect for the monarchy.

Louis had a passion for justice, and his biographer Joinville, who was also his friend and his companion on a crusade, tells us that "often in the summer he went after mass to the wood of Vincennes and sat down with his back against an oak tree, and made us all sit around him. Everyone who had an affair to settle could come and speak to him without the interference of any usher or any official."[3] Great use was made of the king's court as a forum of appeals for all Frenchmen, and for the first time, the court was permanently established in Paris. (Called the *Parlement*, it was staffed by professional jurists.) When complaints reached the king that the *seneschals* and *baillis* were unscrupulous in their behavior towards the provincial population, Louis sent out inquirers to check on them and curtail the abuses of royal authority. His reputation for honesty and fairness was so widespread that even Henry III of England called on Louis to settle a dispute between him and his barons.

Louis was deeply religious, and his life and all his actions were guided by his piety and by what he believed was in accord with the upright Christian life. His zeal had been instilled by his mother who, as Louis himself said, had "given him to understand that she would rather he were dead than have committed a mortal sin."[4] The king visited the sick, gave enormous sums of money to feed the poor and build hospitals, churches, and monasteries, and exhibited altogether a tender and consistent concern for the welfare of his subjects. In many ways, although there was a soft side to him, his was not a sweet saintliness, but a stern one. "The king so loved God and His sweet Mother," Joinville wrote, "that he caused all those to be grievously punished who were convicted of speaking of them evilly or lightly, or with a profane oath." Louis was fanatical in his desire to rid France of heresy, and he

---

3. From Jean de Joinville, *The Life of St. Louis*, trans. R. Hague (New York: Sheed & Ward, 1955), p. 37.
4. This and the following quotations are from Jean de Joinville's "Chronicle of the Crusade of St. Lewis," in *Memoirs of the Crusade*, trans. Sir Frank T. Marzials (New York: E. P. Dutton, 1958), pp. 154, 309.

St. Louis Feeding a Sick Monk, from the Book of Hours of Jeanne d'Evreux, Queen of France, 14th century. (THE METROPOLITAN MUSEUM OF ART, THE CLOISTERS COLLECTION, 1954)

gave strong support—including military aid when necessary—to the inquisitors sent by the papal court to hunt down the remaining Albigensians. With the king's encouragement, the papal inquisitors expanded their activities to include all France. Against the unanimous advice of his councillors, Louis allowed Henry III of England to keep Gascony and that part of Aquitaine which he still owned. Louis did this on the grounds that it was more important to maintain the family relationships between the royal houses than to fight the English. This was a decision for which he has been criticized by historians, who believe that had he fought the English he would have won, thereby preventing the wars of the next century.

Louis undertook two crusades. The plan for the first (which began in 1248, and was officially the seventh crusade) was to go directly to Egypt to attack Muslim power at its source, since the

St. Louis on His Way to the Holy Land, from the Belles Heures of John, Duke of Berry, 15th c. (THE METROPOLITAN MUSEUM OF ART, PURCHASE, 1954, THE CLOISTERS COLLECTION)

sultan controlled Jerusalem.[5] The crusading army was badly defeated, and the king himself was captured and paid a huge ransom for his freedom. Louis spent several years in the Holy Land after he was freed, but the crusade accomplished nothing and Jerusalem remained in Muslim hands. Louis took the cross a second time, even though he was so ill that, as Joinville reported, "he could

---

5. Louis was just as offended by the presence of Jews in his kingdom, and was only restrained from expelling them by his advisors who persuaded him that the Jews had an important economic function to perform.

bear neither to be drawn in a chariot, nor to ride." He got only as far as Tunis, where he died in 1270.

Louis's piety did not in any way mean that he deferred to the church. On the contrary, he kept a strong hand on the French clergy, and on several occasions reprimanded them or interfered with their decisions if he considered they were not behaving properly. He was respectful—but not deferential—to the papacy. He sided with the French clergy when they resisted papal appointments to the French church, and he resisted papal demands for money to support a war in Italy. The French-papal alliance was nevertheless continued, and under this saintly monarch the French expanded into southern Italy and Sicily. The popes, who for several decades had been engaged in a war against the German emperor in Italy, had finally appealed to the English king, Henry III, to come to their aid in Italy. (The prize which the papacy held out was the crown of southern Italy and Sicily.) This scheme did no more than bring down the barons' wrath on Henry's head, and the English plan came to nothing. Louis was then offered the same crown, and when it was clear that it would indeed remain in French hands if the army succeeded in wresting it from the Germans, Louis sent his younger brother, Charles of Anjou, to Italy. This represented an important new stage in French expansion, and one which was to have many repercussions in the future. The close French involvement with the papacy in Italy opened a new chapter in the relations between the two powers which Louis could not possibly have foreseen or liked.

Louis was immovable when he believed that something was morally just. By the time he died, in ways not at all anticipated a century earlier, France had become a kingdom. But unlike England, it was not a kingdom ruled throughout by a common law, and the diversity among its provinces had not been diminished. France's administrative machinery, though elaborated somewhat under Louis, was neither so advanced, nor its governing institutions so impersonal and independent of the monarch, as those of England. But the king of France was known and revered throughout his kingdom and throughout Europe for his devotion to his subjects and the Church, for the quality of his life, and for his

309

adherence to moral principles. Louis was sainted not long after his death—surely the highest mark of respect Christendom could bestow. Under the Capetians, who had labored steadily and hard, "sweet France" had finally become the most important power in Europe.

Germany and the Roman Empire until 1273

The Background to the Hohenstaufen Empire

The consolidation of royal power in Germany had advanced well ahead of both England and France during the tenth and eleventh centuries. But the continued extension of royal government, which had seemed so promising in those early centuries, was considerably retarded by the effects of the investiture controversy. By the end of the eleventh century, royal authority had been undermined because the investiture issue had provided the opportunity for the German nobility to reassert their own power at the expense of the king. As soon as the controversy had begun, Pope Gregory VII found allies among the great German lords for his fight with the emperor Henry IV. When Gregory deposed Henry in 1076, those princes who were opposed to strong central government elected an anti-king in 1077 and thus began the civil wars that—although punctuated by occasional periods of peace—were not finally ended until the mid-twelfth century.

Germany, unlike France, had neither fully developed nor widespread feudal institutions in the eleventh century, but the weakness of the kings during and after the investiture controversy provided the conditions in Germany for the spread of feudal decentralization. The old nobility—the great dukes and barons—were able to add considerably to their territorial holdings. On their enlarged lands they built heavily fortified castles, supported their own armies of vassals, and, having learned from the successful practice of the German kings in the tenth and eleventh centuries, also took over ecclesiastical lands, many of which had once been under royal control. In the course of the confusion and the fighting, many of the free peasants in Germany were reduced to serfdom by the nobility; at the same time the confusion also provided the opportunity for some freemen to rise into the ranks of the lower nobility and become knights, or *ministeriales*.

The alliance between the kings and the clergy, which had been the mainstay of royal power under the Ottonian and early Salian kings, had, as we have seen, been weakened by the investiture controversy. The rapid advance of feudalism robbed the kings of more of their land and authority, particularly since, unlike the Norman rulers in England, the German kings were not recognized as the overlords of the lesser nobility. And then, in the first half of the twelfth century, the feudal lords of Germany returned to the elective principle for selecting their kings.

Although the electoral principle had never in law been formally abandoned, the monarchy had in reality become hereditary in the tenth and eleventh centuries, and the electors had kept the kingship within the ruling family. In 1106 Henry IV's son, Henry V (1106–1125), came to the throne, but his reign was the exception that proved the rule. Henry V had been crowned and recognized as royal heir in 1099, while his father still lived. In 1104 he led a rebellion against his father which ended with Henry IV's death in 1106. The rebellion may have been supported by the pope; it was certainly supported by the princes, since Henry was subject to them, and not the other way around, after he came to the throne. Once installed, Henry made attempts to put the monarchy on a strong footing again, but he was no match for the aristocracy. The princes, secure in their own power in Germany, then supported Henry in his long and complicated negotiations with the papacy, and finally, in 1122, the Concordat of Worms was signed.

Henry had no son to succeed him, so before his death in 1125 he chose a nephew, a member of the Hohenstaufen family, as his designated heir. Although in an earlier period it would have been customary for the electors to have approved the king's choice of a close relative, they now preferred to pass over the Hohenstaufen claim and elected instead a man whom they expected to control.

311

The new king, Lothair (1125–1137), duke of Saxony, was rejected by the Hohenstaufen, and the civil wars began again in 1127. Lothair's son-in-law, a member of the Welf (or, in its more usual, Italianized form, *Guelph*) family, was the king's choice of a successor. Once again the princes passed over the family claim and, at Lothair's death in 1137, turned to a young member of the Hohenstaufen family in the hope that a Hohenstaufen might end the anarchy. But Conrad III's election and rule (1137–1152) only made the situation worse, since now the Guelph family and their supporters reopened the civil wars. At long last, wearied themselves of all the fighting and the attendant disruptions, the princes at Conrad's death chose a man who was a Hohenstaufen on his father's side and a Guelph on his mother's side. In 1152 the princes elected Frederick I Hohenstaufen (Frederick Barbarossa, or Red Beard) "considering," as Frederick's biographer wrote, "not merely [his] achievements and . . . valor . . . but also this fact, that being a member of both families, he might—like a cornerstone—link these two separate walls. . . ."[6]

THE REIGN OF FREDERICK I HOHENSTAUFEN (1152–1190)

Frederick's biographer, Otto of Freising, was the king's uncle, so perhaps his admiration for Frederick was a bit fulsome. "You are known," Otto wrote to the king, "to be so temperate in prosperity, brave in adversity, just in judgment, and prudent and shrewd in courts of law, that these characteristics seem to have taken root in you . . . and [be] granted you by God for the general advantage of the whole world." The undisputed fact, nonetheless, is that Frederick was remarkable in his abilities of leadership; he was an astute politician, a determined man. Even in such excellent company as that of Henry II of England and, later in the century, Philip Augustus of France, Frederick was regarded as the chief statesman in Europe. This was not because his policies were an unqualified success. Frederick suffered many defeats, though by the end of his life, partly due to his ability to change tactics when

6. This and the following quotations are from Otto of Freising, *The Deeds of Frederick Barbarossa*, trans. Charles C. Mierow with Richard Emery (New York: W. W. Norton, 1966), pp. 116, 27, 185, 186.

necessary and partly due to good fortune, he triumphed over his enemies.

Frederick's two ambitions were the restoration of a strong monarchy in Germany and the restoration of the empire. To him these goals were inseparable, although the hope that either—let alone both—might be accomplished seemed slim in 1152. German society had been decentralized in the ways we have so far considered, and there was no turning the clock back. Furthermore, by 1152 the royal territories themselves had been so diminished that the only land over which Frederick had real control was the duchy of Swabia, his family domain. The other royal estates, scattered through Germany, had been effectively removed from royal domination.

To begin with, Frederick accepted what he could not alter. He worked to establish a feudal monarchy by strengthening his control—more accurately by *gaining* control—over the feudal structure of Germany. He officially granted as fiefs the lands held by the nobility and in return received recognition as their overlord. The leader of the Guelph party was Henry the Lion, duke of Bavaria. Henry was Frederick's cousin and second only to the latter in his abilities as a leader and politician. Frederick won Henry's loyalty—at least for a time—by recognizing his claim to the large duchy of Saxony as well as Bavaria. Frederick thus brought peace to Germany, as the electors had hoped. Within a few years of Frederick's election, Otto of Freising could write that "things have changed for the better, and after the time of weeping, the time of laughing has now come, and after the time of war, the time of peace . . . . "

In the tenth and eleventh centuries the German monarch's personal wealth had been in Saxony and the northern part of Germany. Under Frederick that geographical basis, of necessity, shifted southward. The king established his authority securely over Swabia; from there he planned to extend his power into the duchy of Burgundy and then into Italy, over Lombardy. The first part of this plan was implemented in 1156 when Frederick married the heiress to the duchy of Burgundy. That was, as it turned out, by far the easier part of the strategy to fulfill.

313

Much of Frederick's reign was taken up with the problem of Italy, and he has been severely criticized by German historians for pursuing an Italian policy to the neglect (and ultimate detriment) of the cause of a strong German monarchy. But Frederick's idea was to re-establish imperial authority in the Lombard cities of northern Italy and use the revenue from those cities to reassert royal power in the northern kingdom. At the time of Frederick's first Italian expedition (1154–1155), it appeared briefly that his plan had some hope of success, even though the ominous portents were already there.

Italy, like Caesar's Gaul, was divided into three parts: the Norman kingdom of the two Sicilies (also known as the Regno), Rome and the papal states, and the cities of Lombardy in the north. Under ambitious and strong Norman kings, the Regno had become one of the wealthiest and most advanced states in Europe. Sicily was a rich grain-producing area with many industries and an active trade in the Mediterranean; and the mixed population of Normans, Greeks, Muslims, and Jews contributed to the development of bureaucratic institutions, a flourishing economy, and a remarkable literary and artistic culture. (The Norman court at Palermo was splendid in the fashion of the Byzantine rulers.) Over this the Normans ruled with a mixture of tolerance (in return for which the non-Latins paid heavily in taxes) and autocracy.

The Normans held the Regno as a papal fief and were officially papal legates in their country, so they wanted no imperial interference in Italy. However, the central and northern Italian cities, including Rome, had gone through changes which made some of their citizens (including the pope, in 1154) receptive to the emperor. Just as the investiture controversy had freed the papacy from imperial control, it had also freed the Lombard cities. As we have seen, they had used that freedom to pursue their economic interests and grow rich; and they also took advantage of the absence of a strong emperor to establish communes, or government organizations, headed by the merchants and nobles. Although the cities prospered, they were exceedingly competitive with one another, and there were numerous wars among them. To many of the Italians, renewal of imperial authority therefore seemed not a bad thing, since it held out the promise of curtailing this fighting and anarchy. The group who welcomed—at least at first—the emperor's presence in Italian affairs were known as Ghibellines (from the Italianized version of a Hohenstaufen castle, Waiblingen). Those who opposed imperial interference were known as Guelphs. The city which most strongly resisted the emperor was Milan (since the Milanese had begun to expand in Lombardy), so Milan was from the beginning of Frederick's reign a potential threat.

In Rome itself there had been a popular movement to take control of the city, but since Rome was not an economic center, and since its government was run by the pope and a tiny handful of Roman noble families, the movement there had its own special and different peculiarities. This revolution, in its first stages in 1143, was directed by the lower nobility and the citizens who wanted to restore popular rule in accord with the Republican government of ancient Rome. Shortly after it began, the Roman revolution was joined and then taken over by an outsider, the radical reformer Arnold of Brescia.[7] It was Arnold who led the Roman people at the time of Frederick's first trip to Rome, and it was because the pope hoped for Frederick's aid in ridding Rome of Arnold and the revolutionaries that papal policy was friendly— but not unreservedly so—to the emperor. And Frederick, of course, hoped to be crowned Roman emperor by the pope.

By 1155 Arnold of Brescia had been thrown out of Rome, and Frederick had had him killed—an act the latter was said to have later regretted. Frederick was now to be crowned emperor by Hadrian IV, the only Englishman ever to be elected to the papacy. In the course of the preparations for the coronation, the pope and Frederick had their first altercation. Hadrian insisted that as part of the ceremony, Frederick act as the pope's groom and hold his bridle and stirrup when he dismounted from his horse. Frederick refused, but the pope was adamant, and Frederick's advisors finally convinced him that he should comply with what was merely a

---

7. The story of Arnold of Brescia belongs more properly to the history of dissent in the twelfth century and will be referred to again in that context.

formality. This Frederick did, but it was not an auspicious beginning. Hadrian himself was moderate in his attitude toward Frederick, but within the papal court there were men strongly opposed to the emperor's assertion of his rights in Lombardy, fearing that the restoration of imperial power would in the end endanger the papal position in Italy.

In 1157 the pope sent two legates with a letter to be read aloud to the emperor during the course of a council (called a diet) that Frederick was holding at Besançon in Burgundy. In his letter the pope declared that Frederick held the empire as a papal benefice. The word *benefice* (in Latin, *beneficium*) could be translated as simply "benefit," but more usually it meant "fief," the latter, in any event, being the translation chosen by the cardinal-legates. Frederick's response to the letter established an imperial position which, although amplified somewhat by time, remained fundamentally unchanged for the next hundred years. In a letter published throughout his realm and recorded by Otto of Freising, Frederick wrote the following:

And since, through election by the princes, the kingdom and the empire are ours from God alone, who at the time of the passion of his Son Christ subjected the world to dominion by the two swords, and since the apostle Peter taught the world this doctrine: 'Fear God, honor the king' [1 Peter 2:17], whosoever says that we received the imperial crown as a benefice from the lord pope contradicts the divine ordinance and the doctrine of Peter and is guilty of a lie.

During the course of his reign, Frederick's lawyers and advisors found further substantiation for the independence of the imperial position in the laws of the ancient Roman Empire.

Pope Hadrian died in 1159, and his successor, Alexander III (1159–1181), had been one of the cardinal-legates at the diet at Besançon and was absolutely opposed to imperial rule in Italy. Frederick did not recognize the validity of Alexander's election and set up an antipope, Victor IV, whose only support and recognition came from Frederick himself. By this time it was clear that the battle lines were drawn for the papal-imperial conflict to resume with full force.

316

Frederick had already had difficulty with Milan in 1158, and by 1162 the resistance of the Milanese government persuaded him that he should crush the city, and so he did. In the meantime, however, Pope Alexander III had been arranging an alliance between himself and the king of Sicily, and this was now enlarged to include Milan and the Lombard cities, many of which in the recent past had fought against one another. In 1167 the Lombard League was formed, and the combined armies of the allies defeated Frederick's army in a great battle at Legnano in 1176. The next year Frederick recognized Alexander as the only pope. Soon afterward, the emperor made temporary treaties with Sicily and the Lombard cities and finally, in 1183, signed a permanent peace treaty with them. After protracted negotiations, Lombardy recognized the nominal overlordship of the emperor, and even paid him revenues; but Frederick was forced to make such concessions that on balance, his plan to profit from his power over the northern Italian cities was a failure.

Frederick considered his cousin, the Guelph leader Henry the Lion, responsible for the defeat at Legnano because Henry had refused to come to his aid. In 1180–1181 Frederick held a feudal trial at which Henry was deprived of the duchies of Saxony and Bavaria. Even this, however, was only a partial success and, as much as anything, illustrates the weakness of the German monarchy. Instead of allowing the king to absorb those two strong duchies into the royal domain, the nobility insisted that Frederick divide them among the princes. The entire event is significant because the fact that Frederick was able to hold a feudal court and, under feudal law, find Henry guilty of not fulfilling his obligations indicates Frederick's success in establishing the basis of his monarchy within the framework of the feudal society. But it was a limited basis still, since Frederick could not use his power to absorb the two duchies into the royal domain. Frederick received the support of the princes because he accepted the principle that a vacant fief with no inheritor would be given out to another noble, or nobles, rather than reverting to the king.

In spite of all his difficulties, Frederick was able to hold a celebration in Mainz in 1184, marking several occasions: his defeat of Henry the Lion, the knighting of his eldest sons, and the engagement of his heir, Henry, to a princess of the royal family in Norman Sicily. The engagement was a diplomatic coup that came about at least partly because of the high esteem in which Frederick was held even by his former enemies. The marriage, which took place in 1186, sealed the peace treaty between Frederick and the Normans. It did not, at the same time, give promise of anything more, since Princess Constance was not in line to inherit the Sicilian throne. In 1189, however, through a series of deaths in her family Constance became queen of the Regno. The following year Frederick took the cross and went off to lead the third crusade; he died in 1190 before reaching the Holy Land.

Frederick I had realistically evaluated the possibilities for strengthening the monarchy in Germany and had achieved a good deal, though within the limitations described. His particular Italian policy had not succeeded, but when he died he left the possibilities for a new and much greater Italian policy in the hands of his son. And Frederick had succeeded in having the princes recognize Henry as his heir, so the hereditary principle had for the moment been accepted again.

HENRY VI (1190–1197)

Henry had a short, tumultuous, and—in some respects—remarkable reign. During his few years as ruler, he changed and expanded his father's vision of a Hohenstaufen empire to include not only northern Italy and the papal states, but—as the cornerstone of his policy—the kingdom of the two Sicilies.

The German crown passed without event to Henry, since that had been assured before Frederick I had died. Henry's rule was not without opposition, however, since the Guelph family was once again opposed to the continuation of the Hohenstaufen line and now had strong allies outside Germany. Henry the Lion had married the daughter of Henry II of England, and this close familial connection between English royalty and the Guelphs provided English money and arms to support the Guelph rivalry with the Hohenstaufen for many years (up until the battle of Bouvines).

There were rebellions against Henry in Germany, which he was able to quell by 1193. He also made concessions to the German princes which undermined the monarchy his father had established (though the damage may not have been lasting). But Henry had two goals early in his reign (and eventually a third) for which he needed the help of the nobility. First, because he had a rival claimant for the throne in Sicily he needed to be assured that he could leave Germany to the nobility without danger to his position. Secondly, he wanted to make the Hohenstaufen dynasty and the monarchy itself hereditary, not subject to election and approval by the princes. And third, he ultimately would need the aid and loyalty of his nobles because he planned a crusade to the Holy Land.

By 1194 Henry had at last secured the throne of Sicily; and in that year his son was born. Since the throne of Norman Sicily was hereditary, it seemed certain that, barring upheavals, Henry's son Frederick would one day rule Sicily. But Henry's dream was to unite Sicily, Germany, and all Italy in between, into a grand Hohenstaufen empire. To ensure the continuation of that empire he needed to persuade the princes that the German monarchy ought to be hereditary, and he also needed to convince the pope to allow him to control the papal states. In the meantime, in preparation for a crusade to the East, he amassed a huge fleet off the coast of Sicily. (He seems to have hoped to conquer Constantinople too—a scheme inherited from the Normans who had had designs for a Mediterranean empire.)

In spite of the many concessions Henry offered the German lords, they refused to make the German kingship hereditary, although they did elect his infant son Frederick to the throne in 1196. To the papacy Henry offered revenues from all the churches in his huge empire in return for overlordship of the papal states. The pope of course refused, and then lived in fear of the Hohenstaufen threat in Italy. Before Henry took sick and died (in 1197) he had an army in the papal states, so his unexpected death at thirty-three was for the papacy a not even thinly disguised blessing, and all the more so because the royal heir, Frederick II, was only three years old.

Germany, the Empire, and the Papacy (1197–1216)

During the months immediately following Henry's death, the German nobles remained loyal to the Hohenstaufen dynasty and proposed that Philip of Swabia, Henry's younger brother, act as regent for his young nephew. Then, fearing the potentially divisive effects of a long regency, the princes offered Philip the crown. He accepted, and became king in 1198. The Guelph opposition then came forward with their own candidate, Otto of Brunswick, the youngest son of Frederick I's former enemy, Henry the Lion. Otto was the nephew of King Richard the Lionhearted, had been raised in England, and had the full support of the English in his fight for the German throne. Since the English were involved, the French, now ruled by Philip Augustus, rose to champion the Hohenstaufen cause. Within a year of Henry's death the civil wars had begun once again.

The Sicilian situation was even more chaotic because there were rebellions against the German nobles brought to Sicily by Henry to help administer the southern kingdom. Henry's widow Constance solved her difficulties by dying within a year of her husband's death. Before she died Constance had made the young Frederick a ward of the papacy, although he remained in Sicily, where he had been born, and was raised by Sicilian princes.

Pope Innocent III (1198–1216) and the "Imperial Business"

In 1198 the college of cardinals elected Innocent III to the papal throne. At the age of thirty-seven, Innocent III was the youngest member of the college of cardinals. He came from an old, aristocratic Roman family and had an exceptional aptitude for canon law, which he had studied at Bologna. The new pope was a man of many talents. A cool, worldly, and astute diplomat, he was involved in every political issue and major event in Europe and suffered few reversals. He was also sincerely devoted to reform and to spiritual renewal. The high point of Innocent's pontificate

North Sea

Baltic Sea

Lübeck

Elbe

SAXONY

POMERANIA

KINGDOM
OF
POLAND

Rhine

Cologne

BRANDENBURG

River

LORRAINE

River

NASSAU

Mainz

Worms

Bamberg

BOHEMIA

MORAVIA

Toul

FRANCONIA

Waiblingen

AUSTRIA

SLOVAKIA

ALSACE

Freiburg

Augsburg

Besançon

SWABIA

Constance

BAVARIA

Danube

Cluny

TRANSJURANA

BURGUNDY

KINGDOM OF HUNGARY

Legnano

KINGDOM
OF
BURGUNDY

Cortenuova

Milan

Brescia

LOMBARDY

Roncaglia

River

PROVENCE

Alessandria

ROMAGNA

Pisa

PAPAL

TUSCANY

MARCH OF ANCONA

STATES

SPOLETO

Adriatic

Sea

Rome

Sutri

Anagni

DUCHY OF ROME

San Germano

Naples

Benevento

Malfi

Salerno

KINGDOM OF SICILY

Mediterranean

Palermo

Sea

4. The Hohenstaufen Empire in the Late Twelfth Century

321

and of the medieval Church was the Fourth Lateran Council, which he summoned in 1215, and which dealt primarily—though not exclusively—with reform.

Innocent's election indicated a shift in attitude among the cardinals as to the position they felt should be taken in dealing with the imperial problem. Innocent was known to be tough-minded and aggressive in his insistence on the independence of the papacy and the papal states. His theory of papal power was made clear in a sermon early in his reign: "To me is said in the person of the prophet, 'I have set thee over nations and over kingdoms, to root and to pull down . . . . ' [Jeremiah 1:10] To me also is said in the person of the apostle, 'I will give to thee the keys of the kingdom of heaven . . . . ' Thus the others were called to a part of the care but Peter alone assumed the plenitude of power."[8] The important phrase is "plentitude of power," for Innocent never departed from his belief that the pope alone had been given the "fullness of power." He often compared papal and secular authority to the sun and the moon (the sun, which lights up the day, being, of course, the greater power). And Innocent regularly reminded his subjects that he had the authority to judge and penalize them "by reason of sin."

For a man of Innocent's conviction, courage, and skill, the situation in the empire when he became pope afforded the perfect opportunity to recover the papal lands which Henry VI had seized, to restore Sicily as a papal fief (as it had been under the Normans) and, above all, to prevent a revival of the Hohenstaufen plan to unite Germany and Sicily into a single empire and suffocate the papacy in the middle.

Innocent began by claiming that he alone had the right to decide between the claimants to the German throne on the ground that whoever became king would also become emperor and it was therefore the papal prerogative to determine which man he believed suitable for the imperial crown. Innocent at first delayed making any decision, so the civil wars dragged on, to the detriment of the royal power in Germany. Finally, in 1200 he gave his

8. Quoted in Brian Tierney, *The Crisis of Church and State: 1050–1300* (New Jersey: Prentice-Hall, 1964), pp. 131–132.

support to Otto of Brunswick, after extracting from Otto the promise of restoring the papal states to the pope and the guarantee of freedom from secular interference to the German church. But even Innocent could not make Otto a popular candidate in Germany. Gradually, some of Otto's original adherents began to give their loyalty to the Hohenstaufen candidate, Philip of Swabia, and eventually Innocent himself changed sides. He was ready to crown Philip when the latter was assassinated in 1208 (for personal, not political, reasons). So Innocent went back to Otto again. Before Otto was crowned he had to renew his promises to the pope. Once he was actually crowned, however, the emperor began an invasion of northern Italy and also went so far as to prepare an invasion of Sicily. Otto had become as much a Hohenstaufen as Henry VI had ever been, and it was at this juncture (in 1210) that Innocent turned to his ward, Frederick II, who was then only sixteen.

In return for Innocent's support, Frederick had to guarantee that he would relinquish the crown of Sicily as soon as the German throne was securely his. Like Otto, he also had to pledge non-interference with the papal states and freedom for the German church. Above all, he had to give assurance that he would not return to the Hohenstaufen plan to unite Germany and Italy. All these conditions were agreed to in a document called the Golden Bull of Eger in 1213. Within Germany, Frederick had the support of the Hohenstaufen party, leaderless since the death of his uncle Philip; from outside, he had the support of Philip Augustus of France, who depended on the alliance with the Hohenstaufen party as a counterweight to the alliance between the English and the Guelphs. It was due to these foreign alliances that the last major battle in the German civil wars was fought on French soil at Bouvines in 1214.

Philip Augustus and Frederick, backed by the pope, were victorious. Afterward, Frederick had additional hostilities to face in Germany, and there remained some formalities still to be observed, but the German and imperial crowns were now his. He had promised Innocent that once Germany was at peace he would relinquish the Sicilian throne, and he also took the vow to go on a crusade. Thus, before Innocent died in 1216, he was convinced—as well he might have been—that he had saved the papacy from the threat of Hohenstaufen encirclement and that the integrity of the papal states had been preserved. Nothing could have been further from the truth.

Frederick II: The End of the Papal-Imperial Conflict, 1216–1250

Frederick II was so complex and full of contradictions that he beggars description. He was a gifted man, so much so, and in so many areas, that he was called by his contemporaries *Stupor Mundi* (Wonder of the World). Frederick was in every way different from the other kings of the thirteenth century. Although he wrote theological treatises, he was not a pious man. Nothing in his nature allowed him to be subservient to anyone, and surely not to the papacy. He was severe in punishing heretics when he chose, but he was reportedly a skeptic in religious matters.

Frederick had an extraordinary intellect and the decided advantages of having been raised and educated in a kingdom that was intellectually far in advance of most of the rest of Europe. He had grown up in the Regno, a cosmopolitan world populated with Greeks, Muslims, Latins, and Jews. Frederick learned several languages (all of them well), including Greek and Arabic. He was a skilled mathematician and conducted his own experiments in the natural sciences. He also had a scholar's mastery of zoology, art, architecture, poetry, and philosophy. He was a great statesman and general, and when he settled down in Sicily, he showed himself to be a constructive ruler. But Frederick could also be fanatical, cruel (exceptionally so), and authoritarian. He was altogether a man to be reckoned with.

Frederick had no intention of giving up the Sicilian crown as he had promised the pope he would do. His first love and concern was his southern kingdom, and he seems to have cared little for Germany, which he viewed as merely an appendage to the Italian empire. Frederick defeated the last resistance to him in Germany in 1220 and then returned to the Regno. Before he left, he relinquished many of his royal rights to the nobility and placed his sons, Conrad and Henry, on the throne to act as his regents. Between 1220 and his death in 1250 he returned to Germany only once, and then only out of necessity.

The heart of Frederick's plan for an empire was Sicily, and it was from Sicily, with the help of Sicilian officials, that he intended to control all of Italy and Germany. Frederick's main interest in Germany was merely in preventing any uprising there that might curb his Italian plans. He was therefore ready to make concessions to the German princes in return for support that would free him to pursue his other aims. On one occasion he even supported the nobility against his son, Henry, who wanted to restore the German monarchy to a more solid base. But Frederick would not allow even his son's ambition in Germany to stand in the way of his Italian venture.

Frederick's Italian ambitions were certain to cause conflict with the papacy, but Honorius III (1216–1227) had been a long-suffering man, and the conflict did not break out until a new pope was elected in 1227. Gregory IX (1227–1241), who was anything but long-suffering, insisted that Frederick fulfill his vow to undertake a crusade, partly for the sake of recovering Jerusalem, but also partly because he wanted Frederick out of Italy. Frederick set sail from Brindisi in 1227, but immediately returned home because an epidemic had broken out among his sailors. Gregory, who suspected the epidemic was merely an excuse for postponing the crusade, excommunicated Frederick, and the next year Frederick went to the Holy Land without troubling to have the excommunication lifted. Gregory then excommunicated the emperor all over again. The whole affair of the crusade made the pope angry because by negotiating in Arabic with the sultan of Egypt (who then controlled Jerusalem) Frederick was actually able to recover Jerusalem, Nazareth, and Bethlehem from the Muslims.

In Frederick's absence the pope sent troops to recover Sicily, but when Frederick learned of this he returned (in 1229) and quickly defeated the papal troops to a conclusion of uneasy peace in 1230.

325

The following years were Frederick's most productive as a ruler. His code of laws for the Regno (called the Constitutions of Melfi and influenced by the revived *Codex Justinianus*) was the first secular code in Europe since the ancient Roman Empire. Frederick also encouraged the expansion of agriculture and trade, reformed the coinage, and issued a beautiful gold coin, the *augustales*, designed in imitation of the ancient Roman coins. Frederick's desire for a well-educated group of administrators, coupled with his own passion for learning, led to his founding the University of Naples in 1224.

The hostility between the emperor and the papacy simmered for several years, but neither Frederick's plan to control the northern, Lombard cities (in addition to the Regno) nor Gregory's plan to thwart that aim had been abandoned. By the time warfare broke out again in 1236, the papacy and the northern cities, which had regrouped once again into the Lombard League, joined forces to fight Frederick. At the time of Gregory's death in 1241 Frederick's armies were besieging Rome. Frederick then withdrew his forces and devoted his efforts instead to trying to have a friendly pope elected. This was not to happen. The new pope (whom it took the college of cardinals two years to elect) was Innocent IV (1243–1254) and he was absolutely relentless in his opposition to the emperor.

Innocent decided to hold an ecumenical council at Rome, at which he planned to depose Frederick. Frederick's fleet attacked the ships carrying the prelates to Rome, and two cardinals and more than a hundred other clerics were thrust into jail. Frederick had succeeded in delaying the council; he had also succeeded in convincing the pope—if indeed any convincing were necessary— that the Hohenstaufen had to be eliminated for good. In 1245 Innocent managed to hold his council at Lyons; he absolved Frederick's subjects from allegiance to him, deposed Frederick, and determined to deal wih Sicily himself, as he saw fit.

The papal action was simply a further call to arms for Frederick. It also elicited a letter from Frederick to his fellow monarchs, making clear that his resistance to papal power was in the interests of all secular rulers. "You and all kings of particular regions," he wrote, "have everything to fear from the effrontery of such a prince of priests when he sets out to depose us who have been divinely honored by the imperial diadem and solemnly elected by the princes . . . and this when it is no concern of his to inflict any punishment on us for temporal injuries. . . ."[9]

The war, of course, continued. It was costly and difficult for both sides, and nothing was settled when Frederick died of dysentery in December of 1250. He was buried in the cathedral at Palermo in the country he loved. Still, the war dragged on. The imperial armies were first led by Frederick's son Conrad, who died in 1254. They were then led by an illegitimate son, Manfred, who established himself in Sicily. At this juncture the papacy arrived at an agreement with Louis IX of France, who sent his younger brother, Charles of Anjou, to aid the pope in return for the crown of Sicily. Charles was able to defeat Manfred in 1266, and the next year Manfred was killed. The last of Frederick's male descendants was his grandson Conradin, who, at fifteen, tried to lead the Hohenstaufen forces but was defeated and captured by the French in 1268. The youth was brought to Naples and beheaded, if not by papal order, at least with the pope's certain knowledge.

The Aftermath of the Papal-Imperial Conflict

The period in German history from the death of Conrad IV in 1254 until the election of a new king in 1273 is called, somewhat inappropriately, the interregnum. The problem was that there were too many kings—or at any rate, too many contenders— rather than none. Now it was not only the German princes fighting among themselves but foreign rulers also who tried to seize or purchase the crown. Finally, in 1273 the princes decided to give the throne to Rudolf of Hapsburg, duke of Austria. Their intention was to bring about peace by enthroning a family which could be

9. Ibid.

The Apocalypse: The First Trumpet Sounded: The First Woe. *This illustration from the Revelation of John, is one of a series illuminating a German apocalypse of the fourteenth century. In this scene, the forces of evil are represented as secular rulers. Notice that the figures which are emerging from the furnace and their leader (as well as the horse he rides) are all wearing royal crowns.* (THE METROPOLITAN MUSEUM OF ART, THE CLOISTERS COLLECTION, 1968)

easily controlled, and one which would not attempt to reassert a strong centralized government. This is exactly what was accomplished, and with few exceptions, the Hapsburg dynasty kept its throne throughout all sorts of political changes for centuries.

Under Frederick I it had appeared that the German monarchy would be able to overcome the decentralization and weakness of royal authority that had begun during the investiture controversy. Frederick had worked within the feudal structure that existed in Germany by the mid-twelfth century, but the future of the central government depended very much on the continuance of his policies. The crucial period came during the reign of Frederick II. Brilliant and bold in his imperial venture, the second Frederick dissipated royal power by allowing the princes to rule Germany in his absence. At the same time, the old duchies were broken up into several smaller ones, there were new groupings among the nobility, and there were more noblemen with power.

The failure of the Hohenstaufen to subordinate the princes to royal government did not mean that from then onward Germany was in political chaos. It meant, instead, that authority was asserted within the smaller political units. The monarchy, however, never recovered the power that had once given promise of centralizing and unifying Germany; and until the late nineteenth century Germany was not a united country.

The Hohenstaufen attempts to weld Germany and Italy into a single empire were the last significant efforts to unite even that much of Christendom as a single commonwealth. Now and then a German king dreamed of controlling northern Italy, as some even attempted to do, but by the thirteenth century there was neither the energy nor the popular interest for such an enterprise. The idea of a single Christian commonwealth had ended with the failure of Frederick II's imperial dream. The longing that remained for the empire was expressed mainly in literature. It is as if the more disjointed political life became, the greater was the nostalgia for the Roman imperial unity. But the empire, in political reality, had been eclipsed by the power of the "kings of particular regions." And the failure of the German monarchy meant that the true royal power in Europe now belonged only to the kings of England and France.

Italy was more divided after the papal-imperial struggle than it had ever been before. The northern Italian cities maintained the freedom they had gained in the wars against the empire, and though they often had to struggle hard to keep that freedom, their conflicts were mainly with each other. Whether as a cause or a result of their fierce independence, the northern cities went on to become richer from trade and industry than before, developing, in the fourteenth and fifteenth centuries, a beautiful and artistic culture.

The popes did not regain Sicily, and the Regno itself was divided before the end of the thirteenth century. When Charles of Anjou had brought his French troops into Sicily, he had done so with the understanding that the Regno would become an Angevin possession. And so it was, but not for long. In 1282 there was an uprising against the Angevins, called the Sicilian Vespers. The Angevins lost the island of Sicily, though they were able to retain control of southern Italy, then renamed the Kingdom of Naples. In the course of a complicated political intrigue, the island of Sicily became a Spanish possession.

The papal victory over the Hohenstaufen had been dearly bought, and yielded no material gains; and the papacy had lost more in spiritual prestige than it gained in political security in Italy. The lengths to which the papacy had been willing to go to destroy the Hohenstaufen, the amount spent on the wars, and the allies called into Italy to finish the fight against the Germans, had all caused much European dissatisfaction with the papal office. And the victory surely had not brought about the unity of Christendom under papal leadership. This, then, was a chapter with a sorry ending in the papacy's struggle—similar in many respects to the royal struggles—to bring unity to the church and then to all Christendom.

Religious Life in the Twelfth and Thirteenth Centuries

During the twelfth century, the unity of the church and the papal leadership of all Christendom were closer to being realities than ever before. We have seen how, in the wake of the reform movement at the end of the eleventh century, the papacy established its own administrative system and the institutions through which to govern the churches. Directed by the pope and the college of cardinals and administered by the *curia* and a bureaucracy of officials, the church's functions became more complex and more highly centralized in this later medieval period. These functions were the lifeblood of the church—the monastic orders, missionary activities, orphanages, hospitals, schools, pastoral care, and crusades. All were crucial to the order and well-being of the Christian commonwealth. The developments in canon law led to the codification and uniformity of the church's laws and the growth of ecclesiastical courts throughout Europe. All the great popes from the mid-twelfth through the thirteenth century were trained in canon law, and the papal court became the highest court of appeals in the church, increasingly busy as more and more disputes over appointments, elections, and jurisdictional questions were referred to Rome.

The respect with which the papacy was regarded in Christendom derived, to begin with, from the victory won at the time of the investiture controversy and from papal leadership in the crusading movement. Above all, the papacy's greatest strength during the twelfth century, and culminating in the pontificate of Innocent III (1198–1216), derived from its leadership of the reform movement.

Religious Movements of the Twelfth Century

There was, at the same time, a restlessness in religious life among laymen which led to a great increase of popular religious and reform movements in Europe. At the heart of these new movements was a deep sense of spiritual devotion which found expression in a variety of different ways, some orthodox and some not. The desire for a life of religious purity—the same impulse which had led to the reform movements of the tenth and eleventh centuries—remained strong in the twelfth century and was channeled now in several different directions. Underlying the growing religious diversity was the wish for a rigorous personal spiritual experience which meant for many people a reaffirmation of the past, and a return to the way of life of the early apostles and the desert saints as well as to the separateness, dedication, and poverty of the early Christians. For some the return to the purity of the primitive church and its early saints meant a total renunciation of the world; for others it included an even more extreme puritanism and mortification of the flesh; for still others, it meant a return to preaching as an emulation of the apostles and early missionaries.

Within the church's traditional organization, the best model for the seclusion and asceticism of the desert saints (while serving as a reproach to the less severe orders) was the Cistercian order. This austere order had an impressive growth in the twelfth century: 530 monastic houses within a hundred years. We have seen how these "puritans of the church," as they have been called, sought out wildernesses in order to re-create the hardships of the early saints. In time, however, the world caught up with the Cistercians—or they with the world, it is difficult to know which. They were so successful in their agricultural enterprises that they became wealthy entrepreneurs, and even moneylenders, and in the thirteenth century the order fell away from the uncompromising purity with which it had begun. St. Bernard, who claimed not even to see the beauties with which nature itself is adorned, would have been shocked at the luxury of the order in its later history. But during the twelfth century the Cistercians remained close to their reforming principles.

The spirit of withdrawal found expression in another way which was separate from, though not opposed to, the framework of the church. During the twelfth and thirteenth centuries there were many men and women in Europe who chose to live as recluses, quite alone except for someone nearby to supply them with food and water. Some lived in the shadow of a monastery, and the monks came and fed them. As the towns grew up during this period there were others who lived near the city gates, and still others who lived in cells attached to the town churches. Many of these anchorites and anchoresses were enclosed in their cells for life, and the church had a formal ceremony of enclosure for them, performed by a cleric.

This life of withdrawal within a monastery or an anchorite's cell was not a vocation for everyone, and a less extreme way was found by the men and women who began the orders of canons. These were groups of devoted, selfless men or women who wished to live according to a communal rule while also serving society, caring for the sick, burying the dead, rebuilding churches, and doing whatever seemed to be needed. They adapted a rule which had been written by St. Augustine earlier than the Benedictine Rule, that was neither so specific nor so strict as the latter in its delineation of the monastic life. The followers of the Augustinian Rule formed communities and took vows of poverty, celibacy, and obedience, and then went out into the world to work among the needy. There were many different groups of them, including some clergy attached to the cathedrals who took monastic vows and then continued their work among their parishioners. This recognition of the need to work among the people, especially in the towns, is an indication of the social problems that were emerging in the changing society of this later medieval period.

With the growth of towns there came a new class of urban poor who were suffering in the transition from rural to urban life. The solace and comfort they looked for from their parish priest was in many cases not forthcoming. We know from the evidence of the groups which rose to criticize the clergy (and at the beginning of the thirteenth century, from the attention paid by Innocent III to pastoral care) that the complaints of the poor were often justified. Many upper clergy were wealthy and in every way quite removed from their poorer parishioners. It was not that the clergy were more corrupt or immoral than in previous centuries, but rather that they were often not moral *enough* in an age when people identified the church with the church of the apostles. Here again, the desire for a personal religious experience and for more warmth and humanity from the church became evident. As the century wore on, the criticism grew louder that the clergy were simply not fulfilling their proper functions. Among the middle class the growth of literacy created higher expectations; people hoped for sermons that would help them find their way to a better Christian life within the world. So out of a variety of somewhat differing motives, people grew very responsive to the popular preachers.

Popular preachers became fairly common figures in the towns (and the countryside, as well) in the twelfth and thirteenth centuries. Many preached messages that were not heretical, or at least not to begin with. Some, like Arnold of Brescia in the mid-twelfth century, joined their criticisms of the clergy to the popular revolutionary movements in the Italian cities. Although the case of Rome was particular in the extreme since it was the seat of papal power, Arnold of Brescia's criticisms of the clergy's wealth and secular power—so different from the poverty of the apostolic Church—were not unique.

Heresy in the Twelfth Century

Criticism of the clergy was not in itself heretical. In fact, it came most of all from clerics and monks. Under some circumstances, however, the line between attacking clerical abuses and attacking the sacraments which the clergy performed could be easily crossed. Such was the case of Peter Waldo, a rich merchant of Lyons, who became imbued with the desire to lead a perfect Christian life and in 1173 gave away his worldly goods and began to preach. There was nothing heretical in that. He preached a life of poverty and apostolic simplicity and drew many followers, who were known as the Poor Men of Lyons, or the Waldensians. Then, hoping to discover the message of the Gospels, Waldo had some parts of the New Testament translated into the vernacular and began to preach from the Scriptures. Since he was not learned in theology, he fell into errors of interpretation, and the bishop of his diocese insisted that he stop preaching. Waldo then went before the pope at the Third Lateran Council (in 1179) and, after being examined on doctrinal matters, was permitted to continue living in apostolic simplicity with his adherents, but no longer permitted to preach. Waldo was also subjected to some humiliation at the council: He was ridiculed by some of the learned prelates with whom he could not have hoped to compete on theological grounds.

Peter Waldo's conviction that preaching was a necessary part

334

of the apostolic life led him to continue to preach after he had been forbidden to do so, and in 1184 he was condemned for disobedience. In a sense Waldo was then driven to heresy, because the church did not make room for him and his followers at the point when the Waldensians were critical only of the clergy but not of the whole sacramental system for salvation. It was a simple step, finally, from Waldo's belief that the apostolic church, without an elaborate clergy and without the sacraments, was the only true church, to the view that the Roman church had fallen away from its true origins. The Waldensians now formed their own church, based on the belief that faith and the apostolic life were all that were necessary for salvation. The Waldensians became extremely active and successful missionaries. In spite of the efforts of the church of Rome to stamp out the movement, it spread through Italy and France into Spain, and even to parts of eastern Europe. Through all the travails which the sect endured, the Waldensian church, though very small, has survived to this day.

The Cathars, or Albigensians, as they are popularly known (so-called because of their strength in Albi, in the county of Toulouse) were heretics of a different stamp from the Waldensians. They began as a heretical movement, and defined themselves from the start as a church in opposition to the Roman church and all its teachings. The Cathars were not disaffected reformers, as were the Waldensians, nor were they popular revolutionaries, as the Roman followers of Arnold of Brescia has been. The immediate source of the Catharist heresy was the Bogomils, a sect which began in Bulgaria, spread to Byzantium during the tenth and eleventh centuries, and then to northern Italy and southern France when in the twelfth century trade and contact between East and West became more frequent.

The basic Catharist tenet was the dualist belief in the division between good and evil. In this view, God created only the things of the spirit, and Satan created all material things: Spirit is therefore good, and all material things are evil, and there is a constant battle between the forces of good and the forces of evil, between spirit and matter. For the Catharists, the soul was good, the body evil. The perfect life was one devoid of material things. The Cathars

Propaganda against the Albigensians. *Much of what we know about the Albigensians comes from the opposition. In this medallion from a moralized Bible, the heretics, identified as "Perfecti" by their hoods, are seen seducing Christian women. This scene is used as an allegory of the destruction of Christian dogma by the Cathars. The fox with the burning tail symbolizes the heretics destroying Christianity by fire. The number of women in the illustration, although intended to be unfriendly, attests to the fact that women were greatly attracted to heretical movements in the late Middle Ages.* (MS BODLEY 270[b] FOL. 123[v])

did not eat meat and were altogether very ascetic. They preached sexual abstinence because they believed it sinful to bring more bodies into the world. They rejected the Roman church, believing that the only true church was that of the spirit, and that the visible church was the creation of Satan. They rejected the Incarnation of Christ because they did not believe that the Son of God could be reincarnated as a man. They rejected the sacraments (and of course the clergy who performed them) and believed that salvation could come only through repentence and rejection of the worldly church. The Cathars could then become "perfect," after receiving the *consolamentum*, or "consolation," from one of the "perfected." They were divided into the "perfect" and the "believers." The "believers" could go on living their normal lives until they were on their deathbeds, at which time, if they repented, they could be assured of salvation. The "perfect" followed the ascetic principles of Catharism and formed a kind of priestly group.

The Albigensian heresy had a wide appeal for many different reasons. In southern France, and particularly Toulouse, the church was known for its wealth and the clergy for its lack of spirituality. Thus the lives of the "perfected" were respected all the more in contrast to the worldliness of the local clergy. The Albigensians furnished a community and a fellowship for individuals already dissatisfied with the church. This community was appealing to women because it treated them on an equality with men, and the doctrine of celibacy released them from the burdens of marriage and childbirth. There was also undoubtedly some appeal in the fact that "believers" could live as they wished until close to the end of their lives, when they could then become "perfected" and be assured of the kingdom of heaven. The support of many southern French nobility was an important factor in the long survival of the Albigensian heresy. Some of the nobility joined the Cathars, while many more were protective of them because the heresy accorded with their own desire to divest the churches of their wealth and reduce the power of the local clergy.

It is perhaps true, as some historians have maintained, that the papacy did not recognize the extent of the Catharist heresy until, from the papal point of view, it was too late. The Cathars were condemned in the 1180s, and the papacy attempted by peaceful measures of persuasion to bring them back into the Roman church. At the beginning of his reign, Innocent III still hoped that peaceful measures would succeed, and he sent preachers into southern France to try to convert the heretics. Preaching was not successful, and Innocent appealed to Philip Augustus to wage a crusade against the Albigensians, but Philip refused due to more pressing business with the English.

Finally in 1208, when Innocent's legate to Toulouse was murdered, the pope called for a crusade against the Albigensians. Although Philip Augustus still refused to lead it, he permitted the northern French nobility to participate. Christians as well as heretics were slaughtered. There is a story that before the city of Beziers was attacked by the crusaders, the papal representative present was reminded that there were Christians in the city. He is then supposed to have said, "Kill them all, the Lord will know his own." True or not, this sums up the temper of the moment and the intransigence of the defenders of the faith.

The crusade did not end until 1223, and by the time it was over, the Catharist movement had been almost totally wiped out.[10] Those Cathars still alive were hunted down and brought to trial. Unless they recanted, the Cathars were severely punished and usually condemned to death. Small groups did manage to escape and some continued to practice their religion, which persisted as late as the fourteenth century. But the strength of the heresy had been broken once and for all.

One of the by-products of the Catharist heresy was the establishment of special courts, responsible solely to the papacy, for trying heretics. This task was not left to local ecclesiastical authorities because they had been neither reliable nor successful in ferreting out the heretics, and also because the trials required special training in theology. Although as a regular procedure the Inquisition was not formalized until shortly after 1231, these courts set up to exact confessions from the heretics in southern France were its beginning. Incontrovertibly, the Inquisition was an unsavory institution since, among other things, it allowed torture and people could be accused without being allowed to confront their accusers. To those who operated the Inquisition, however, the method seemed of course less important than the possibility that it would restore individuals to the "right" belief and save their souls.

The Orders of Friars:
St. Dominic and St. Francis

Throughout the twelfth century there was a great increase in the numbers of traditional monastic houses. The increase was so large that an act of the Fourth Lateran Council, held by Innocent III in

10. The decisive defeat of the Cathars had taken place at the battle of Muret in 1213.

1215, prohibited the founding of any new orders. There were two exceptions, however. These were the orders of friars, the Dominicans and Franciscans, both of which brought a new spirit into the church.

St. Dominic (1170–1221) was a well-educated Spanish cleric who found his life's work in the fight against the Catharist heresy in southern France. The first—and accidental—encounter between Dominic and the heretics occurred when he passed through southern France on a mission for the Spanish church. At some point between 1200 and 1207, Dominic returned to France with his purpose clearly in mind and set out to win back the heretics by the force of his preaching and his arguments. He gathered followers, and though they were still few in number at the time of the Fourth Lateran Council, he went to appeal for confirmation to the pope. Two factors were against Dominic's confirmation. The council had decided that no new orders would be founded, and more important, Dominic's plan for his order was a departure from monastic tradition.

Dominic envisioned that his order would carry on his own work, and that instead of being cloistered, the monks would be preachers in the world, fighting heretics and also teaching the believers. It was the wandering nature of the preachers more than anything else which set the Dominicans apart from the traditional orders. The order was confirmed after much discussion, and it grew quickly thereafter, attracting to it men who wanted to combine an ascetic life with an intellectually demanding one, all in the service of the church. The Dominicans were eventually placed in charge of the Inquisition in southern France (and sometimes elsewhere in Europe as well) from which they received the unfortunate appelation which is a play on the word *Dominican* in Latin: They were called *Domini canes,* or "hounds of God."

The Dominicans adopted the Franciscan ideal of poverty, although they did not adhere to it in the strict and literal sense in which Francis himself had done. The Franciscans, for their part— as we shall see—became divided themselves, as the order grew during the thirteenth century, over the question of the practicality and validity of maintaining the rule of absolute poverty.

339

In 1210 a slight, barefoot man in a brown robe tied with a cord around the waist came before Innocent to ask for confirmation of the rule he had written for himself and his twelve followers. He was St. Francis, the sweetest and, surely, the best loved of all the medieval saints (and most likely of all the church's saints). Innocent gave verbal approval to the rule, thus drawing into the church a movement which for the magnanimity of its spirit has no equal.

St. Francis (1181–1226) was born in the northern Italian hill town of Assisi. His father was a wealthy cloth merchant who fully expected Francis to carry on the family business and perhaps even become a knight. Francis' youth was similar to that of the other young men from wealthy families with whom he grew up. It was an easy life, and Francis was spirited and loved wine, women, and song as much as anyone. But then, in stages, he began his conversion to a life devoted to God. The most important, and final, incident was in the chapel of the church of San Damiano in Assisi, where he heard a voice telling him to repair the building. Francis went home, took some cloth from his father's business, sold it to raise money, and then gave the money for the necessary repair to the church. Francis' father was so enraged when he learned what his son had done that he demanded the return of the money and went so far as to bring Francis before the bishop of Assisi. When the bishop told the young man to obey his parent, Francis took off all his clothes and returned them to his father.

From that time on Francis obeyed only his "father" in heaven. That was in 1208, and by the following year Francis had begun to preach and to gather around him his twelve companions. The essence of Francis' spirit and his calling is contained in particular in two passages in the Bible. One is from St. Matthew (19:21), in which Jesus says, "If thou wouldst be perfect, go, sell what thou hast, and give to the poor, . . . and come and follow me." The other is from St. Luke (9:1–6) and tells how Jesus called the apostles together and "sent them to preach the kingdom of God and to heal the sick. And he said unto them, take nothing for your journey. . . ." A life devoted to preaching the word of God to all God's creatures, and a life of absolute poverty were the bases

Innocent III Approving the Rule of St. Francis. Fresco in the Upper Church of St. Francis of Assisi. (ALINARI/EDITORIAL PHOTOCOLOR ARCHIVES, INC.)

341

of the simple rule which Francis presented to Pope Innocent III in 1210, and which the pope in his wisdom allowed.

Francis had no intention of founding an order. He wanted only to devote himself to a life of apostolic simplicity, poverty, and preaching. The most lovable thing about Francis is that his devotion to God and poverty was joyful. He threw off the shackles of the world's goods to love God and His flock with greater freedom, and to go among them with the utmost humility. Hence the name of his little group of followers from the beginning was *frateres minores*, or "lesser brothers." Nothing is more beautiful than the story that St. Francis preached to the birds in perfect faith that all God's creatures could understand the word of God. And if the many lovely legends surrounding Francis' life are to be believed, he was perfectly understood.

Francis resisted the formation of an order as much as possible, but he attracted a large number of followers and one was formed and officially confirmed in 1223. Three years later Francis died, having supposedly received on his body the stigmata, the wounds which Christ sustained when being nailed to the Cross.

The Dominicans and Franciscans represent a new and different spirit within the church because they reflect the popular reform movements during the twelfth century. The Franciscan ideal, particularly, is an outgrowth of the popular desire for a closer communion with God and for more humanity and compassion for the human condition. The essence of the traditional monastic spirit is withdrawal and contemplation, but the orders of friars were formed for preaching and teaching, for work among the people, and—in the case of the Franciscans—as an example of poverty and humility. The Franciscans and Dominicans modified one another's character. The Franciscans adopted the Dominican devotion to education and in the thirteenth century contributed many important intellectual leaders to the universities.

The Dominican order was officially approved at the Fourth Lateran Council in 1215, and although the Franciscans were confirmed later (in 1223), it was Innocent III who decided that the church would embrace St. Francis. Both decisions were in accord with the pope's intention to maintain control over the reform

An early (mid-13th c.) drawing by Matthew Paris, *representing St. Francis preaching to the birds.* (BY PERMISSION OF THE MASTER AND FELLOWS OF CORPUS CHRISTI COLLEGE, CAMBRIDGE)

movement, and it was the spirit in which Innocent called the Fourth Lateran Council.

The Fourth Lateran Council of 1215

"[O]f all the desires of our heart," Innocent wrote to the prelates whom he summoned to the Council, "we long chiefly for two in this life, namely, that we may work successfully to recover the Holy Land and to reform the Universal Church. . . ."[11]

The problem of the Holy Land was pressing because the third crusade (1189–1192) had failed to recover Jerusalem and the fourth crusade (1204) had never even reached its destination (resulting instead in the capture of Constantinople). So Innocent preached the fifth crusade, and at the Council Frederick II took crusader's vows and promised to set off for Jerusalem as soon as he could settle his affairs in Germany.

The Council approved all the political decisions Innocent had taken during his pontificate and then set out to enact laws, or canons, which had as their main purpose the uniformity of practice and belief within the Roman church. During the twelfth century, as the discipline of canon law had evolved, much work had been done by the canonists to codify the church's laws and make them uniform. Now, at the Fourth Lateran Council, that work was continued and new laws were enacted, designed, as Innocent said, "to uproot vices and implant virtues, to correct abuses and reform morals. . . ."

Of the seventy canons adopted, a few deserve special attention. The number of the sacraments, which had not been formalized before, was established at seven, as they remain today. As a discipline, all Christians were required to confess their sins to a priest at least once a year and then receive the sacrament of the Eucharist. The miracle which occurs during the performance of the Eucharist was also formally defined; it is the doctrine of transubstantiation,

11. The quotations from Innocent III and the Fourth Lateran Council are from Marshall Baldwin, *Christianity Through the Thirteenth Century* (New York: Harper and Row, 1970), pp. 293, 294, 308.

and it means that, although the bread and wine used to commemorate the Last Supper remain outwardly the same, they miraculously become the body and blood of Christ.

Innocent was deeply concerned with the pastoral functions of the clergy because he recognized the need for that compassion and understanding which St. Francis and the friars had brought into the church. Many laws were enacted to instill in the clergy a devotion to the flock entrusted to their care, and to keep them free of the abuses which had elicited so much criticism since, as one of the canons states, "Nothing is more injurious to the church of God than the selection of unworthy prelates for the direction of souls."

The council enacted several laws with regard to the Jews. Innocent expressly discouraged—or tried to discourage—their overt persecution, as well as their forced conversion. But the second-class status of Jews was clearly defined, as was the necessity for Christians to refrain from close relations with them. The most famous—or infamous—law was the one which required Jews to wear special dress to set them apart from the Christian community. (This law applied also to Muslims, although their presence in Christian lands was so restricted as to present little danger of their not being identified.) A Catholic historian, commenting on these laws, says that "Innocent saw his world as one without neutrals; to the point that Jews were not fully a part of that world, they were thought of as its enemies."[12] Considered in the light of this statement, the crusades against Muslims and heretics and the legislation against the Jews are all of a piece with the insistence on unity—the effort, as Innocent himself put it, "to allay differences."

At his death in 1216 Innocent had seemingly accomplished most of the "desires of his heart"—reform, the promise of a crusade against Islam, and uniformity of the church's laws and Christian practices. The Fourth Lateran Council can thus be considered the culmination of papal leadership of the reform movement: All the reforming elements that had arisen had been either incorporated

12. Edward A. Synan, *The Popes and the Jews in the Middle Ages* (New York: Macmillan, 1965), p. 87.

into the church or anathematized, all differences now outwardly allayed. But the events following Innocent's death show how precarious was the balance he had so skillfully maintained.

The Decline of Papal Leadership

Innocent had stressed the urgency of the need for reform which, along with the recovery of Jerusalem, he declared required "attention so immediate as to preclude further apathy or delay unless at the risk of great and serious danger." Although there is some rhetoric in this statement, there is also truth in it. There was risk for the church in the thirteenth century: a loss of confidence in the papacy, and a widening cleavage between the clergy and the laity.

Its desire to direct society according to Christian laws, and the insistence on unity—"a world without neutrals"—led the papacy to become increasingly legalistic and increasingly involved with "treasures on earth." From the pontificate of Innocent III onward, there was a steady growth of papal financial assets and of papal concern with the *camera*, the department in charge of all church revenues. The papacy's financial exactions in the thirteenth century had two aspects: One was the means devised to raise money; the other was the purpose for which money was used.

Soon after Innocent III's death, the church began its protracted and bitter struggle against the Hohenstaufen, and the need for money to wage those wars was great. Innocent III had levied the first income tax on the clergy to raise money for a crusade; from then on the tax became a regular assessment. But this was not enough to support the extraordinary expenses incurred in the thirteenth century, so other, smaller taxes were levied on the churches of Europe. One of the important new devices was to "reserve" to itself the right to make appointments to the higher ecclesiastical offices in churches and monasteries. In other words, the pope retained the right to "provide" (appoint) an ecclesiastic to fill a certain archbishopric or bishopric as that office became vacant. The tax on these "reserved" benefices was customarily as high as

346

the entire income for the first year of the appointment. This use of "reservations" and "provisions" was begun slowly but became more frequent as the thirteenth century went on, and by the fourteenth century it had become a regular practice.

There was now no check on the pope's authority to centralize the papal monarchy, raise taxes, or take over the right of appointing local ecclesiastical officials. This "plenitude of power" meant, from a legal point of view, that there was nothing the pope could not do (though there might be some things he would not do), that there were no legal limitations on his sovereign power.

There was more than a hint in the 1250s and 1260s, however, of where the attacks on this sovereignty were to come from. The first signs were in the objections to papal policy in England during the reign of Henry III and, in France, during the reign of St. Louis. When Henry's barons revolted, it was in no small measure because he had allowed the clergy to be taxed excessively by the pope, because he himself had willingly drained money from England to pay for the papal wars against the Hohenstaufen, and because he had allowed himself to be beguiled into trying for the crown of Sicily. In France, King Louis IX himself supported the French clergy in their objections to the papal policy of "reservations" to the French church.

That so much money was being used to fight the Hohenstaufen was not lost upon the laity of England and France. There were two aspects, in particular, of that bitter struggle which did not go unnoticed or uncriticized. The popes themselves had diverted the crusading ideal in proclaiming a crusade against the Hohenstaufen. For a crusade against the Albigensians there had been at least some justification because the latter were heretics and counted, therefore, as enemies no less than the Muslims. But the Hohenstaufen were papal enemies because they had challenged papal supremacy and because they threatened the foundations of the church's temporal power in the papal states. The cynical use of a crusade to wipe out the Hohenstaufen and the lengths to which the papacy was willing to go to preserve its possessions aroused many criticisms, one of the loudest criticisms being that the papacy's possessions were its curse. The gulf between the papal monarchy, with its vast bureaucracy administering its legal and financial business, and the apostolic church was becoming wider.

The breach between the clergy and the laity was also widening. The intention of the reforming popes, starting with Gregory VII, had been to disengage the laity from the internal affairs of the church. In the process, the clergy as a group became more distinct from the laity than they had ever been. This need not have been a negative factor in the church's relations with the laity, but in the twelfth century, as we have seen, the gulf was not so tolerable to the laity. It was just this gap which Innocent III had hoped to close by legislating, at the Fourth Lateran Council, on the duties and character of priests engaged in pastoral care. And it was precisely this gap which the Franciscans in particular had been brought into the church to close. But here another paradox developed to trouble the church.

The essence of the Franciscan spirit lay in the joyful devotion to preaching and to poverty, and in the compassion with which the Franciscans approached those whom they served. The papacy had no intention of changing that motivation; on the contrary, the papal hope was that this spirit would work to bring the laity closer to the church. Two developments grew out of the fact that the friars became the good right arm of the papacy. The secular clergy resented the friars, who were able to preach and to do other good works without approval or supervision of the local ecclesiastical authorities. Papal support of the friars against the secular clergy, when there was conflict, led to dissension between the clergy and the friars and between the clergy and the papacy. The latter development was of even greater fundamental importance.

Once the Franciscan order had been confirmed and the Franciscans had begun to teach, preach, and become missionaries to distant Eastern lands, they were confronted with the need for houses, and then by the need for revenue to support their activities. The situation became more complex as the order increased in size. While the main body of the Franciscans accepted the necessity of having houses, and of having what income seemed necessary, there developed a rift between those who insisted on observing the rule of absolute poverty (as St. Francis had done in his lifetime) and those who saw the need to modify the original rule. The strict adherents of "Lady Poverty" were known as the Fraticelli (Little Brothers), or the Spirituals. They wanted the order to rid itself of its houses and return to begging for whatever was required. This individualistic and otherworldly spirit was much admired, though the Spirituals convinced neither the other Franciscans (the Conventuals) nor the papacy of their position.

To add to their difficulties, the Spirituals adopted the heretical ideas of the monk Joachim of Flora, who had died in 1202. Joachim had been a mystic and a believer in the millennium. He had interpreted prophecies in the New Testament, predicting that a new age was to come about when the visible church would pass away and the Holy Spirit would reign supreme. The Spirituals believed that the herald of this new age was St. Francis, and that the year of the crisis which would usher in the era of the Holy Spirit was 1260. The crisis did not, of course, arrive—at least not in the sense anticipated. At about the same time, however, the rift within the Franciscan order became greater, and the last Franciscan General— that is, the head of the order—who was genuinely sympathetic to the Spirituals was overthrown. From about the 1260s onward, the Spirituals became more extreme in their insistence on poverty, wanting it not only for themselves, but advocating and then insisting on it for the papacy and the entire church.

The Spirituals were symptomatic and representative of several changes that were occurring in religious life. They were forced out of the church for the very reasons the Franciscans had in the first place been welcomed into it. St. Francis and his adherents had originally represented the heart of the reforming movement— the desire to return to a life of apostolic simplicity. This devotion to the apostolic life, which carried with it the wish for a personal experience of God, became stronger than ever in the thirteenth century. It was not yet, in the middle decades of the century, a direct attack on the papacy, but it was a criticism of the papal temporal power and the wealth of the church. That the Spirituals were rejected and then repeatedly attacked by the church points up the changed attitude of the papacy toward criticism and dissent. As that criticism became louder, the papacy grew firmer in the

The Apocalypse; St. John's vision of the New Jerusalem, from a German manuscript, 14th c. *The new age, heralded by Joachim of Flora, was equated in popular imagination with the coming of the "new Jerusalem," as foretold in the Revelation of St. John 21:1–2: "Then I saw a new heaven and a new earth, for the first heaven and the first earth had vanished, and there was no longer any sea. I saw the holy city, new Jerusalem, coming down out of heaven from God . . ."* (THE METROPOLITAN MUSEUM OF ART; THE CLOISTERS COLLECTION, 1968)

assertion of its own orthodoxy and more determined to resist diversity.

The period from the Fourth Lateran Council to the 1270s was an important stage in ecclesiastical history because in those decades the papacy lost its leadership of the reforming movement. The papal insistence on uniformity had led the Church to become less

350

and less flexible in its attitude towards those who wished for a personal experience of God (separate from, but not necessarily in opposition to, the Church). Perhaps the most serious lesson learned from the papal struggles to quiet the Spirituals was that to resist diversity was to encourage it.

Nor was the papacy any more flexible in its behavior toward the "kings of particular regions." Innocent III had been quite wise when he had tied together in equal importance the necessity for reform and the crusade to recover Jerusalem. The ecclesiastical leadership of the crusade had been perhaps the best indication of the papacy's international character and the crusades had transcended—at least initially—nationalism. But at the time of the first crusade there had been no firm boundaries and no strong monarchies (or none strong enough to resist papal claims to universality). The papacy's belief in a unified Christian commonwealth, centered in the See of St. Peter, remained as firm after the wars with the Hohenstaufen as it had been at the start. But by then, the political world had changed. The canon lawyers still could legislate for unity, but these laws became harder to implement as the resistance to the universal authority of the pope became stronger. By the 1270s Europe had arrived at the last stages before the final dissolution of medieval unity.

Epilogue:
The Great Crisis

The hundred years from the 1270s to the 1370s was a period of crisis and change—in certain clear ways the end of the medieval experience. The essential character of medieval civilization during the twelfth and most of the thirteenth century was its unitary nature—one church, governed from Rome, and the belief in a single Christian society. This framework, within which medieval culture had so luxuriantly flourished, began, in the last decades of the thirteenth century, to show signs of dissolution.

As the century drew to a close, the indications became stronger and more insistent that the papacy was having difficulty controlling religious unrest and tension. Confronted by strong monarchies, the international hegemony of the pope was harder to maintain and, in the last decade of the century, became the object of an attack so severe that it never completely recovered. By the 1270s it was apparent that reason and revelation would go their separate ways and that the synthesis so carefully constructed by St. Thomas would not last. And one of the most cherished assumptions of the Middle Ages—that all knowledge could be brought into harmony with Christianity—was shattered.

Underlying these changes were a serious economic contraction and a decline in population which began slowly in the closing decades of the thirteenth century and gained momentum during the fourteenth. The accomplishments and innovations of the later medieval period had been sustained and encouraged by an expanding economy and a growing population. Prosperity had given

353

people a new lease on life, and an abundance of energy had been poured into every human endeavor. This pattern of growth was now replaced by one of decline, and fourteenth-century Europeans entered into a period of prolonged hardship.

The Castastrophes of
the Fourteenth Century

Two major changes in agriculture had led to the increased production and expanding population of the later Middle Ages. The first was that more land was put under cultivation; the second was that qualitative advances were made, particularly the triennial system of crop rotation. For more than two centuries Europeans lived off these improvements, and the steady increase in prosperity and population continued. But no new technological advances were made, and once the intense period of colonization within and outside Europe had passed, no new land could easily be put under cultivation. By the mid-thirteenth century signs of an imbalance between Europe's population and its food supply began to appear, and by the last decades of the century there was no longer sufficient food.

The earliest signs of the declining food supply were the settlements made on very poor soil where yields were low. These had to be given up quickly because, after a few harvests, the ground simply did not produce enough to make it worth cultivating. By the early fourteenth century the problem of food supply could not, in any event, have been solved by trying to wrest crops from infertile soil.

There were acute shortages of grain, one of the most severe occurring in 1315–1317. Poor grain yields had certainly not been unknown, even at the peak period of prosperity in the preceding centuries, but insufficient harvests now became a regular feature of agricultural life. There were many famines, and large numbers of people starved. It appears likely that the shortages were due in part to a climatic change in Europe (particularly, more rainfall in the north) which adversely affected the grain crop and in England made it finally impossible to cultivate vineyards.

Although we know that during times of famine the poorer peasants in the rural areas surely starved, the townspeople were even worse off. The latter had to rely on imported grain, and in periods of food crisis not enough was available and prices rose exorbitantly. Several catastrophes then piled one on top of the other, with disastrous effects on the economy and populations of Europe. The first of these was war.

The fourteenth was a century of warfare. The Hundred Years War between France and England began officially in 1337, but in reality it started in the 1290s when Philip IV of France invaded Flanders. During much of the century there were also wars among the Italian city-states, wars in Sicily, and civil wars in Germany. These conflicts, especially between the French and English, lasted longer than any Europe had experienced internally during the preceding two hundred years and, moreover, the character of warfare itself had changed. The wars were now fought mainly by mercenaries. These soldiers for hire could fight for longer periods of time than the vassals of kings, whose tenure of service was limited by feudal law. The mercenaries were also greater in number, and they were professionals whose entire lives were devoted to fighting. They had not been trained to be chivalrous, and their warfare was brutal. In intervals of peace, the mercenary companies did not disband, having no land of their own and no other work for which they were trained. Instead, they pillaged and robbed the countryside, as much a scourge as any of the other pestilences of the century.

Another of the features of fourteenth-century warfare was the deliberate destruction of crops and land. Invading armies, such as the English in France, lived off French soil—or intended to. To prevent this the French would sometimes burn their own crops and slaughter their own animals. For whatever reason, the food did not reach the French people, and this pattern was repeated wherever there was fighting in Europe, so that after every major battle or every army's march through the countryside, land and crops lay ruined.

The new warfare was expensive in another way. The mercenaries were costly, so the rulers who hired them had continually to raise taxes and find new ways to exact money from their subjects. When taxes and other aids were not sufficient, the kings began to debase the coinage, adding to the overall financial instability that had already been evident before the mid-fourteenth century. And then another terrible crisis hit Europe.

In 1348–1349 the Black Death, or bubonic plague, was brought into Europe by Genoese sailors who had contracted it in a port on the Black Sea. The total figure for the death rate from the plague in Europe is difficult to confirm, but it was at least as high as a quarter of the population and may have been as high as a third. The disease struck Italy first. Then, from the port of Marseilles, it spread through France and the rest of continental Europe to England, and eastward to Russia. The effects varied considerably from city to city. In some cities, such as Siena, fifty percent of the population died; in others, such as Bruges and Hamburg, the death rate was even higher. Some towns escaped, while some sustained losses of twenty or twenty-five percent. Altogether, the mortality rate was extremely high, especially among the most vulnerable—the very young and the aged. The rural population was devastated, too, though the effects were probably not quite so catastrophic in less densely populated areas. And the psychological effects were terrible in town and country alike, because the causes of the disease were not understood at all, nor how it was contracted, and certainly not what precautions might be taken. There was widespread panic.

So great was the fear of contact with the bodies of those who had died of the plague that many dead were left unburied. People ran, leaving families, homes, all, in the hope of escaping the contagion. Many others, of course, stayed behind to care for the sick and bury their kin. Besides fear, the plague engendered a variety of other reactions. There was a renewed religious fervor, in the hope of expiating the sins that had brought on disease. Groups of people called Flagellants went about the countryside and from town to town, whipping themselves and each other because they believed that if they punished themselves sufficiently they would

Tanoe p̄ stragem lomm maxinā luct ieiunia et
p̄ñas graues p̄ p̄ocessionalr eunti p̄ romā eum
humila pleto et clero apparet angelus sanguino
lentani ense inagina reponens sup palacui mag͂

**The End of the Plague in Rome, from the Belles Heures of Jean, Duke of Berry
(15th c.).** *The survivors are shown burying their dead, while the Angel symbolizes
the end of the pestilence. This illustration was done early in the fifteenth century
when the horrors of the plague were still fresh in peoples' minds.* (THE METROPOLITAN
MUSEUM OF ART, THE CLOISTERS COLLECTION, 1954)

Procession of Flagellants from the Belles Heures of Jean, Duke of Berry (15th c.). (THE METROPOLITAN MUSEUM OF ART, THE CLOISTERS COLLECTION, PURCHASE, 1954)

achieve purification. Rumors spread that the Jews had caused the plague by poisoning the water, and there were massacres of the latter in many German towns.

The mortality rate from the Black Death was even higher than it might otherwise have been because the plague descended on a population already suffering from lack of sufficient food. The immediate and abrupt drop in the population was accompanied by every misery imaginable. Everywhere survivors were left without families, friends and homes; in the countryside, entire villages were deserted, and land simply abandoned; in the towns, businesses completely wiped out. Although in some parts of Europe there were people without jobs, in most places there was a serious shortage of labor.

As soon as the worst shock of the Black Death had passed, the birth rate rose slightly as people tried to re-establish their lives. But recovery was extremely short-lived. The Black Death was the worst and the most terrifying European plague, but it was by no means the last. There were successive epidemics throughout the century, and the population continued to decline rapidly until the 1370s. After this the decline, though steady, was less rapid; and the trend did not begin to reverse itself until the mid-fifteenth century.

The labor shortage was acute in the rural parts of Europe, where the need to cultivate the land and produce the all-important grain was most pressing. In the face of the labor shortage, many lords found it impossible to keep their serfs working the land without providing them with better conditions. This brought about a rapid rise in the emancipation of serfs and a new pattern of relationships between the nobles and their newly freed tenants. The manorial system which had for so long characterized much of northern Europe began to break down. Tenant farmers were able to buy their plots of land and pay rents in kind or in money rather than in labor. In the preceding centuries the opportunity for serfs to buy their freedom had always existed, but it had not affected large numbers of the peasant population and had not gone hand-in-hand (as now) with the other changes in people's status.

There was now a widening gap between the rich and the poor

peasants. Those who had enough land to produce even a small surplus of grain to sell were able to accumulate capital to buy more land, and land was cheap and available. The poor peasants, however, became poorer. Many were displaced at the time of the plague; many others had to vacate those small settlements made in desperation on infertile soil. And in some parts of Europe the labor shortage produced an adverse reaction among the landlords, who became far more repressive than before in the fear that without serfs to work the land, there would not be enough to eat. Though there were many local variations, in general the pattern was one of greater freedom for peasants of Western Europe and greater oppression for those of Eastern Europe.

The difficult economy, the warfare which devastated land and crops, the increasing burden of taxation imposed by rulers, and the struggle between lord and peasant under which new arrangements were sometimes worked out—all these conditions provoked a great number of peasant uprisings during the fourteenth century. We have seen signs of the discontent among the poor of Europe in the twelfth and thirteenth centuries. The religious movements, particularly the heresies, had certainly contained elements of social unrest, but none of this had ever been so clearly focused as in the movements of the fourteenth century. And even then the protests against the oppression of kings and nobles do not seem to have been well-organized, or to have included effective remedies.

The three major insurrections were a revolt in Flanders (1323–1328), the uprising of the Jacquerie near Paris (1358), and the Peasants' Revolt in England (1381). The Flanders revolt began as a protest against the ruler's tax collectors and quickly directed itself against the nobility in general. It started among the peasants and was soon joined by the urban poor, and its duration is an indication of the difficulty which the nobility—and finally, the king—had in suppressing it. The Flanders revolt was violent as well as prolonged, and there is evidence, not just of hostility between the classes, but of real hate and fear.

The Jacquerie (from the common peasant name Jacques) were provoked by a combination of intolerable circumstances produced partly by the warfare in the Île de France, partly by the ravages of the Black Death, and partly by the brigandage of the mercenary companies. The final fuse which touched off the revolt was a royal order demanding that the castles and fortifications in the Île de France be repaired, which meant more taxes and forced labor. The record of brutality on both parts, even if exaggerated, is horrifying. Once again, it is a record of hate and intolerable pain. By the time the revolt was suppressed by the nobility, some 20,000 peasants has been massacred.

The Peasants' Revolt in England was the best organized of these three uprisings, and the one with the clearest program. In essence, the peasants of England wanted the abolition of their serfdom and of forced labor, as well as a reduction in taxes. Their revolt was also a long time in coming, which is why it is briefly included here, even though it takes us beyond the chronological limit for the period of change in the fourteenth century. The English movement had another characteristic which was shared by some of the other revolts in Europe but was most pronounced in England. During its course, the movement was influenced by a large heretical group, called the Lollards, who were anticlerical and highly critical of the church's organization. This combination of social and religious protest on a larger scale than before was another aspect of the attack on the medieval order.

There continued, throughout the fourteenth and fifteenth and into the sixteenth centuries, revolts and uprisings too numerous to count. Most were apparently spontaneous and leaderless—outcries against poverty, social inequities, and misery, without real direction and, for the most part, without lasting consequences. These were the very real manifestations of the changing social conditions of Europe—the "labor pains" felt by nearly all who were trying (or being forced) to break out of the traditional framework of the European Middle Ages.

During the fourteenth century the countryside for all the reasons we have noted—war, disease, and starvation—became once again thinly populated. Much land, in a shorter time than it had taken to bring it under cultivation, returned to forests and meadows. And rural society became more isolated than it had been at any time during the preceding two hundred years. Another factor which led to the depopulation of the countryside was the large migration of peasants into the towns. This began early in the fourteenth century and became a much larger movement immediately following the Black Death. The labor shortage in the towns had caused wages to rise, and peasants went in the hope of finding opportunities for employment and good salaries. They also went because they had simply been displaced, their land was no longer worth farming, and because they hoped for protection from warfare and brigandage behind city walls. But the peasants came into cities which were suffering from all the disasters which had devastated the rural areas, as well as from a decline in trade and manufacture.

The volume of trade and manufacture, and the profits therefrom, had begun to level off in the last half of the thirteenth century mainly for two reasons. The earlier commercial boom had encouraged many new businesses and industries, and competition had lowered prices and profits. In addition, there was a contraction of the Eastern markets, the result of circumstances beyond European control, which adversely affected Europe's international commerce.

Then, in the fourteenth century, grain shortages also raised prices considerably; the kings taxed the cities heavily to pay for their wars, and the instability of the economy led to the ruin of many businesses, large and small. Rulers borrowed from banks when they were hard-pressed for money and, if they defaulted, as they often did, banks and entire banking fortunes were wiped out. When the peasants came into the towns to find employment, they swelled the labor pool, and wages dropped. In response, the guilds restricted their memberships and became closed corporations. The ultimate effect of these changes was to enlarge the ranks of the urban poor and unemployed. The contracting markets for goods encouraged cutthroat competition among businessmen with the result that some who were successful became wealthy, but others were forced out of business entirely.

The population decline alone—and it was not the only factor—

resulted in smaller markets for manufactured goods, and so there was a general decline in production. Merchants who had money were not encouraged to continue investing it in business, and they began to buy land, which was now available. Those who had money were eager to spend it on luxuries, so the trade in luxury goods remained profitable. The tendency during the fourteenth century—and it continued into the next—was for the rich to become richer. There were fewer fortunes, but they were usually large. The gap between rich and poor widened in the towns, and there, too, were uprisings that broke out all through the century. Poor workers rose up against the wealthy merchants who controlled the political power in the cities, the competition between guilds led to movements of protest, and, as in the countryside, there were cries of rage against economic and social injustices.

Decline in trade and depression in many cities were balanced by the emergence of new trade routes and new commercially important areas in Europe. Some of the main centers of northern European commerce of the earlier period, particularly Flanders, went into a marked decline, but the trade in woolen cloth was taken over by England. Many of the old overland routes were closed, and the great fairs once held at Champagne were eclipsed; but commerce and industry prospered further north in the German cities along the Rhine, the Baltic, and the North Sea. The Hanseatic League, a group of nearly eighty towns, including Bremen, Hamburg, and Lubeck, was formed precisely to regulate and control trade.

Italy, still the center for Mediterranean trade, was struck no less forcibly than other centers by the contraction of markets, declining population, warfare that ravaged the countryside, and plagues. With great difficulty, Italian trade was able to stabilize and then recover. (One contemporary observer in the fourteenth century—Petrarch—thought the world was almost coming to an end before his eyes, so grave were the Italian problems.) Although recovery was slow and opportunities for great commercial fortunes were no longer so many or varied, Italy managed to hold the eastern Mediterranean market until the beginning of the seventeenth century. Elsewhere the old commercial centers were not so resilient: All Europe suffered an economic depression from which it did not really recover until after the middle of the fifteenth century.

It is easy to paint a picture of the gloom and disaster of the fourteenth century. It began with an economic regression and population decline of about one-half, which was caused by the catastrophe of the Black Death. Yet, although the picture was dismal, it was by no means unrelieved. The effects of the wars, famines, and epidemics that marred people's lives for so many generations were quite varied. Trade and industry provide good examples because it is possible to point out in them that what was happening was the emergence of a new pattern. Although Flanders was quite ruined, England began the woolen industry that was to become the economic staple of the country for centuries. The cities of France which had been rich and prosperous, situated as they were along the old trade routes, became poor, but the towns of northern Germany prospered. Businessmen were less willing to take the huge financial risks that had brought so many fortunes to the Italians during the early twelfth century. Instead, they were encouraged to invest conservatively in land and to try to find better and more economical means of production. In the countryside, the vacating of the land began with abandoning the poorest soil, so that eventually farming was done only on the most fertile and productive ground in Europe. The economy was unstable, due to the continuing decline of the population and the constant shortage of labor, but wages remained high. And the recession of the European economy as a whole never approached the bare subsistence level of the central medieval period. When Europeans eventually began to reverse the decline in their economy, they were not forced to start all over again because they had the accumulated experience of the later medieval period to draw upon.

The effects of the plagues, the shrinking economy, and the warfare of the fourteenth century cannot, in any event, be measured solely in terms of population loss, reduced agriculture, and contraction of markets. Other deleterious changes occurred that are more difficult to measure objectively. We know, for example, that the Black Death caused a high rate of mortality among the clergy, who were exposed to it unduly in the course of their work among their parishioners. Ecclesiastics at the highest level were not immune, either. Half the college of cardinals died of the plague. The result was that in the years following the plague and subsequent epidemics, of necessity the qualifications for the clergy were lowered in order to replenish their numbers. The same was true, although to a slightly lesser extent, for the learned professions and the nobility. This does not mean there were not individuals of dedication in the clergy or men of intellectual prominence among the learned. That there were fewer of them is a fact, and that generally people were not quite so well-fitted, either by training or birth, for their positions in life is also true. The number of talented and well-trained people during the twelfth and thirteenth centuries, and the extent of literacy and learning, had been genuinely impressive. These qualities did not disappear during the troubles of the fourteenth century, but they were altogether appreciably diminished.

The Dissolution of
Christian Unity

At the same time that the economic foundation of medieval Europe was being weakened, several factors converged to threaten the traditional religious framework of medieval Christendom. The first of these was the attack on papal sovereignty and the international character of the papacy by the secular monarchs. Well before the final decades of the thirteenth century, papal claims to leadership over a unified Christian society had become difficult to translate into reality. Religious unrest and dissent were increasingly difficult to contain, and the church had shown itself less and less tolerant of criticism. Even before the papacy's struggles with the Hohenstaufen emperors had ended, those conflicts had acquired the air of an outmoded cause. Yet the popes and their lawyers reiterated their claims for supremacy despite the growth of kingdoms no longer willing to brook ecclesiastical interference.

365

The attack on the papacy, when it finally occurred, came from the kings of both England and France, but the real fight was between Philip IV of France and the pope. And the first skirmish, which broke out in 1295, was only a bellwether of the major assault on papal power.

The issue which ignited the initial conflict was the taxation by Edward I of England (1272–1307) and Philip (the Fair) of France (1285–1315) of their respective churches to raise money for war against one another in Gascony. The French and English clerics protested to the pope, who was then Boniface VIII (1295–1303), a brilliant canon lawyer, an able administrator, and a man who easily made enemies. Boniface's reaction, when the clergy protested to him, was to issue a papal bull forbidding royal taxation of the church without prior consent of the pope and threatening anyone who continued such taxation with excommunication.

This was no stronger a stand than Innocent III had taken on several occasions a century earlier, but the world had changed, even though the commonplaces of the canon lawyers had not. Boniface's threat only served to harden royal resistance to papal interference, and Edward outlawed those English clerics who would not contribute to the monarchy. Philip went even further, forbidding the export of gold, silver, and other valuables from France, a move which struck at the heart of the papal financial structure. Boniface backed down and issued a bull undoing the first one.

The peace between Boniface and the French king did not last long, however, and the next phase of the conflict came close to violence. This time the issue was the problem of jurisdiction over clerics accused of crimes. It specifically involved a bishop of the French church whom Philip had arrested and was preparing to bring to trial in the royal court. Boniface let loose a shower of papal bulls against Philip, his actions, and his right to tax and to try the clergy. The basis for this reaction was Boniface's conception of papal authority and its relationship to secular power. The pope was simply rehearsing the old lessons recited so effectively by Innocent III a hundred years earlier. In the bull *Unam Sanctam*, issued in 1302, Boniface said of the two powers, "Both are in the power of the church, the spiritual sword, and the material. But the latter is to be used for the church, the former by her. . . . The one sword, then, should be under the other, and temporal authority subject to spiritual."[1] Old lessons, not well-received by a forward-looking king. And at the end, Boniface added his most extravagant claim for papal authority—extravagant, that is, in the context of the early fourteenth century: "Furthermore we declare, state, define and pronounce that it is altogether necessary to salvation for every human creature to be subject to the Roman pontiff."

At Philip's court the reaction was to prepare a list of charges against Boniface, accusing him of everything from buying and selling church offices to heresy. The king's plan was to send a contingent to capture the pope and bring him to France to stand trial. In September of 1303 a group of Frenchmen, joined by some of Boniface's Italian enemies, went to the Italian town of Anagni where Boniface was residing, to seize the pope. All but one of his cardinals had deserted him, but the townspeople stood by him, drove the troops out, and rescued the pontiff. Boniface then returned to Rome and died there the following month.

In the years that followed, Philip was exonerated of all responsibility, although a small number of his inner circle of advisers did not escape so lightly and were actually excommunicated by the succeeding popes. The victory clearly belonged to the French king, however, as the next stage in papal history demonstrated. The pope elected soon after Boniface's death lived less than a year, and in 1305 the college of cardinals elected the bishop of Bordeaux, who took the name Clement V. Clement (1305–1314) was a compromise candidate, and a clever compromise, whose election demonstrated the eagerness of the cardinals not to offend the French king. Clement was a native of Bordeaux, which was then subject to England, but in all other respects, he was French and was regarded by France as pro-French.

Boniface's death had not closed the chapter for Philip and, from 1303 on, he pressed for a posthumous trial against the pope. His

1. This and the following quote are from Henry Bettenson, *Documents of the Christian Church* (New York and London: Oxford University Press, 1943), pp. 162–163.

lawyers and advisors were meanwhile collecting—and perhaps faking—evidence against Boniface. There then emerged a long list of accusations against the latter, including charges that he had been a heretic. The verdict, when the trial was actually held (in 1311–1312), was the result of a bargain struck between Philip and Clement V. The Knights Templar, the order founded during the early crusading period, had grown rich in France, and Philip wanted the Templars condemned in order to confiscate their considerable money and property. Clement to some extent saved Boniface, but at the expense of the Knights Templar. The trial against Boniface reached no verdict: Although he was not cleared, the pope was not found guilty. The charges against him were simply not proved. But the Templars in France were dissolved, and their wealth was confiscated.

Clement V had been in France at the time of his election, and he was installed into office at Lyons and never went to Rome. In 1309 he moved his court to Avignon, and from then until 1377 seven consecutive popes governed the church from there. The papacy purchased the city (which was imperial territory), and a beautiful papal palace was built, surrounded by lovely gardens. Nearby, the cardinals created their own palaces.

The prolonged absence of the papacy from the See of St. Peter was not altogether a matter of deliberate policy. During the fourteenth century Italy was in constant turmoil: There were wars among the city-states and several invasions, so the trip into the central part of the peninsula was fraught with physical danger for the popes. The Italians—particularly the Romans—were furious with the popes for staying away and hostile when they attempted to return. It was therefore easier for the pontiffs to remain at Avignon, and the longer they did, the harder it was for them to come back to the problems of Rome. Although Rome depended for its financial well-being on the presence of the papal court and the visitors to the Holy See, during the fourteenth century the city was nearly deserted, and cattle were actually seen wandering in and about many abandoned churches.

To contemporaries, the period of the Avignonese papacy was known as "the Babylonian Captivity," a reference to the impris-

Palace of the Popes at Avignon. (COURTESY OF THE FRENCH GOVERNMENT TOURIST OFFICE)

onment of the Jews in ancient Babylon. The widespread belief was that the papacy had become the slave of the French monarchy and the fact that the seven Avignonese popes were all French seemed to substantiate the accusation. This was not entirely the case, however. The popes were in many respects independent, although they were by no means above suspicion in their political leanings.

The Avignonese popes centralized the administration of the church and the papal court in a more efficient manner than had ever been done before. This was particularly true in the matter of the apostolic treasury. The popes at Avignon were expert at devising new taxes as well as new ways of collecting old ones., They greatly extended their right to make appointments to ecclesiastical benefices all over Europe by "reserving" those benefices and then "providing for" (filling) them systematically, thereby ignoring the local ecclesiastical groups responsible for electing bishops, abbots, and other church officials. In addition, there were various ways in which this system could be—and was—further abused. The pope might leave a bishopric vacant for a year, and take all the income from the territory, including the part that would have supported the bishop and his work. There was absenteeism, since it sometimes happened that a wealthy cleric would be appointed to more than one position; and the Avignonese popes were also accused of simony, or the buying and selling of church offices.

The Avignonese popes, in fact, seem basically not to have been corrupt. By and large, they took an interest in reform and very much wanted to launch a crusade to recover Jerusalem from the Muslims. They were, however, unusually preoccupied with their finances. In a period of inflation and hardship, the ecclesiastical court was the most luxurious in Europe, and the popes and their cardinals were excessively involved—for any period in history—in their temporal affairs.

Opposition to papal authority during the Avignonese period was particularly fierce in England and Germany, although the most blatant attack had, of course, come first from the king of France. In England, a series of antipapal laws was enacted during the last half of the fourteenth century. These laws, known as the Statutes of Provisors and Praemunire, were intended to do away with papal rights of appointment to the English church, thereby reducing papal intervention in English ecclesiastical affairs in general.

German opposition to papal authority led to yet another papal-imperial conflict, between the emperor Lewis of Bavaria (1314–1347) and Pope John XXII (1316–1334). The conflict need not detain us long. The issue arose from the pope's anger at not being consulted in determining the outcome of a disputed election in Germany. John XXII took the familiar position that the imperial title was the pope's to give or not, as he saw fit. Once again a pontiff was rehearsing the old lesson, and once again that lesson was not well received. The electors took the occasion to reject completely the papal claims to authority over the empire. The German position, simply stated, was that the imperial power was descended directly from God, not from the pope. The German clergy took this quarrel—indeed took the whole Avignonese period—as the opportunity to assert a great deal of independence from direct papal control over the German church. So the hostility of the secular governments, and of the local clergies of Europe, simmering during the last half of the thirteenth century, now finally boiled over. This overt hostility toward the papacy was undoubtedly aggravated by the long absence of the popes from Rome, and by the stringent control they tried to maintain over the institutions of the church.

Of all the charges leveled against the popes of Avignon, the gravest was that their tenure had been merely a prelude to an even more deplorable chapter in papal history. In 1377 Gregory XI (1370–1378) made the official papal return to Rome, but found conditions there so difficult, and the animus towards the papacy so high, that he was on the verge of leaving for Avignon when he died (in 1378). The cardinals then elected an Italian to the papacy. Almost immediately many of them regretted their decision, and, returning to Avignon, they elected a second pope. A certain number of cardinals, however, remained in Rome with the Italian pope, and for nearly forty years Christendom had two rivals and at one point even three, each claiming to have been legally elected.

Nothing, therefore, had been solved by the return in 1377 of the last of the undisputed line of Avignonese popes, and all the forces which had been released in opposition to the papacy and the organized church at the beginning of the fourteenth century now grew more confident and courageous.

The secular states did not find their theorists until the fourteenth century; then, the realities of political life, the anger engendered by the papacy, and the careful study of Aristotle's *Politics*, combined to produce a new way of understanding the state and the relations between the church and the state. One of the best examples of this is the work *Defensor Pacis*, or *Defender of the Peace*, by Marsiglio of Padua (ca. 1280–1342), published in Paris in 1324. Italian by birth, Marsiglio's intellectual career was mostly at Paris, where he became rector of the university in 1313. His book is the most radical of the political treatises written in the early part of the century.

The *Defensor Pacis* is a political theory in support of the state as an entity unto itself, with its own nature and its own reasons for being, none of which have to do with spiritual ends. After a detailed and cogent explanation of the functions of the state and a discussion of how it should best be governed, Marsiglio dealt with the church, and it was here that he overturned, in theory, the existing order. He believed that the church was a department of the state and that the clergy had no power to legislate or to intervene in temporal matters, but existed solely to minister to the spiritual needs of the faithful. Even in its own internal affairs, the church was to be controlled by the secular government, and the clergy were to be paid by the state, like any other functionaries. In addition, Marsiglio attacked the very foundation of the papacy's spiritual and temporal authority by denying the Petrine doctrine. According to his view, the papal position was the result of its historic development, and not divinely ordained. Marsiglio's work was condemned by the church.

The radicalism of this assault on papal authority and the church is an indication of the general impatience with the old order. Although Marsiglio's ideas were too radical to have immediate application, they influenced a handful of other intellectuals and their traces appear in the writings of the most important heretics from then until the time of Martin Luther.

The attacks on the papacy came from many different sources

and sprang from many different impulses. It is once again not surprising to find that given the great attention the Avignonese popes paid to their fiscal policies, the loudest protests came from that wing of the Franciscan order which was devoted to strict poverty. Earlier, as we have seen, the Spirituals insisted on absolute adherence to St. Francis' doctrine of poverty—for themselves. By the early years of the Avignonese papacy they had taken the theological position that Christ and his disciples had no possessions whatever, either individually or in common. They believed that the poverty of Christ was a dogma of the faith. The controversy between the Franciscans and the rest of the church came to a head during the pontificate of John XXII, who declared that the perfect Christian life consisted in doing charity instead of living a life of total poverty. In 1323, Pope John issued a bull in which he declared the doctrine of Christ's poverty heretical. Among the Spirituals, those who refused to accept the papal ruling separated themselves permanently from the main order of Franciscans and devoted themselves thereafter to a life of absolute poverty. Their condemnation did not end the movement, and they, too, remained part of the religious picture, as more and more religious groups began to take root and thrive outside the church.

We have seen the upsurge of popular religious movements all through the late twelfth and the thirteenth centuries. We have also seen that these movements were—although sometimes with great effort—largely contained within the church. By the fourteenth century, however, although there was some effort by the Avignonese popes to direct church reform, the papacy had effectively lost the leadership of the reform movement from which it had derived so much strength and respect.

The groups which now appeared all over Europe developed from two impulses deeply imbedded within Christianity. One was the impetus for reform, which seems always to reassert itself once the need becomes apparent. The other was the desire for a personal experience of God. The longing for a subjective union with God is, of course, as old as the Christian religion, and the yearning for a spiritual experience apart from any organized institutional framework had always been a part of medieval Christianity. Mysticism now came to the fore as the most pronounced "new" development of the fourteenth century. The difference between the "modern devotion" and earlier mysticism was precisely the fact that it now became a *movement*, and a lay movement, rather than the preserve (as more usually it had been) of monks and clergy. The great mystics of the preceding centuries, such as St. Bernard of Clairvaux, had, in a real sense, been professionally trained. Now mystical groups began to appear everywhere, though most of the largest were in northern Europe. These groups were led by individuals who were able to convey to others the essence of their own spiritual experience. Some of these groups were heretical, others not, but all, from the church's point of view, were at least dangerously close to heresy because they were usually anticlerical and always a reproach to the wealth and institutional aspects of the church.

One of the best examples of this "modern devotion" was the Brethren of the Common Life, founded in Holland by Gerard Groote (1340–1384) and his followers, which spread throughout Europe. Groote's followers included some clergy, but mainly this was a lay movement whose members took simple vows and lived communally. They believed that the good Christian life consisted of emulating the life of Christ and in living with one another in love and humility. The great book which grew out of the teachings of the Brethren was written by Thomas à Kempis after the close of this period, but it exemplifies the spirit of the movement. Its title, the *Imitation of Christ*, is the clearest statement of the fundamental beliefs of the Brethren and, indeed, of all the mystical groups. The Brethren of the Common Life founded schools in which they provided training in simple piety and gave an excellent education besides. The mind and the heart both were instructed in brotherly love and the pure love of God. There were many other mystical groups, and many individual mystics all over Christendom, and this kind of devotion was becoming popular in the fullest sense of the word.

We have already seen how the Black Death, and the epidemics which followed during the remainder of the century, encouraged the growth of popular piety, and the longing for a spiritually satisfying experience apart from the organized church. A specter hung over Europe, and it is hardly strange that there was a greater preoccupation than there had been for centuries with death and the macabre. The outward exuberance of the twelfth and thirteenth centuries gave way to the inward concern with death and redemption. The world and its ills were more difficult to understand and harder to cope with than they had been in a long while, and the spiritual cares of men and women in the fourteenth century became more serious, and more urgent.

Finally, the medieval intellectual synthesis, which had reached its fulfillment with St. Thomas Aquinas, was broken apart. The thrust of intellectual life in the thirteenth century, culminating in the career of St. Thomas, had been to reconcile Aristotle and the dogmas of the Christian faith. This was the goal toward which the main currents of medieval thought had been moving. Yet that harmony was no sooner achieved than it was broken.

In the years following the death of St. Thomas in 1274, scholars who had been doubtful of the possibility of synthesizing faith and reason emerged as the leading intellectuals of their time, and by the mid-1300s the two most brilliant post-Thomist philosophers had succeeded in "separating" reason and faith. Duns Scotus (1266–1308), a Scottish Franciscan who studied and taught at the universities in Paris and Oxford, began to develop the position that the truths of the Christian faith cannot be illuminated by reason. This was carried much further by William of Ockham (ca. 1300–1349), who was also a Franciscan and who also taught at Paris and Oxford. He argued more clearly than Duns Scotus— and with more impact on his contempories—the necessary separation of reason and faith. Ockham and many of his followers no longer believed that the human mind could comprehend the majesty of God and the mysteries of faith. In his view, reason could not prove the dogmas of faith. There had been an optimism in St. Thomas's writings, which was now gone.

This new position was both a break with the past and a beginning. Looking backward, from the vantage point of centuries, it is possible to see that once the arguments which separated faith from reason had been persuasively offered (as they were by Ockham), the changes which followed over time could not be halted. Separated from one another, reason and faith could each follow its own natural direction. Reason, or the method of rational inquiry, could take all knowledge within its province (all, that is, except revelation), and from the fourteenth century on, a fresh impetus was given to the study of the natural world and progress in the areas of scientific thought. On the other side, those who were no longer so concerned to explain their faith were free to experience it more open-heartedly. Thus the dissolution of the medieval framework of society gave rise to new ideas about religion and the state, and new ways of thinking about man and nature. The way was being prepared for the Protestant Reformation of the sixteenth century and the final sundering of Christian unity. Until then the attacks on the traditional medieval assumptions continued, particularly in northern Europe, where the familiar frames of reference did not quickly or easily disappear. In Italy, however, by the beginning of the fourteenth century, a new attitude was being formed, and a new cultural outlook was developing.

A New Beginning:
The Return to Rome

Of this new cultural outlook, Dante Aligheri (1265–1321) was the herald, and Francesco Petrarca, known as Petrarch (1304–1374), was the father. Italy had in two respects always been closer to its classical Roman past than had northern Europe. Italy had remained more urbanized throughout the Middle Ages, and the learning and literature of pagan Rome were at the same time more firmly rooted in Italian soil and closer to the surface. And there was, of course, the city of Rome itself.

During the papal-imperial struggles of the twelfth and thirteenth centuries, the northern Italian cities had struggled with great determination to keep from being swallowed up by either the empire or the papacy. In the course of those battles, these cities had generally sided with one or the other power, as we have seen. In the long aftermath of these conflicts, there were revolutions in northern Italian cities against the representatives of either the pope or the emperor, depending on which power claimed ultimate overlordship at the time. In their desire to gain freedom the revolutionaries were abetted, unintentionally, by the papacy's long absence from Rome which provided an opportunity for anti-papal sentiment to run rampant. The papacy had acted as a political arbiter and had tried to maintain a political balance in Italy, but during the fourteenth century this balance was lost, and the Italian cities became independent and closer, or at any rate felt themselves to be closer, to the city-states of Roman antiquity. There was even an attempted restoration, led by Cola di Rienzi, of the ancient Republic in Rome in 1347.

In his youth, Cola had been impressed by the ruins of the ancient city, and he collected classical manuscripts and became a good historian of Rome's ancient past. Completely caught up in a vision of the grandeur of ancient Rome, he dedicated himself to restoring the Republic. At the time, Rome was torn by strife among the noble families, and when di Rienzi summoned the Roman people to the Capitoline hill and announced the reconstruction of the ancient constitution, his plan seemed capable of succeeding. Cola threw the nobles out of the city temporarily, but then did nothing. When the nobility returned, Cola fled. The sequel to the story occurred several years later in 1354, when Cola returned, tried once more to reconstitute the ancient system, and was finally killed by the Romans.

Every literary Italian was caught up in Cola di Rienzi's attempt to return to the past. Between his two attempts in Rome, Cola had been brought (in 1352) to the papal court at Avignon to be tried, and Petrarch, who was visiting at Avignon, saw his arrival as a prisoner and wrote of it to a friend. Petrarch was as disappointed as all Cola's other supporters that his plan had failed. Although Petrarch understood that to some extent the responsibility had indeed been Cola's, he pointed out that di Rienzi was not charged with "those errors that all good men reprove in him. His crime clearly is that he dared to imagine and to bring about that the Republic should be safe and free, and that the affairs of Rome and its empire should be managed in Rome."[2] Cola was saved (or managed to save himself) by claiming that he was a poet, although in Petrarch's opinion he was unworthy to be considered one—a strange irony, since Cola's dream of restoring ancient Rome was the political counterpart to the literary revival of classical antiquity.

It was Dante Aligheri who was the herald of the literary revival. Dante's greatest work, *The Divine Comedy* (*La Commedia Divina*), takes the form of an allegorical visit to the next world. In briefest outline, it is the story of Dante's passage from Hell through Purgatory, until finally he reaches Heaven. In this long narrative poem, in verse of unsurpassing beauty, Dante conveys the medieval synthesis of reason and faith. In the beginning, going up through the stages of Hell, the author is led by his guide, the Roman poet Virgil. Dante chose Virgil as his mentor for several reasons. Firstly, Virgil was the most perfect poet, the finest in the Latin language. In addition, he wrote extensively about suffering ("the tears of things") and about wisdom learned through suffering. Virgil loved Italy as Dante did, and he depicted nature and the Italian countryside. In one of his poems Virgil had foretold the birth of a savior. To the ancient Romans this had been their first emperor, Augustus; to the Christians, however, Virgil had predicted the birth of Christ. So for a mixture of reasons, classical and Christian (medieval), Virgil was elected to guide Dante through the paths of reason and through Hell as far as Purgatory, where Dante was then guided by Beatrice, the woman he loved. Beatrice represented the next stage in the ascent toward God; she personified Divine Grace and the church, with its sacraments for salvation. For the last, exalted stage of his journey, Dante chose St. Bernard, the mystic, to lead him to his final personal vision of God and Heaven.

Dante wrote *The Divine Comedy* in Italian and, more precisely, in the language of his native Tuscany, thereby elevating the Tuscan dialect to literary status. By using Tuscan he exercised an unusual

2. Morris Bishop, ed. and trans., *Letters From Petrarch* (Bloomington: Indiana University Press, 1966), p. 117.

choice. The more usual would have been to write in Latin; failing that, it would have been expected that Dante would use French, the language of the romances, epics, and, in the thirteenth century, still the dominant vernacular in Christendom. Dante's innovation began the shift from medieval Latin, the medium of the scholastics, to the vernacular for poetry and other—though by no means all—creative writing.

From Dante's many writings, we know that he was familiar with every author of Greek and Latin antiquity whose works were available. He knew the Greeks in translation, and he also knew many Roman authors, and knew them so well that he could readily judge their merits. In the generation beginning with Dante's younger contemporary, Petrarch, large numbers of newly discovered classical manuscripts became known in Italy, but a new attitude was formed towards them. In Dante's works, however much he loved ancient Rome and its writers, all the classical themes were within the medieval framework. Virgil, representing the pagan world, did not reach Heaven.

The figure most responsible for the new intellectual current in northern Italy was Petrarch (1304–1374), who devoted himself to finding manuscripts of classical authors, copying them, and writing about them to his many, many friends in order to publicize their special value. Petrarch's family was Florentine, but had left its native city and settled near Avignon; Petrarch was sent to study law at Montpellier. He disliked law so intensely that his father, in order to remove all distractions, actually burned most of Petrarch's other books (mainly classical authors), and did this in spite of the fact that it was he who had introduced his son to Cicero, whom he especially loved. His father died in 1326, and Petrarch immediately gave up law. By this time he was already gaining a reputation as a poet and, indeed, his literary fame today rests on his lyric poetry in Italian, especially the sonnets to his beloved Laura.

Petrarch professed to look down on his sonnets, regarding them as "trifles," but he worked at them steadily, and he perfected the sonnet form. (They are like perfect gems, in fact.) In Petrarch's own view his most important contribution was his missionary

Portrait of Petrarch, 14th c.   *This realistic portrait shows the humanist wearing the laurel wreath given him by the King of Naples. The laurel wreath was chosen because it was the symbol used first by the Greeks and then adopted by the Romans to celebrate triumph and outstanding achievement. In Greek tradition, laurel was associated with Apollo, who was believed to be the god of poets.* (ALINARI/EDITORIAL PHOTOCOLOR ARCHIVES)

380

work for the classics. His family had been well-off, and he was educated, extremely well-traveled, and constantly corresponded with an extraordinarily wide circle of friends. Petrarch's background, connections, and environment provided him with unlimited opportunities to search out manuscripts, to write about them, to encourage his friends to study them, and to discuss the value of the literature.

Petrarch and his fellow lovers of the classics were searching for something different from either scholasticism or mysticism, something more in keeping with their urban world in the fourteenth century. Although Petrarch's brother was a monk, and Petrarch regarded the monastic life as the highest form of devotion, asceticism was not the answer for him, nor was the world of university scholars, who, in Petrarch's view, were locked in endless disputations in logic that seemed arid and fruitless.

Petrarch turned to the Latin classics; and in the works of the three authors he most loved he found ideas about man, education, and living in the world which shaped his intellectual development.

In the writings of Virgil, the poet of the Augustan age, of Livy, its historian, and of Cicero, its orator, statesman, and philosopher, Petrarch and a small literary group, who would now be considered humanists, rediscovered—or believed they rediscovered—and were inspired by the values the Romans held most dear.

They found in Livy's *History of Rome* a guide to selfless patriotism to one's country and responsibility to one's fellow citizens. Most of all, the humanists also rediscovered what the Romans had believed were the humane purposes of an education. These they learned from Cicero. In several of his works, Cicero discussed not only how a Roman should be prepared to participate in civic life, but what his education should do for his character. The ultimate value of the Roman literary education was to transmit the Roman values—understanding of civilization and what it means to be a civilized human being. Cicero used the word *humanitas*, for which there is no simple equivalent. It was intended to convey a sense of the dignity of human beings and the human condition—the sense of one's personal dignity, and that of others. The best in Roman literature was used to teach *humanitas*, because in the

381

fullness of that idea resides the highest form of culture and civilization to which humans can, and must, aspire. For, as Cicero said, "it is important to remember how far the nature of man transcends the nature of beasts."[3] And it is by devotion to the "*studia humanitatis*," or "studies of humanity," that we are elevated and taught that concern for the "welfare of humanity which should be nearest to the heart of every man." Through literature we learn the examples of great men and the wisdom of great minds; their influence "is not conveyed by the living voice alone; it is transmitted to posterity in written works."

Petrarch, who wrote continuously to everyone involved in this new intellectual movement, more than anyone in his generation, bent all his energies to spreading Ciceronian ideas and to searching out manuscripts of Cicero and all the other Latin authors. He begged manuscripts from friends who possessed ones he did not have, and he copied out an immense number himself. He also had a lovely habit of addressing letters to the great Roman figures he admired, speaking to them as if they were his contemporaries (as indeed to him they seemed), so congenial were their ideas to him.

Petrarch rightly deserves the title accorded him by posterity. He was surely the father of that humanist movement which is the chief characteristic of the period beginning in Italy in the fourteenth century and known as the Renaissance. "Renaissance" means "rebirth" and the term is used, by custom now, to describe the era in Italy, following the Middle Ages, in which the *studia humanitatis* and the revival of classical literature were emphasized.

It was Petrarch himself who first used the term "medieval," with its deliberately pejorative connotation, to describe the thousand years of history which we have now reviewed. On the one hand he was correct to recognize that the older order was indeed changing and that one of the signs of change was a new approach to the study of the classics. The humanists studied manuscripts they treasured without reference to any standard except their intrinsic value to human experience. So we have come nearly full circle, back to Virgil and the story of Aeneas' trials and sufferings

3. This and the following quotations are from Cicero, "On Moral Duties," in *The Basic Works of Cicero*, ed. Moses Hadas (New York: Random House, 1951), pp. 41, 58.

to "found the Roman people." Aeneas' devotion to his homeland, to family, and to the mission given him to reach Italy—all these qualities which the Romans cherished now found an immediate response in the fourteenth century. Those virtues, so beautifully expressed in Virgil's *Aeneid*, now acquired a new meaning because they signified a responsibility in the world and a duty to one's fellow human beings.

We have seen, however, that, after all, the Roman inheritance was woven into the fabric of European thought as it developed throughout the medieval period. Certainly, the continuing influence of Rome remained one of the chief unifying forces in the formation of Europe for a thousand years. But as persistent and important as Rome had always been, the yardstick by which Roman values and ideas had formerly been measured was the extent to which, and the way in which, they could illuminate the Christian faith.

Petrarch and his fellow humanists understood the difference between *their* view and that of the men and women living in the period we call the Middle Ages. So the humanists turned away from their immediate past, disparaging it in *all* regards—or nearly all—because they rejected it in favor of their present, not understanding (nor caring about) the diversity and creativity of the preceding thousand years. The framework of medieval civilization was surely changed during the fourteenth century, and the assumptions of the medieval world were gradually transformed. But the foundations of European culture and civilization were laid during the Middle Ages and those, of course, endure.

A Selected Guide to Further Reading

General

Bark, William C., *Origins of the Medieval World*, New York, 1960.

Barrow, R. H., *The Romans*, Harmondsworth, 1949.

Brooke, Christopher, *Europe in the Central Middle Ages*, New York, 1971.

Brown, Peter, *The World of Late Antiquity*, London, 1971.

Dawson, Christopher, *The Making of Europe*, Meridian edition, New York, 1956.

Dawson, Christopher, *Medieval Essays*, New York, 1954.

DeMolen, Richard L., ed. *One Thousand Years: Western Europe in the Middle Ages*, Boston, 1974.

Heer, F., *The Medieval World*, New York, 1962.

Pearsall, D. and E. Salter, eds., *Landscapes and Seasons of the Medieval World*, New York, 1967.

Pounds, N., *An Historical Geography of Europe 450 B.C.–A.D. 1330*, Cambridge, 1973.

Southern, R. W., *The Making of the Middle Ages*, New Haven, 1961.

Wood, Charles T., *The Quest for Eternity: Medieval Manners and Morals*, Garden City, New York, 1971.

Zacour, Norman P., *Medieval Institutions*, 2nd ed., New York, 1976.

Social and Economic History

Abrahams, I., *Jewish Life in the Middle Ages*, New York, 1969.

Adams, J., *Patterns of Medieval Society*, Englewood Cliffs, 1969.

Aries, Philippe, *Centuries of Childhood*, trans. Robert Baldick, New York, 1962.

Bautier, R. H., *The Economic Development of Medieval Europe*, New York, 1971.

Bennett, H. S., *Life on the English Manor*, Cambridge, 1960.

Boase, T., *Death in the Middle Ages*, New York, 1972.

385

Brooke, Christopher, *The Structure of Medieval Society*, London, 1971.
Cheyette, F., *Lordship and Community in Medieval Europe*, New York, 1967.
Cipolla, C., ed., *The Fontana Economic History of Europe: The Middle Ages*, London, 1972.
Duby, Georges, *The Early Growth of the European Economy*, trans. B. Clark, Ithaca, 1974.
Duby, Georges, *Rural Economy and Country Life in the Medieval West*, trans. C. Postan, London, 1968.
Gimpel, Jean, *The Medieval Machine: The Industrial Revolution of the Middle Ages*, Harmondsworth, 1976.
Hodgett, Gerald A. J., *A Social and Economic History of Medieval Europe*, London, 1972.
Homans, George C., *English Villagers of the Thirteenth Century*, New York, 1970.
Latouche, Robert, *The Birth of Western Economy*, trans. E. M. Wilkinson, London, 1967.
Leighton, A., *Transport and Communication in Early Medieval Europe*, Newton Abbot, 1972.
Lewis, A. R., *Naval Power and Trade in the Mediterrean*, Princeton, 1957.
Lopez, R., *The Commercial Revolution of the Middle Ages*, Englewood Cliffs, 1971.
Lopez, R. and I. Raymond, *Medieval Trade in the Mediterranean World*, New York, 1967.
Miskimin, Henry A., *The Economy of Early Renaissance Europe, 1300–1460*, Cambridge, 1975.
Morewedge, R., ed., *The Role of Women in the Middle Ages*, Albany, 1975.
Mundy, John H. and Peter Riesenberg, *The Medieval Town*, Princeton, 1958.
Pirenne, Henri, *Economic and Social History of Medieval Europe*, New York, 1956.
Riché, Pierre, *Daily Life in the World of Charlemagne*, trans. Jo Ann McNamara, Philadelphia, 1978.
Roisling, M., *Life in Medieval Times*, New York, 1973.
Roth, C. and I. Levine, eds., *The Dark Age: Jews in Christian Europe*, New Brunswick, 1966.
Rorig, Fritz, *The Medieval Town*, Berkeley, 1969.
Sapori, Armando, *The Italian Merchant in the Middle Ages*, New York, 1970.

Stuard, Susan M., ed., *Women in Medieval Society,* Philadelphia, 1976.
Thrupp, Sylvia L., ed., *Early Medieval Society,* New York, 1967.
White, Lynn, Jr., *Medieval Technology and Social Change,* London, 1962.
Ziegler, P., *The Black Death,* New York, 1969.

Political History
Baker, Timothy, *The Normans,* London, 1966.
Barraclough, G., *Origins of Modern Germany,* New York, 1963.
Bloch, Marc, *Feudal Society,* 2 vols., Chicago, 1964.
Bronsted, Johannes, *The Vikings,* trans. K. Skov, Harmondsworth, 1965.
Brooke, Christopher, *The Saxon and Norman Kings,* London, 1974.
———, *From Alfred to Henry III,* New York, 1966.
Bullough, P., *The Age of Charlemagne,* New York, 1972.
Douglas, David, *William the Conqueror,* Berkeley, 1964.
Evans, Joan, *Life in Medieval France,* New York, 1968.
Fawtier, Robert, *The Capetian Kings of France,* London, 1962.
Fichtenau, Henrich, *The Carolingian Empire,* New York, 1964.
Gabriel, Jackson, *The Making of Medieval Spain,* London, 1972.
Ganshof, F., *The Carolingian and the Frankish Monarchy,* Ithaca, 1971.
———, *Medieval Feudalism,* trans. Philip Grierson, 3rd ed., New York, 1964.
Heer, F., *The Holy Roman Empire,* trans. J. Sandheimer, New York, 1968.
Henneman, J., *The Medieval French Monarchy,* Hinsdale, Illinois, 1973.
Holt, J. C., *Magna Carta,* Cambridge, 1965.
Hyde, J., *Society and Politics in Medieval Italy,* London, 1973.
Lasko, P., *The Kingdon of the Franks,* New York, 1971.
Mack Smith, Denis, *Medieval Sicily, 800–1713,* New York, 1968.
Morrall, John B., *Political Thought in Medieval Times,* New York, 1962.
Morris, John, *The Age of Arthur,* New York, 1973.
Munz, Peter, *Frederick Barbarossa,* Ithaca, 1969.
O'Callahan, Joseph, *A History of Medieval Spain,* Ithaca, 1975.
Petit-Dutaillis, Charles, *The Feudal Monarchy in France and England From the Tenth to the Thirteenth Century,* New York, 1964.
Strayer, Joseph, *Feudalism,* Princeton, 1965.
———, *On the Medieval Origins of the Modern State,* Princeton, 1970.
Ullmann, Walter, *A History of Political Thought: The Middle Ages,* Harmondsworth, 1965.

Wallace-Hadrill, J. M., *The Barbarian West, 450–1000*, 3rd ed., London, 1967.

Religious and Cultural Life

Baldwin, John W., *The Scholastic Culture of the Middle Ages, 1000–1300*, Lexington, 1971.

Baldwin, Marshall W., *Christianity Through the Thirteenth Century*, New York, 1970.

Barraclough, G., *The Medieval Papacy*, London, 1968.

Bolgar, R., *The Classical Heritage*, New York, 1964.

Brooke, Christopher, *The Twelfth Century Renaissance*, London, 1969.

Cobban, A. B., *The Medieval Universities: Their Development and Organization*, London, 1974.

Crombie, A. C., *Medieval and Early Modern Science*, New York, 1959.

Dales, Richard C., *The Intellectual Life of Western Europe in the Middle Ages*, Washington, 1980.

Dales, Richard, *The Scientific Achievement of the Middle Ages*, Philadelphia, 1973.

Daly, L. J., *The Medieval University, 1200–1400*, New York, 1961.

Deansley, Margaret, *History of the Medieval Church, 590–1500*, London, 1974.

Diringer, D., *The Illuminated Book: Its History and Production*, New York, 1967.

Grant, E., *Physical Science in the Middle Ages*, New York, 1971.

Grodecki, Louis, *Gothic Architecture*, New York, 1977.

Holmes, G., *Dante*, Oxford, 1980.

Knowles, David, *Christian Monasticism*, New York, 1969.

———, *The Evolution of Medieval Thought*, New York, 1964.

———, *Saints and Scholars*, Cambridge, 1963.

Monter, William E., ed., *European Witchcraft*, New York, 1969.

Morrison, K., *Tradition and Authority in the Early Church*, Princeton, 1969.

Prawer, Joshua, *The Latin Kingdom of Jerusalem*, London, 1972.

Russell, F. H., *The Just War in the Middle Ages*, Cambridge, 1975.

Russell, J. B., *A History of Medieval Christianity*, New York, 1968.

Smalley, B., *The Study of the Bible in the Middle Ages*, Notre Dame, 1964.

Southern, R. W., *Western Society of the Church at the Middle Ages*, Baltimore, 1970.

Tellenbach, J., *Church, State and Christian Society at the Time of the Investiture Contest*, Oxford, 1948.

Thompson, J. W., *The Medieval Library*, New York, 1967.

Tydeman, William, *The Theater in the Middle Ages*, Cambridge, 1978.

Von Simson, Otto, *The Gothic Cathedral*, 2nd ed., rev., New York, 1965.

Waddell, H., *The Wandering Scholars*, New York, 1968.

Byzantium and Islam

Andrae, Tor, *Mohammed, the Man and His Faith*, New York, 1960.

Daniel, N., *The Arabs and Medieval Europe*, New York, 1960.

Diehl, C., *Byzantium: Greatness and Decline*, New Brunswick, 1957.

Gabrieli, F., *Mohammad and the Conquests of Islam*, New York, 1968.

Geanakoplos, Deno J., *Byzantine East and Latin West*, New York, 1966.

Hitti, P. K., *History of the Arabs*, 6th ed., London, 1958.

Hussey, Joan M., *The Byzantine World*, New York, 1961.

Lewis, Bernard, *The Arabs in History*, New York, 1960.

Peters, F. E., *Allah's Commonwealth*, New York, 1973.

Von Grunebaum, G., *Medieval Islam*, Chicago, 1961.

Vyronis, Speros, *Byzantium and Europe*, New York, 1967.

Watt, W., *Muhammed, Prophet and Statesman*, London, 1965.

Index

Figures in italics indicate illustrations.